T0122877

Get the eBook FREE!
(PDF, ePub, Kindle, and liveBook all included)

We believe that once you buy a book from us, you should be able to read it in any format we have available. To get electronic versions of this book at no additional cost to you, purchase and then register this book at the Manning website.

Go to https://www.manning.com/freebook and follow the instructions to complete your pBook registration.

That's it!
Thanks from Manning!

SPA Design and Architecture

Understanding single-page web applications

EMMIT A. SCOTT, JR.

MANNING

SHELTER ISLAND

For online information and ordering of this and other Manning books, please visit
www.manning.com. The publisher offers discounts on this book when ordered in quantity.
For more information, please contact

> Special Sales Department
> Manning Publications Co.
> 20 Baldwin Road
> PO Box 761
> Shelter Island, NY 11964
> Email: orders@manning.com

Manning Publications Co.
20 Baldwin Road
PO Box 761
Shelter Island, NY 11964

Development editor:	Dan Maharry
Technical development editor:	Joel Kotarski
Technical proofreaders:	Andrew Gibson
	Jean-François Morin
Copyeditor:	Sharon Wilkey
Proofreader:	Linda Recktenwald
Typesetter:	Marija Tudor
Cover designer:	Marija Tudor

ISBN: 9781617292439
Printed in the United States of America

To my three beautiful children, Ana Carolina, David, and Sofía.
Thanks for all the smiles, hugs, and unconditional love.
You are forever in my heart.

brief contents

contents

foreword

In 1991, Tim Berners-Lee launched the world's first website, which ran on a program he named the WorldWideWeb. Two years later, he would release the source code for the WorldWideWeb and the world itself would never be the same. You can still see that first web page at info.cern.ch.

Since 1991, the web has experienced unprecedented popularity. At 24 years old, it's still the most widely used technology in the world. It runs on all operating systems, all hardware platforms, and nearly all mobile devices in some form or fashion. The program that makes this all possible is the almighty web browser.

Traditionally, web browsers were simply middlemen. They would fetch data from a server, display it, take data back to the server, and get more data to display. But today's web browsers, while still true to the original principals of the web, are far more complex than anyone could ever have imagined back then.

The humble browser has graduated into a full-fledged runtime for applications of all sizes. These are applications that don't have to be installed, can be accessed from anywhere, and run everywhere. This is the holy grail for developers. Being able to deploy one codebase that runs everywhere and is always up to date is an opportunity too good to pass up. No other technology can make this boast.

Riding on the success of the web platform is the ubiquity of JavaScript—a language created in 10 days that's now the most used programming language in the world. Developers have embraced JavaScript, and that has opened up doors to new types of applications that we never would have dreamed possible in a web browser.

These new applications, often called single-page applications (SPAs), run almost entirely in the browser, and they introduce a whole new set of principles, patterns, and problems. The broad appeal of the web has resulted in a Cambrian explosion of JavaScript and CSS frameworks; so many that it is daunting at best to try to find the needle of success in the haystack of frameworks.

That, dear reader, is why this book is so important.

For the past four years, I've worked at Telerik as a developer advocate focusing on the Kendo UI JavaScript library. I've watched countless JavaScript frameworks come and go. The hype reaches critical mass, and then the next big thing shows up, and the developers who are actually building solutions on these fads are left to pick up the pieces. It often leaves me wondering when it will settle down and we can focus on the one "right way" to build this new generation of rich client applications.

The raw truth is that there is no "right way" to do anything. There is only the way that works for your project and your skill set. There is only the way that makes you most productive and, ultimately, most successful.

In order to find that way in the world of SPAs, it's imperative to understand the fundamental principles behind the SPA concept itself. Learning a framework will not be sufficient and will ultimately leave you short and wanting more. A deep understanding of the core concepts on which a successful SPA rests will enable you to make the right decisions with confidence and to know how to build the last 20% when your JavaScript framework of choice takes you only 80% of the way there.

This book will be your guide. It's for experts and novices alike. While reading it, I found myself learning basics that I had hastily glossed over, as well as getting new insight into terminology that I thought I had a good grasp of but only partially (and in some cases incorrectly) understood. The insight and explanations contained in these pages are not just academic but also practical and hands-on, showing you how to build an SPA and addressing real-world implementations head-on while discussing relevant SPA frameworks.

I'm generally skeptical of books that try to tackle a concept as big as that of SPAs, but this is one of the few reads that somehow manages to take a very complex topic and break it down into easily understandable and digestible pieces.

It is without hesitation that I provide my full recommendation for this book—each and every page.

BURKE HOLLAND
DIRECTOR OF DEVELOPER RELATIONS
TELERIK

preface

Many of the projects I've worked on have been long-running efforts taking a year or more to build. Then, of course, there were updates and additional phases to complete after that. Because these types of projects take so long, technology grows by leaps and bounds in the meantime. By the time I was ready to start the next project, I'd have to reevaluate my tech stack because things had changed so much.

It was when my team and I were gearing up for our most recent single-page application project that I had the idea to write this book. My director had given us the green light to research the "best of breed" for the technologies we wanted to use. So we began evaluating various solutions and creating small proof-of-concept applications.

While going through this process again, I was reminded of the difficulties in sifting through the sheer volume of information available to us these days. It also occurred to me how daunting this must be for those new to creating single-page applications.

So I set out to write a book that would not only summarize what's involved in building an SPA but also give a nice introduction to some of the libraries and frameworks used to create them. Additionally, I wanted the book to be straightforward and easy to digest, yet give enough technical details so that you can actually build an SPA when you've finished reading it.

Thanks for taking this journey with me. I hope you'll find this book to be an indispensable guide to single-page application development.

acknowledgments

This is my first book, so as you can imagine it was quite overwhelming at times. I was very fortunate, though, to have three extraordinary people in my corner who consistently went above and beyond the call of duty to help mold and shape this book: Dan Maharry, my development editor; Joel Kotarski, my technical development editor; and Andrew Gibson, my technical proofreader. They are an amazing team to work with and I can't thank them enough.

Thank you, too, Sharon Wilkey, for the wonderful job as copyeditor, and Jean-François Morin, for lending a hand as the Java/Spring technical proofreader.

I'd also like to thank the numerous other people at Manning who made this book possible: Marjan Bace, Michael Stephens, Bert Bates, Maureen Spencer, Kevin Sullivan, Mary Piergies, Candace Gillhoolley, Rebecca Rinehart, Ana Romac, Toni Bowers, and Linda Recktenwald, as well as the unsung heroes who worked so hard to bring this effort to fruition.

Special thanks to Burke Holland for writing the book's foreword. I'm a huge fan of Burke's work and his writing and feel honored that he agreed to write this.

Thanks to the reviewers who read this book in its various stages of development: Alain Couniot, Anirudh Prabhu, Bruno Sonnino, David Schmitz, Fernando Monteiro Kobayashi, Johan Pretorius, John Shea, Maqbool Patel, Philippe Vialatte, Rajesh Pillai, Shrinivas Parashar, Trevor Saunders, Viorel Moisei, and Yogesh Poojari.

Thanks also to my family: my wife Rosalba, my daughter Ana Carolina, my son David, my other daughter Sofía, and my mom Lucy. Words just aren't enough to thank you for all the love, support, and encouragement you gave me throughout this endeavor.

To all my friends and colleagues, both at work and elsewhere, thank you for your encouragement and support as well.

about this book

This book was written to give you an introductory look at what it takes to create a single-page application. The book not only introduces you to frameworks and technologies for creating an SPA but also shows you how to unit test them and how to automate client-side development and build-related tasks.

Because part of the process of creating an SPA is deciding what your technology stack will look like, the book compares various approaches used by today's leading JavaScript frameworks. One of the reasons why so many frameworks exist is that there's no single correct way to build an application. By comparing different frameworks, you can better decide what's right for you and your next project.

Each chapter of the book includes a complete, working application. I've tried to keep things interesting yet not overwhelming. I'm not a fan of long-running examples that fill half a book with pages and pages of source code to wade through. So I decided to create a separate project for each chapter. I also tried to keep each example as small and to the point as possible while still being interesting and relevant to the concepts and topics for the chapter.

Roadmap

Part 1: The basics

- Chapter 1 introduces you to the overall SPA concept. From the beginning you'll start learning important concepts and how SPAs are different from traditional web applications. You'll get a clear, concise definition accompanied by an overview of how the various pieces and parts of an SPA fit together.
- Chapter 2 dives deeper, introducing you to a family of JavaScript frameworks known as MV* frameworks and their role in the creation of a single-page application. The chapter talks about the commonalities among frameworks, as well

as how they're different. The end-of-chapter project is written three different ways, each with a different MV* framework so you can see different architectural styles in practice.

- In chapter 3, you'll get acquainted with modular programming. You'll see first-hand through examples and the chapter's project the reasons you should be using modules in your SPA. We'll also break down the module pattern's syntax and walk through it step by step. We'll top off the chapter with an introduction to module loading and AMD modules.

Part 2: Core concepts

- Chapter 4 gives you a crash course on client-side routing. You'll get a break-down of how routing works under the covers and see how various frameworks approach routing. You'll also get an understanding of how client-side routing affects the application's state.
- Chapter 5 introduces you to layout design and view composition in an SPA. We'll start with simple designs and work our way up to more complicated ones with complex routes. Additionally, we'll touch on advanced layout topics, like working with nested views and sibling views.
- In chapter 6 we'll talk about inter-module communication. What's the good of creating modules if they can't talk to each other, right? You'll not only see different approaches to inter-module communication but also get a feel for modular application design.
- Chapter 7 looks at the role of the server in an SPA environment. Although the client is still the focus, you'll see how your SPA communicates with the server and how to handle results from your server calls. The chapter examines result handling from the standpoint of both callbacks and the use of promises. You'll also see how MV* frameworks help you with these tasks. At the end of the chapter, you'll get a brief introduction to REST and see how your SPA can consume RESTful services.
- Chapter 8 is an overview of unit testing JavaScript applications, specifically SPAs. Don't worry if you've never done any unit testing on the client. We'll take this slow and easy and go through the basics step by step.
- Finally, in chapter 9, you'll see how client-side task automation helps you both in development and in creating a build process. You'll get clear pictures of the most common types of tasks for each scenario and see them in action in the code for the end-of-chapter project.

The appendices are meant to complement the chapters. Appendix A is a walk-through of the complete source code for all three versions of the project for chapter 2. Appendix B and appendix C complement chapter 7. Appendix B is an overview of the XMLHttpRequest API, and appendix C is a summary of the server-side calls for the chapter's project. Although the chapter is written deliberately so that you can use the server-side language of your choice, appendix C additionally includes a guide to the Spring MVC code that was used in the downloadable source. Appendix D is a simple guide for installing Node.js and Gulp.js, which you'll need if you want to try out the code for chapter 9.

Audience

This book assumes you have at least basic knowledge of JavaScript, HTML, and CSS. It's also helpful if you have some level of web development experience, although this isn't a requirement. This book does, however, target those who have little or no experience in the development of single-page applications or have created SPAs but not using the technologies described in this book.

Code conventions and downloads

Source code in listings or in text appears in a `fixed-width font like this` to separate it from ordinary text. Code annotations accompany the listings, highlighting important concepts.

Source code for the examples in this book can be downloaded from the publisher's website at www.manning.com/books/spa-design-and-architecture.

Software and hardware requirements

If you're using a recent Mac OS X or Windows computer and a modern browser (for example, Firefox, Safari, or Chrome), you should have no trouble with any of the examples. For any special software requirements, you'll find directions in the chapter/appendix itself.

Because most of the examples dynamically fetch HTML files, you may need to set certain privileges in your browser if you're running the example locally (versus using a server). Please see the readme.txt file in the downloadable source for the project for details.

If you want to try the example for chapter 7, you'll need to use some type of server and some type of server-side language. Everyone has their preferences, so it's left to you to decide what you want to use. I used Java/Spring MVC and include a mini guide to getting that set up. If you're using something else, I describe the server-side calls and objects conceptually so you can re-create them using the technology of your choice.

Author Online

Purchase of *SPA Design and Architecture* includes free access to a private web forum run by Manning Publications where you can make comments about the book, ask technical questions, and receive help from the author and from other users. To access the forum and subscribe to it, please go to www.manning.com/books/spa-design-and-architecture. This page provides information on how to get on the forum once you've registered, what kind of help is available, and the rules of conduct on the forum.

Manning's commitment to our readers is to provide a venue where a meaningful dialog between individual readers and between readers and the author can take place.

It's not a commitment to any specific amount of participation on the part of the authors whose contribution to the Author Online forum remains voluntary (and unpaid). We suggest you try asking the author some challenging questions lest his interest stray!

The Author Online forum and the archives of previous discussions will be accessible from the publisher's website as long as the book is in print.

About the author

 Emmit Scott is a senior software engineer and architect with more than 17 years of experience in creating web-based applications. He's developed large-scale applications for education, banking, and telecommunications. His hobbies include reading (especially Jim Butcher novels), playing the guitar (was a head banger back in the day), and spending as much time as possible with his children.

about the cover illustration

The figure on the cover of *SPA Design and Architecture* is captioned "Habit of a Young Turk of Quality in 1700." The illustration is taken from Thomas Jefferys' *A Collection of the Dresses of Different Nations, Ancient and Modern*, London, published between 1757 and 1772. The title page states that these are hand-colored copperplate engravings, heightened with gum arabic. Thomas Jefferys (1719–1771), was called "Geographer to King George III." He was an English cartographer who was the leading map supplier of his day. He engraved and printed maps for government and other official bodies and produced a wide range of commercial maps and atlases, especially of North America. His work as a mapmaker sparked an interest in local dress customs of the lands he surveyed and mapped, and which are brilliantly displayed in this four-volume collection.

Fascination with faraway lands and travel for pleasure were relatively new phenomena in the late 18th century and collections such as this one were popular, introducing both the tourist as well as the armchair traveler to the inhabitants of other countries. The diversity of the drawings in Jefferys' volumes speaks vividly of the uniqueness and individuality of the world's nations some 200 years ago. Dress codes have changed since then and the diversity by region and country, so rich at the time, has faded away. It is now often hard to tell the inhabitant of one continent from another. Perhaps, trying to view it optimistically, we have traded a cultural and visual diversity for a more varied personal life. Or a more varied and interesting intellectual and technical life.

At a time when it is hard to tell one computer book from another, Manning celebrates the inventiveness and initiative of the computer business with book covers based on the rich diversity of regional life of two centuries ago, brought back to life by Jeffreys' pictures.

Part 1

The basics

This part of the book will get you acquainted with some basic concepts you'll need to know before developing your first single-page web application.

In chapter 1, we'll talk about what an SPA is in very clear terms. It's important to know what this type of architecture involves and why you might choose it over that of a traditional web application.

Keeping your application's code base clean and maintainable becomes critical when working within the context of a single page. Chapter 2 compares different styles of JavaScript framework that help you achieve that goal. The chapter frames the discussion with an introduction to the three architectural patterns that heavily influenced these frameworks: MVC, MVP, and MVVM. The chapter then progresses into how the same application must change based on the style of framework that's implemented.

In chapter 3, you'll get a crash course on the module pattern and how it will change the way you think about organizing your JavaScript code. Using this pattern, you'll be able to create functions and variables as you normally would but within the cozy confines of a structure that mimics classic encapsulation in other languages. As you'll find out in this chapter, modular programming is crucial for a successful SPA.

What is a single-page application?

This chapter covers

- The definition of a single-page application (SPA)
- An overview of the basic elements of an SPA
- The benefits of SPAs over traditional web applications

Developers have been chasing the dream of delivering web applications with the look and feel of native desktop applications for about as long as they've been writing them. Various solutions for a more native-like experience, such as IFrames, Java applets, Adobe Flash, and Microsoft Silverlight, have been tried with varying degrees of success. Though different technologies, they all have at least one goal in common: bringing the power of a desktop app to the thin, cross-platform environment of a web browser. The single-page (web) application, or SPA, shares in this objective, but without a browser plugin or a new language to learn. The idea that a native-like experience can be realized using only JavaScript, HTML, and Cascading Style Sheets (CSS) is a tantalizing thought, but what is an SPA under the covers, and where did this idea begin?

The stage was set in the early 2000s. A brand-new way of thinking about web-page design came about when the AJAX movement started to gain steam. It began with an interesting, yet obscure, ActiveX control in Microsoft's Internet Explorer browser, used to send and receive data asynchronously. These humble beginnings eventually led to a revolution, when the control's functionality was officially adopted by the major browser vendors as the *XMLHttpRequest (XHR)* API.

Developers who began to merge this API with JavaScript, HTML, and CSS obtained remarkable results. The blending of these techniques became known as *AJAX*, or Asynchronous JavaScript and XML. AJAX's unobtrusive data requests, combined with the power of JavaScript to dynamically update the Document Object Model (DOM), and the use of CSS to change the page's style on the fly, brought AJAX to the forefront of modern web development.

Piggybacking off this successful movement, the SPA concept takes web development to a whole new level by expanding the page-level manipulation techniques of AJAX to the entire application. Additionally, the patterns and practices commonly used in the creation of an SPA can lead to overall efficiencies in application design, code maintenance, and development time. Having a successful implementation of a single-page application, though, will be greatly impacted by your understanding of SPA architecture.

As with most emerging solutions, single-page application design comprises a variety of approaches. Varying opinions by today's experts, plus a multitude of competing libraries and frameworks, can make finding the right solution for your SPA project challenging. The more you know going into it, the more successful you'll be in finding the implementation that's right for you and your development goals. That's why I'll start by providing a clear understanding of an SPA and its benefits. Over the course of the book, you'll examine each facet of SPA development by using a style of JavaScript frameworks commonly called *MV* frameworks*.

> **Not everything is MV***
>
> Our discussion of SPAs in this book is limited to MV* frameworks (and you'll learn more about them in chapter 2). It's important to make this distinction up front, however, because other approaches can be used to create an SPA, including using React (https://facebook.github.io/react) or Web Components (a W3C specification for a set of standards for component-based web development), for example.

1.1 SPA in a nutshell

In an SPA, the entire application runs as a single web page. In this approach, the presentation layer for the entire application has been factored out of the server and is managed from within the browser. To get a better idea of what this looks like, you'll review a couple of illustrations.

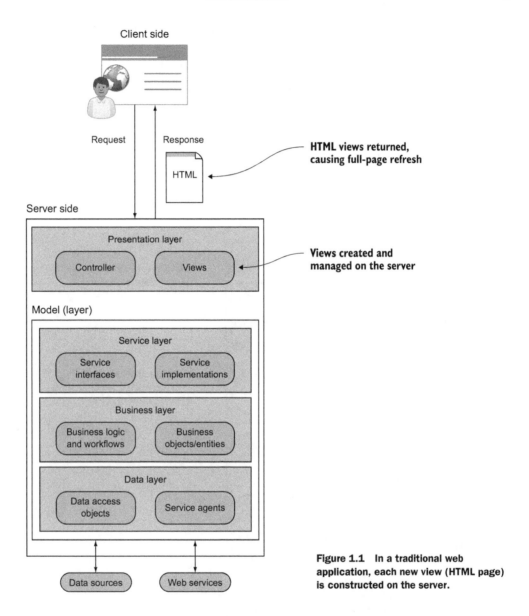

Figure 1.1 In a traditional web application, each new view (HTML page) is constructed on the server.

First, let's take a look at a web application that's not an SPA. Figure 1.1 shows a large web application that uses a traditional server-side design.

With this design, each request for a new view (HTML page) results in a round-trip to the server. When fresh data is needed on the client side, the request is sent to the server side. On the server side, the request is intercepted by a controller object inside the presentation layer. The controller then interacts with the model layer via the service layer, which determines the components required to complete the model layer's task. After the data is fetched, either by a data access object (DAO) or by a service agent, any necessary changes to the data are then made by the business logic in the business layer.

Control is passed back to the presentation layer, where the appropriate view is chosen. Presentation logic dictates how the freshly obtained data is represented in the selected view. Often the resulting view starts off as a source file with placeholders, where data is to be inserted (and possibly other rendering instructions). This file acts as a kind of template for how the view gets stamped whenever the controller routes a request to it.

After the data and view are merged, the view is returned to the browser. The browser then receives the new HTML page and, via a UI refresh, the user sees the new view containing the requested data.

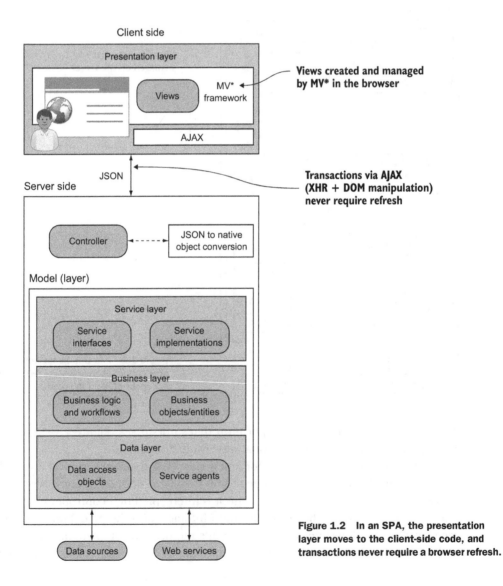

Figure 1.2   In an SPA, the presentation layer moves to the client-side code, and transactions never require a browser refresh.

Figure 1.2 demonstrates how this design could look as an SPA. Notice what has happened with the presentation layer and our transactions.

Moving the process for creating and managing views into the UI decouples it from the server. From an architectural standpoint, this gives the SPA an interesting advantage. Unless you're doing partial rendering on the server, the server is no longer required to be involved in how the data is presented.

The overall SPA design is nearly the same as the traditional design. The key changes are as follows: no full browser refreshes, the presentation logic resides in the client, and server transactions can be data-only, depending on your preference for data rendering.

1.1.1 No browser refreshes

In an SPA, views aren't complete HTML pages. They're merely portions of the DOM that make up the viewable areas of the screen. After the initial page load, all the tools required for creating and displaying views are downloaded and ready to use. If a new view is needed, it's generated locally in the browser and dynamically attached to the DOM via JavaScript. No browser refreshes are ever needed.

1.1.2 Presentation logic in the client

Because our presentation logic is mostly client side in an SPA, the task of combining HTML and data is moved from the server to the browser. As on the server side, source HTML contains placeholders where data is to be inserted (and possibly other rendering instructions). This client-side template is used as a basis for stamping out new views in the client. It's not template HTML for a complete page, though. It's for only the portion of the page the view represents.

The heavy lifting of routing to the correct view, combining data with the HTML template, and managing a view's lifecycle is typically delegated to a third-party Java-Script file commonly referred to as an *MV* framework* (sometimes called an *SPA framework*). Chapter 2 covers templates and MV* frameworks in detail.

1.1.3 Server transactions

In an SPA, several approaches can be used to render data from the server. These include server-side partial rendering, in which snippets of HTML are combined with data in the server's response. This book focuses on an alternative approach, in which rendering is done on the client and only data is sent and received during business transactions. This is always done asynchronously via the XHR API. The data-exchange format is typically JavaScript Object Notation (JSON), though it doesn't have to be. Even using client-side rendering, though, the server still plays a vital role in the SPA. Chapter 7 reviews the role of the server in more detail.

Even if you're already using a server-side design pattern such as Model-View-Controller (MVC) to separate views, data, and logic, reconfiguring your MVC framework for use with SPAs is relatively easy. Therefore, frameworks such as ASP.NET MVC or Spring MVC can still be used with an SPA.

1.2   *A closer look*

Now that you have a bird's-eye view of the SPA, let's break it down a little further. Let's talk about what's going on in the presentation layer now that it's moved to the browser. Because upcoming chapters provide more detail, I'll keep this discussion at a high level.

1.2.1   *An SPA starts with a shell*

The *single-page* part of the SPA refers to the initial HTML file, or *shell*. This single HTML file is loaded once and only once, and it serves as the starting point for the rest of the application. This is the only full browser load that happens in an SPA. Subsequent portions of the application are loaded dynamically and independently of the shell, without a full-page reload, giving the user the perception that the page has changed.

Typically, the shell is minimal in structure and often contains a single, empty DIV tag that will house the rest of the application's content (see figure 1.3). You can think of this shell HTML file as the mother ship and the initial container DIV as the docking bay.

The code for the shell has some of the basic starting elements of a traditional web page, such as a HEAD and BODY. The following listing illustrates a basic shell file.

Listing 1.1   Example SPA shell

```
<!DOCTYPE html>
<html>
<head>
    <title>Shell Example</title>
    <link rel="stylesheet"
        type="text/css"              Load the application's style sheets
        href="app/css/default.css">
</head>
<body>
    <div id="container"></div>       Initial container DIV
</body>
</html>
```

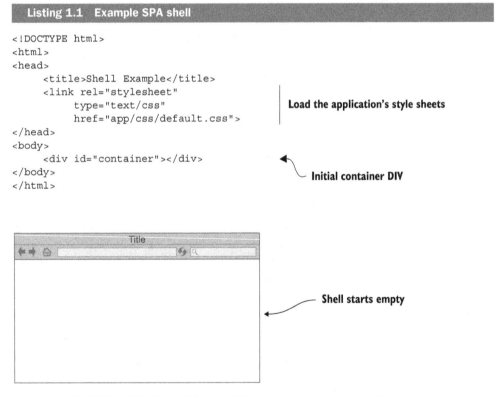

Figure 1.3   The HTML shell is the beginning structure. It has no content yet, only an empty DIV tag.

The initial container DIV can have child containers beneath it if the application's viewable area is divided into subsections. The child containers are often referred to as *regions*, because they're used to visually divide the screen into logical zones (see figure 1.4).

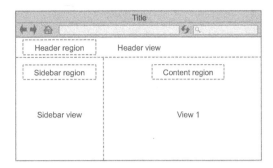

Regions help you divide the viewable area into manageable chunks of content. The region container DIV is where you tell the MV* framework to insert dynamic content. It's worth noting, though, that other paradigms are used by frameworks not covered in this book. React, for example, uses DOM patching rather than the replacement of particular regions.

Figure 1.4   Subsections of the shell are called regions. A region's content is provided by a view.

1.2.2   *From traditional pages to views*

The "pages" of the application aren't pages at all, at least not in the traditional sense. As the user navigates, the parts of the screen that appear to be pages are actually independent sections of the application's content, called *views*. Chapter 2 covers views in detail. For now, it's enough to know that the view is a portion of the application that the end user sees and interacts with.

Imagining the difference between the average web page and the view of an SPA can be difficult. To help you visualize the difference, take a look at the following figures. Figure 1.5 shows a simple website composed of two web pages. As you can see, both web pages of the traditional site contain the complete HTML structure, including the HEAD and BODY tags.

page1.html

```
<!DOCTYPE html>
<html>
<head>
      <title>Page 1</title>
      <link rel="style
      type="text/css"
      href="app/css/de
</head>
<body>
      <h1>page 1</h1>
</body>
</html>
```

page2.html

```
<!DOCTYPE html>
<html>
<head>
      <title>Page 2</title>
      <link rel="stylesheet"
      type="text/css"
      href="app/css/default.css">
</head>
<body>
      <h1>page 2</h1>
</body>
</html>
```

Figure 1.5   In traditional site design, each HTML file is a complete HTML page.

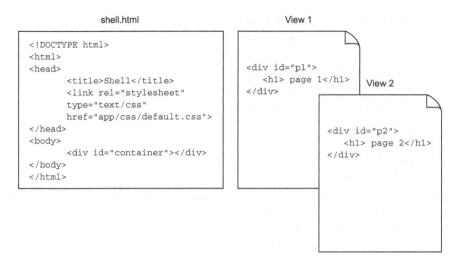

shell.html

```
<!DOCTYPE html>
<html>
<head>
        <title>Shell</title>
        <link rel="stylesheet"
        type="text/css"
        href="app/css/default.css">
</head>
<body>
        <div id="container"></div>
</body>
</html>
```

View 1

```
<div id="p1">
    <h1> page 1</h1>
</div>
```

View 2

```
<div id="p2">
    <h1> page 2</h1>
</div>
```

Figure 1.6   In an SPA design, one complete HTML file contains placeholders for the HTML fragments stored in view files.

Figure 1.6 shows the same website as an SPA. The SPA "pages" are only HTML fragments. If the content of the viewable area of the screen changes, that's the equivalent of changing pages in a traditional website.

When the application starts, the MV* framework inserts view 1. When the user navigates to what appears to be a new page, the framework is swapping view 1 for view 2. Chapter 4 covers SPA navigation in detail.

1.2.3   The birth of a view

If sections (or views) of the application aren't part of the initial shell, how do they become part of the application? As mentioned previously, the various sections of the SPA are presented on demand, usually as a result of user navigation. The skeletal HTML structure of each section, called a *template*, contains placeholders for data. JavaScript-based libraries and frameworks, commonly referred to as *MV**, are used to marry data and at least one template. This marriage ultimately results in the final view (see figure 1.7). All the screen's content beyond the shell gets placed into separate views.

```
{"firstName":"Karen",
"lastName":"Tate"}
```

```
<div>
        First Name: {{firstName}} <br>
        Last Name: {{lastName}}
</div>
```

First Name: Karen
Last Name: Tate

Server   Data   Template   View

Figure 1.7   A view is the marriage of data and one or more templates.

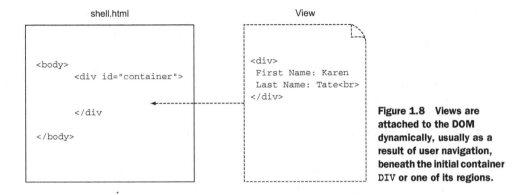

Figure 1.8 Views are attached to the DOM dynamically, usually as a result of user navigation, beneath the initial container DIV or one of its regions.

The completed view is attached to the DOM, as needed, either directly under the initial container DIV, as illustrated in figure 1.8, or in one of the regions if there are any.

1.2.4 View swapping for zero reload navigation

All of this happens without having to refresh the shell. So instead of getting served a new static page for every navigation request, the SPA can display new content without a disruption for the user. For a particular part of the screen, content of one view is merely replaced by the content of another view. This gives the illusion that the page itself is changing as the user navigates (see figure 1.9). Navigation without a reload is a key feature of the single-page application that gives it the feel of a native application.

MV* library/framework

shell.html

```
<!DOCTYPE html>
<html>
<head>
        <title>Shell</title>
        <link rel="stylesheet"
        type="text/css"
        href="app/css/default.css">
</head>
<body>
        <div id="container"></div>
</body>
</html>
```

View 1

```
<div id="p1">
  <h1> page 1</h1>
</div>
```

View 2

```
<div id="p2">
  <h1> page 2</h1>
</div>
```

Figure 1.9 Views in an SPA are seamlessly swapped (through DOM manipulation) for a given area of the screen, giving the user a more desktop-like feel.

The interesting thing about navigation in an SPA is that, to the user, it looks like the page is changing. The URL will look different, and even the Back button can be used to take the user to the previous "page."

Keep in mind that the heavy lifting of creating and managing the views in the client is handled by MV* frameworks. In chapter 2, you'll dissect their various parts to get an even clearer picture.

1.2.5   *Fluidity through dynamic updates*

Another defining aspect of the SPA is how data from the server can be retrieved asynchronously and inserted dynamically into the application. So not only does the page not reload during navigation, it also doesn't reload while requesting and receiving server data. This, too, gives the appearance and feel of a native application. The techniques of AJAX make this all possible. I began this chapter by talking about the natural evolution of web development and how AJAX played a pivotal role in the development of the SPA concept. So I'd be remiss if I didn't include AJAX as part of the SPA definition.

Previously, I explained in great detail how the page, or view, is swapped dynamically during navigation. Domain data from the server, or from cache, can also be added and removed in the same fashion. The retrieval of the data, which happens silently in the background, can happen in parallel with other data requests. After the data is fetched, it's combined with the HTML template, and the view is updated in real time. The ability to update the page right in front of the user's eyes without even as much as a flicker gives the application a certain fluidity and sleekness that can't be attained with a traditional web application. Chapter 7 covers accessing data in greater detail.

1.3   *Benefits of SPAs over traditional web applications*

The web browser is still a great way to distribute software because of its "thinness," ubiquity, and standardized environment. End users will already have a web browser. It's also great for software updates, because the updates happen on the server instead of users having to worry about the installation process. Unfortunately, jarring, full-page reloads, content being duplicated with every request, and heavy transaction payloads have all diminished the benefits of browser-delivered content.

Web-based customer interactions are far from over, though. Just the opposite is true, and SPAs are at the forefront of this user-experience revolution. The idea of the single-page application was born out of our desire to give end users the best experience possible. Here are some reasons you should consider single-page application architecture:

- *Renders like a desktop application, but runs in a browser*—The SPA has the ability to redraw portions of the screen dynamically, and the user sees the update instantly. Because the SPA downloads the web-page structure in advance, there's no need for the disruptive request to get a new page from the server. This is similar to the experience a user would get from a native desktop application;

therefore, it "feels" more natural. An advantage over even the desktop application, the SPA runs in the browser, making its native-like, browser-based environment the best of both worlds.

- *Decoupled presentation layer*—As mentioned previously, the code that governs how the UI appears and how it behaves is kept on the client side instead of the server. This leaves both server and client as decoupled as possible. The benefit here is that each can be maintained and updated separately.

- *Faster, lightweight transaction payloads*—Transactions with the server are lighter and faster, because after initial delivery, only data is sent and received from the server. Traditional applications have the overhead of having to respond with the next page's content. Because the entire page is re-rendered, the content returned in traditional applications also includes HTML markup. Asynchronous, data-only transactions make the operational aspect of this architecture extremely fast.

- *Less user wait time*—In today's web-centric world, the less time a user has to wait for the page to load, the more likely the person is to stay on the site and return in the future. Because the SPA loads with a shell and a small number of supporting files and then builds as the user navigates, application startup is perceived as being quick. As the previous points state, screens render quickly and smoothly, and transactions are lightweight and fast. These characteristics all lead to less user wait time. Performance isn't just a nice-to-have. It equates to real dollars when online commerce is involved. A study by Walmart that was published in *Web Performance Today*[1] indicated that for every 100 ms of performance improvement, incremental revenue grew by up to 1%. In Walmart terms, that's huge.

- *Easier code maintenance*—Software developers are always looking for better ways to develop and maintain their code base. Traditionally, web applications are a bit of a Wild West kind of environment, where HTML, JavaScript, and CSS can be intertwined into a maintenance nightmare. Add in the ability to combine server-side code with the HTML source (think Active Server Pages or JavaServer Pages scriptlets) and you've got a giant, steaming pile of goo. As you'll see in upcoming chapters, MV* frameworks like the ones covered in this book help us separate our code into different areas of concern. JavaScript code is kept where it needs to be—out of the HTML and in distinct units. With the help of third-party libraries and frameworks (for example, Knockout, Backbone.js, and AngularJS), the HTML structure for an area of the screen and its data can be maintained separately. The amount of coupling between the client and the server is dramatically reduced as well.

---

[1] www.webperformancetoday.com/2012/02/28/4-awesome-slides-showing-how-page-speed-correlates-to-business-metrics-at-walmart-com

1.4   *Rethinking what you already know*

In a single-page web application, you use the same languages that you normally use when creating a web application: HTML, CSS, and JavaScript. There's no browser plugin required and no magic SPA language to learn. HTML and CSS continue to be the primary building blocks for the UI's structure and layout, whereas JavaScript is still the cornerstone for interactivity and UI logic (see figure 1.10).

The difference to the user is in how the application will feel using SPA architecture. The navigation feels more like a native desktop application, delivering a smoother, more enjoyable experience. This difference for you, the developer, is that to create an application

SPA client

CSS: styles and layout

HTML: structure

JavaScript: behavior

Figure 1.10   CSS, HTML, and JavaScript are the building blocks for the single-page application. There's no special language to learn and no browser plugins required.

that functions within a single HTML page, you'll need to rethink your normal approach to web development.

As mentioned in the previous section, in an SPA, the application is broken into independent sections, or views. So you'll no longer create entire pages in which common elements, such as a header or a main menu, are repeated. Even the common sections are views in an SPA. You'll also have to stop thinking about the layout of individual pages and start thinking in terms of view placement in the available real estate of the screen. As it turns out, this is easy after you get the hang of it. Global layout areas, such as a main menu, remain fixed throughout the user experience. Shared areas of the screen, such as the center content well, are reused by the application to swap the various views (as well as entire regions) during user navigation.

To the end user, though, the application can *look* exactly like a traditional web application. As figure 1.11 illustrates, it can have a header, a sidebar, or any other typical web-page element.

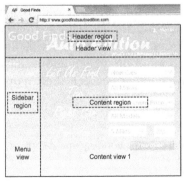

Figure 1.11   Using regions, an SPA's views can be placed so that it looks exactly like a traditional web page.

On the JavaScript side, you'll continue to code as you normally would, with one major exception. Because you're dealing with a single page that doesn't refresh, simple global scope for variables and functions won't suffice. You'll divide your code into workable units and house it in special functions called *modules* that have their own scope. This frees you from having to create all your variables and functions in the global namespace.

Communication with the server in an SPA is via AJAX. Though the name implies XML, most modern SPAs use AJAX techniques but use JSON as the preferred data-exchange format. It's an ideal format for the SPA because it's lightweight and compact, and its syntax is well-suited for describing object structure. But AJAX should be nothing new to most developers. Even traditional web applications typically use at least some AJAX.

Your overall design will revolve around keeping all the SPA code easily manageable and decoupled from other areas of concern. But don't worry about any extra complexity. Once you get the hang of the unusual syntax of the module pattern, your life as a developer will get easier. I present modular programming in detail later in the book and use variants of the module design pattern in all the examples. So no worries—you'll see it so much that by the end of the book it'll be second nature to you!

1.5 Ingredients of a well-designed SPA

If you researched the topic of single-page applications before picking up this book, you may have felt a little overwhelmed at your choices. As you've seen so far, the SPA isn't a single technology. It's a federation of technologies that work together to create the finished product. There are almost as many libraries and frameworks as there are opinions about the correct approach to take. So admittedly, trying to find the pieces of the puzzle that not only fit together but also fit the needs of your project and the preferences of your team can be rather daunting.

The good news is that there's a method to the madness. If you look at the single-page application concept as a whole, it can be broken into a list of categories that can fit any style of solution you adopt as your own.

1.5.1 Organizing your project

Having a well-organized project isn't complicated, but it does require some thought and shouldn't be taken for granted. Fortunately, no hard-and-fast rules apply to directory structures. The general rule of thumb is that you should use whatever style works for the development team. A couple of common ways to organize your files are by feature and by functionality.

Grouping similar files by feature is somewhat akin to organizing code in a compiled language, such as Java, into packages. It's clean, discourages the cross-referencing of features, and visually segments files related to a particular feature within the project's file structure. The following listing illustrates how the client code for an application might be arranged using this style.

Listing 1.2 Sample directory structure (by feature)

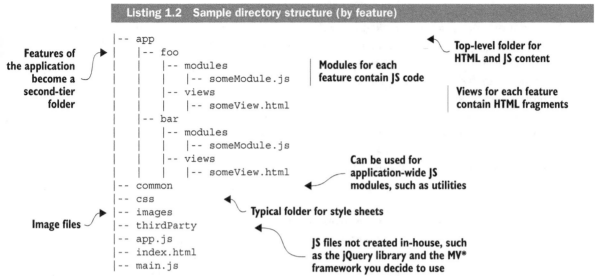

A modified version of the *by feature* directory structure was proposed in the AngularJS style guide.[2] It favors a simplified version of listing 1.2, which eliminates the named functionality folders under each feature. The blog entry is a good read and has several variations based on the size and complexity of the application; the gist of the structure is specified in the following listing. In this version, boundaries are removed from the various file types within a feature. The style guide argues that this simpler version still groups things by feature but is more readable and creates a more standardized structure for AngularJS tools.

Listing 1.3 Simplified "by feature" directory structure

Alternatively, you and your development team might elect to organize the project by functionality (see listing 1.4). This is perfectly acceptable as well. Most SPA libraries and frameworks aren't that opinionated when it comes to directory structure. The choices come down to preference. If you do choose to organize your directory by functionality, it's still a good idea to include the name of the feature as a subfolder under the functionality. Otherwise, under each functionality folder, you'll end up

---

[2] http://blog.angularjs.org/2014/02/an-angularjs-style-guide-and-best.html or http://angularjs.blogspot.co
.uk/2014/02/an-angularjs-style-guide-and-best.html

having many unrelated files together. That might be all right for smaller applications, but for large applications, this leads to a sort of "junk drawer" effect.

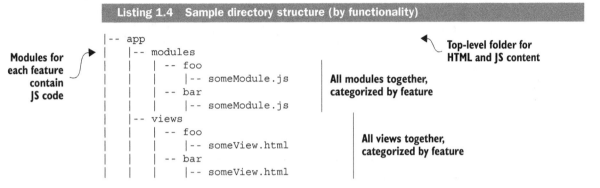

Listing 1.4 Sample directory structure (by functionality)

```
|-- app
|   |-- modules
|   |   |-- foo
|   |   |   |-- someModule.js
|   |   |-- bar
|   |   |   |-- someModule.js
|   |-- views
|   |   |-- foo
|   |   |   |-- someView.html
|   |   |-- bar
|   |   |   |-- someView.html
```

Modules for each feature contain JS code

Top-level folder for HTML and JS content

All modules together, categorized by feature

All views together, categorized by feature

The preceding two listings are pretty basic, to give you the idea. The size of the application, architecture choices, and personal preferences also influence the types of folders used and their names. The term *modules* might be labeled *js* or *scripts*. Instead of *views*, you might choose *templates*. Even the type of framework you incorporate might influence the way you choose to create your directory structure. If you're creating an AngularJS project, for example, you might also have other folders such as *controllers*, *directives*, and *services*.

However you choose to stack it, having an agreed-upon file structure and sticking to that organizational model will greatly enhance your chances for a successful project.

1.5.2 *Creating a maintainable, loosely coupled UI*

Having clean, organized JavaScript code is a step in the right direction for building scalable, maintainable single-page applications. Layering the code so that the JavaScript and HTML can be as loosely coupled as possible is another tremendous step. This approach still allows HTML and JavaScript to interact but removes the need for direct references in the code.

How are these separate layers achieved? Enter MV* patterns. Patterns to separate data, logic, and the UI's view have been around for years. Some of the most notable ones are Model-View-Controller (MVC), Model-View-Presenter (MVP), and Model-View-ViewModel (MVVM). In recent years, these patterns have begun appearing in the form of JavaScript libraries and frameworks to help apply these same concepts to the front end of web applications. The basic idea is that a framework or library, outside your own logic, manages the relationship between the JavaScript and the HTML. The MV* libraries and frameworks allow you to design the UI such that domain data (the model) and the resulting HTML "page" the user interacts with (the view) can communicate but are maintained separately in code. The last component of the MV* pattern, the controller or ViewModel or presenter, acts as the orchestrator of all this.

MV* library/framework

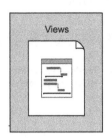 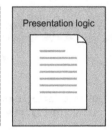 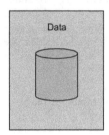

Figure 1.12   Keeping the presentation layers segregated based on their purpose allows designers and developers to work in parallel. It also allows developers to test, maintain, and deploy code more effectively.

Keeping the view, logic, and data separated, as in figure 1.12, is an effective tool in the design of a single-page application.

Achieving this level of separation in your SPA has the following advantages:

- Designers and developers can more effectively collaborate. When the view is void of logic, each resource can work in parallel toward the same goal without stepping on each other's toes.
- Separate view and logic layers can also help developers create cleaner unit tests, because they have to worry about only the nonvisual aspect of a feature.
- Separate layers help with maintenance and deployments. Isolated code can more easily be changed without affecting other parts of the application.

It's OK if this facet of SPA development still seems a little murky at this point. This is one of the harder concepts to grasp. Don't worry, though. Chapter 2 covers the MV* patterns thoroughly.

1.5.3   *Using JavaScript modules*

Having an elegant way of allowing all your JavaScript code to coexist harmoniously in the same browser page is a necessity in an SPA. You can achieve this by placing the functionality of your application into modules. Modules are a way to group together distinct pieces of functionality, hiding some parts while exposing others. In the ECMAScript 6 version of JavaScript, modules will be supported natively. Meanwhile, various patterns, such as the module pattern, have emerged that you can use as a fallback.

In a traditional web application, whenever the page is reloaded, it's like getting a clean slate. All the previous JavaScript objects that were created get wiped away, and objects for the new page are created. This not only frees memory for the new page but also ensures that the names of a page's functions and variables don't have any chance of conflicting with those of another page. This isn't the case with a single-page application. Having a single page means that you don't wipe the slate clean every time the user requests a new view. Modules help you remedy this dilemma.

The module limits the scope of your code. Variables and functions defined within each module have a scope that's local to its containing structure (see figure 1.13).

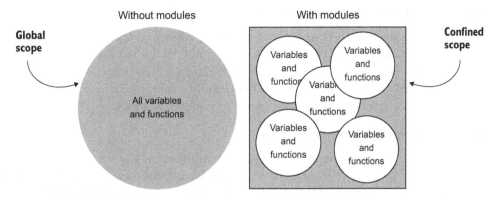

Figure 1.13 Using the module pattern limits the scope of variables and functions to the module itself. This helps avoid many of the pitfalls associated with global scope in a single-page application.

The module pattern, combined with other techniques to manage modules and their dependencies, gives programmers a practical way to design large, robust web applications with single-page architecture.

This book covers the topic of modular programming with JavaScript quite extensively. Chapter 3 provides an introduction. You'll also explore the topic of script loaders, which help manage the modules and their dependencies. Throughout the entire book, you'll rely on the module pattern to help build your examples.

1.5.4 *Performing SPA navigation*

Chapter 4 provides an in-depth look at client-side routing. To give users the feeling that they're navigating somewhere, single-page applications normally incorporate the idea of *routing* in their design: JavaScript code, either in the MV* framework or via a third-party library, associates a URL-style path with functionality. The paths usually look like relative URLs and serve as catalysts for arriving at a particular view as the user navigates through the application. Routers can dynamically update the browser's URL, as well as allow users to use the Forward and Back buttons. This further promotes the idea that a new destination is reached when part of the screen changes.

1.5.5 *Creating view composition and layout*

In a single-page application, the UI is constructed with views instead of new pages. The creation of content regions and the placement of views within those regions determine your application's layout. Client-side routing is used to connect the dots. All of these elements come together to impact both the application's usability and its aesthetic appeal.

In chapter 5, you'll look at how to approach view composition and layout in an SPA, tackling both simple and complex designs.

1.5.6   Enabling module communication

Modules encapsulate our logic and provide individual units of work. Although this helps decouple and privatize our code, we still need a way for modules to communicate with each other. In chapter 6, you'll learn the basic ways in which modules communicate. In doing so, you'll also learn about a design pattern called *pub/sub*, which allows one module to broadcast messages to other modules.

1.5.7   Communicating with the server

I began our definition of a single-page application by discussing the metamorphosis that web pages have undergone since the introduction of the XMLHttpRequest API. The collection of techniques, called AJAX, that revolve around this API is at the heart of the SPA. The ability to asynchronously fetch data and repaint portions of the screen is a staple of single-page architecture. After all, in an SPA we create the illusion for users that, as they navigate, the screen is somehow changing smoothly and effortlessly. So what would this feat of showmanship by the application be without the ability to acquire data for our users?

Chapter 7 focuses on using our MV* frameworks to make calls to our server. You'll see how these frameworks abstract away a lot of the boilerplate code used in making requests and processing results. In doing so, you'll learn about something called a *promise* and a style of web service called a *RESTful service*.

1.5.8   Performing unit testing

An important but overlooked part of designing a successful single-page application is testing your JavaScript code. We test our back-end code to smithereens. Unfortunately, JavaScript unit tests aren't always performed so religiously. Today, many good unit-testing libraries are available. In chapter 8, you'll get an introduction to basic JavaScript unit testing with a framework called QUnit.

1.5.9   Using client-side automation

In chapter 9, you'll learn about using client-side automation not only to create a build process for your SPA but also to automate common development tasks.

1.6   Summary

Here's a quick recap of what you've learned about SPAs so far:

- SPAs are an approach to web development in which the entire application is housed in a single page.
- In an SPA, no full-page refreshes occur after the application loads. Instead, presentation logic is loaded up front and presented in terms of view swapping within content regions.
- SPAs communicate with the server asynchronously. Often the data format used in this communication is JSON-formatted text.

- MV* frameworks provide the mechanism used by SPAs to marry data from our server requests with the views the user sees and interacts with. There are alternatives to MV* not covered in the book, particularly when using technologies such as React or Web Components.
- Instead of relying on global variables and functions, the JavaScript code in an SPA is organized using modules. Modules provide state and/or data encapsulation. They also help code stay decoupled and more easily maintained.
- Some of the benefits of an SPA include a desktop-like feel, a decoupled presentation layer, faster and lighter payloads, less user wait time, and easier code maintenance.

The role of MV* frameworks

This chapter covers

- An overview of UI design patterns
- An introduction to MV* in the browser
- Exposure to core MV* concepts
- Benefits of MV* libraries/frameworks
- A list of considerations when choosing a framework

Probably one of the most difficult tasks a web developer faces is creating a code base that can grow gracefully as the project grows. The larger and more complicated a project becomes, the more difficult the task. Shaping a project's code base in a way that makes troubleshooting, maintenance, and enhancements easier, not harder, is no small feat, though. This is true for even traditional web projects.

In an SPA, keeping your code segregated based on its functionality is more than just a good practice. It's critical to being able to successfully implement an application as a single page. The key to this is creating a separation of concerns within your application. Having a separation of concerns within your code base means that you're making a concerted effort to separate the various aspects of the application's code based on the responsibility it has.

```
<button style="background-color: #ccc;" onClick="if(formValid && !formChanged){showConfirmation();}">
      Confirm
</button>
```

Figure 2.1   Indiscriminately interweaving JavaScript, HTML, and CSS makes your project more difficult to manage as it grows.

We can break the overall SPA into many application layers, on the server side as well as in the client. Within the browser space, we can begin our quest for creating a separation of concerns in a fundamental way by first remembering the roles of our three primary languages: HTML, CSS, and JavaScript:

- *HTML*—This is the scaffolding of your application. This code is primarily concerned with the elements that provide placeholders for content, give the UI its structure, and offer controls the user can interact with.
- *CSS*—Style sheets describe the design of the UI, giving it its look and formatting.
- *JavaScript*—In a general sense, the code in this layer represents the application's presentation logic. This layer is used to give a web application its dynamic nature, providing behavior and programmatic control over the other two layers.

We've all worked with these three languages and understand the role of each. Even so, because these three languages can easily be mixed together, your code can quickly turn into spaghetti (see figure 2.1). This can make your project extremely challenging to manage.

It's possible, however, to produce code written in a decoupled manner but still achieve the same level of interactivity between each layer. Each part of your code can be compartmentalized based on the purpose it serves.

Additionally, this compartmentalization can be extended to encompass the application's data versus its presentation to the user. Data and events can be assigned to your UI via mapping, instead of direct assignment in your business logic. The UI and the data can both be observed for changes, allowing them to stay in sync and giving your logic a means to react appropriately. So not only can the code itself be segregated based on its responsibility, but your UI's presentation and the data it represents can be disjoined. This achieves yet another level of separation in your application (see figure 2.2).

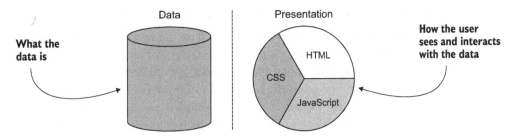

Figure 2.2   The data of your application can be separated from its representation in the UI.

Although it's entirely possible for you to create a homemade solution to manage all these layers of separation, it's probably not where you want to spend your development time. Thankfully, though, a myriad of libraries and frameworks are ideal for just such a task. If used in your application, they can play a key role in creating a successful separation of concerns by externally managing the relationship between your logic, data, and the UI. In varying degrees, they also provide many other features to assist you in building your SPA.

This chapter defines JavaScript MV*, briefly discusses its evolution from traditional UI design patterns, and discusses what these frameworks do for us. The chapter also breaks down some common MV* concepts, using three MV* frameworks to illustrate different approaches to the same objective. As mentioned in chapter 1, not everything is MV*. My focus in this book, however, is on the MV* style of frameworks.

To further demonstrate how the same concepts are prevalent in MV*, even though the approach may differ, you'll create a small but reasonably realistic online directory project with each framework. I'll abbreviate the code samples in the text so the concepts don't get lost in the code. (The code for all three versions is available in appendix A, with a complete code walk-through. And the code for each is available for download online.)

The end of the chapter includes a list of things to consider when selecting a framework that's right for you. Because all MV* implementations are different approaches to the same problem, you'll ultimately have to decide which one is the right fit for you. There's no clear right or wrong answer that fits all situations. Once you understand the role of MV* and its underlying patterns, though, you'll be able to select one that best fits your environment. After all, no one knows your situation better than you do. You know the factors that affect your project, your end users, your budget, your timelines, and your development resources.

2.1   *What is MV*?*

The term *MV** represents a family of browser-based frameworks that provide support for achieving a separation of concerns in your application's code base, as discussed in the introduction. These frameworks have their roots in traditional UI design patterns, but the degree to which they follow a pattern varies from implementation to implementation.

In MV*, the *M* stands for *model* and the *V* stands for *view*. Section 2.2 covers them in depth, but for this discussion let's briefly summarize each term:

- *Model*—The model typically contains data, business logic, and validation logic. Conceptually, it might represent something like a customer or a payment. The model is never concerned with how data is presented.
- *View*—The view is what the user sees and interacts with. It's a visual representation of the model's data. It can be a simple structure that relies on other parts of the framework for updates and responses to user interactions or it can contain logic, again depending on the MV* implementation.

As you'll see in section 2.1.1, traditional UI design patterns include a third component, which helps manage the relationship between the model and the view, as well
their relationship with the application's user. Although most modern browser-based
UI design frameworks based on MVC/MVVM have some notion of a model and a view,
it's the third component that varies, in both name and the duty it performs. Therefore, people have generally settled on the wildcard (*) to represent whatever the third
component might be.

Section 2.1.2 presents a lot more about MV* in the browser. First, though, let's find
out a little about traditional UI design patterns, which form the roots of MV*. Knowing
how we got here will help you get a better idea of why things work the way they do.

2.1.1 Traditional UI design patterns

Using architectural patterns to separate data, logic, and the resulting representation
of the output is a notion that has been around for a long, long time. Central to these
design patterns is the idea that an application's code is easier to design, develop, and
maintain if it's segmented based on the type of responsibility each layer has.

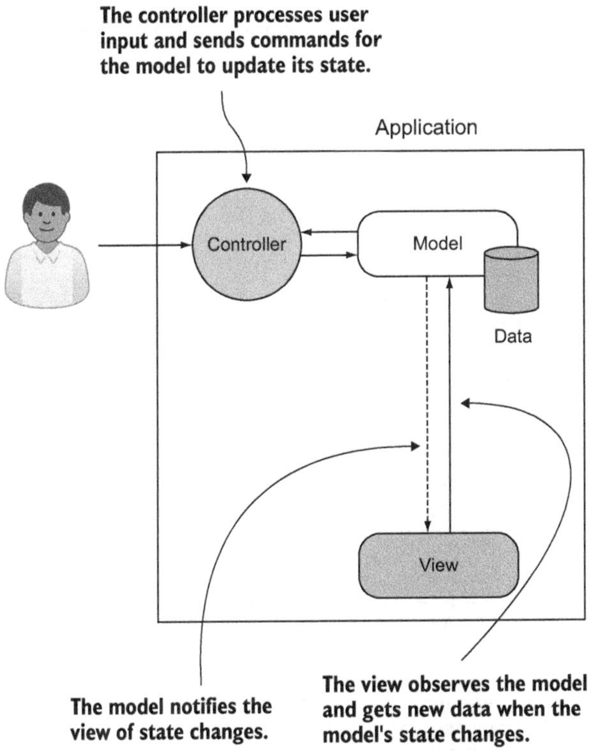

This section details the three patterns that have had the most influence
on client-side approaches: Model-
View-Controller (MVC), Model-View-
Presenter (MVP), and Model-View-
ViewModel (MVVM). After a proper
introduction to these design patterns,
you'll see in section 2.1.2 how they
relate to the MV* frameworks we see in
the browser today.

MODEL-VIEW-CONTROLLER

Model-View-Controller (MVC) is one of
the oldest patterns to try to separate
data, logic, and presentation. MVC
was proposed by Trygve Reenskaug
and later implemented in the Small-
talk programming language in the
1970s.

MVC was instrumental in the design
of graphical user interfaces then and
still is today. Since its inception, it and
its variants have become common
design patterns for all types of software development. The MVC pattern
includes the model, the view, and a
controller (see figure 2.3):

The controller processes user
input and sends commands for
the model to update its state.

The model notifies the
view of state changes.

The view observes the model
and gets new data when the
model's state changes.

**Figure 2.3   The MVC design pattern has been used for many
years in the development of graphical user interfaces.**

- *Controller*—The controller is the entry point for the application, receiving signals from controls in the UI. It also contains the logic that processes the user input and sends commands to the model to update its state based on the input received.

The interactions with the controller set off a chain of events that eventually lead to an update of the view. The view is aware of the model in this pattern and is updated when changes are observed.

MODEL-VIEW-PRESENTER

In 1996, a subsidiary of IBM called Taligent came up with a variation of MVC called *Model-View-Presenter*, or *MVP*. The idea behind this pattern was to further decouple the model from the other two components of MVC. Under MVP, a controller-like object and the view would jointly represent the user interface, or *presentation*. The model would continue to represent data management. As noted in figure 2.4, in MVP, there's no controller acting as a gatekeeper. Each view is backed by a component called a presenter:

- *Presenter*—The presenter contains the view's presentation logic. The view merely responds to user interactions by delegating responsibility to the presenter. The presenter has direct access to the model for any necessary changes and propagates data changes back to the view. In this way, it acts as a "middleman" between the model and the view.

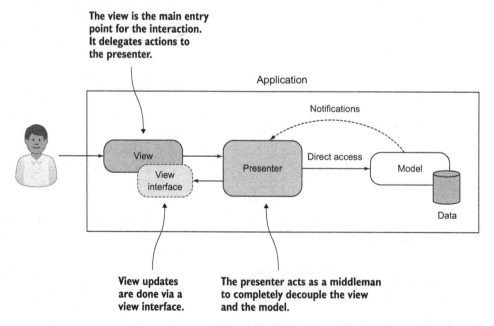

Figure 2.4   MVP is a variation of MVC. With this pattern, the view is the entry point, but its logic is in the presenter.

The presenter takes on the task of keeping the view and model updated. Having an object in the middle allows the view and model to have more-focused responsibilities.

MODEL-VIEW-VIEWMODEL

Model-View-ViewModel (MVVM) was proposed by John Gossman in 2005 as a way to simplify and standardize the process of creating user interfaces for use with Microsoft's Windows Presentation Foundation (WPF). It's another design pattern that emerged to try to organize the code associated with the UI into something sensible and manageable, while still keeping the various components of the process separate.

As in MVP, the view itself is the point of entry. Also like MVP, this model has an object that sits between the model and the view (see figure 2.5). The third component in this pattern is called the ViewModel:

- *ViewModel*—The ViewModel is a model or representation of the view in code, in addition to being the middleman between the model and the view. Anything needed to define and manage the view is contained within the ViewModel. This includes data properties as well as presentation logic. Each data point in the model that needs to be reflected in the view is mapped to a matching property in the ViewModel. Like a presenter in MVP, each view is backed by a ViewModel. It's aware of changes in both the view and the model and keeps the two in sync.

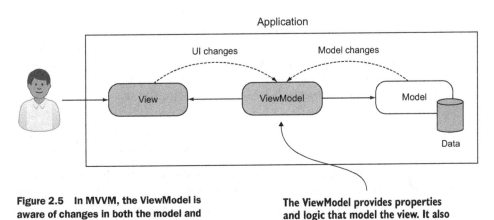

Figure 2.5   In MVVM, the ViewModel is aware of changes in both the model and the view and keeps the two in sync.

The ViewModel provides properties and logic that model the view. It also keeps the model and view in sync.

Now that you know a little about traditional UI design patterns, you can better understand browser-side MV* approaches. Let's fast-forward, then, and talk about the MV* we see in the browser.

2.1.2   *MV* and the browser environment*

Just like application code running on the server or natively as a desktop application, code running in the browser can benefit from using good architectural design patterns. In recent years, many frameworks have cropped up, aiming to fulfill this need.

Most are based on MVC, MVP, or MVVM to some degree. The browser is a different sort of environment, though, and we're dealing with three languages at once (JavaScript, HTML, and CSS). Therefore, it's difficult to perfectly match a browser-side MV* framework with a design pattern. Trying to pigeonhole them into one category or another is, in most cases, a fruitless undertaking. Design patterns should be malleable strategies, not inflexible directives.

One of the reasons why the term *MV** sprang up in the first place is that it's often hard to nail down what the third concept in the framework is. The term represents sort of a compromise, to cease the endless disputes about whether particular frameworks are more this pattern or more that pattern.

The remnants of the traditional patterns are there but are loosely interpreted. Each one has some form of the data model, whether it's in the form of a *POJO* (plain old JavaScript object) or some model structure dictated by the implementation. Each also has some notion of a view. The third cog in the machine might be a little more elusive, though. The framework might employ an explicit controller, presenter, or ViewModel. But it might have some sort of hybrid or not have the third part at all!

Derick Bailey, creator of Marionette.js for Backbone.js, put things rather eloquently in one of his online posts, titled "Backbone.js Is Not an MVC Framework":

> *Ultimately, trying to cram Backbone into a pattern language that doesn't fit is a bad idea. We end up in useless arguments and overblown, wordy blog posts like this one, because no one can seem to agree on which cookie-cutter pattern name something fits into. Backbone, in my opinion, is not MVC. It's also not MVP, nor is it MVVM (like Knockout.js) or any other specific, well-known name. It takes bits and pieces from different flavors of the MV* family and it creates a very flexible library of tools that we can use to create amazing websites. So, I say we toss MVC/MVP/MVVM out the window and just call it part of the MV* family.*
>
> Source: http://lostechies.com/derickbailey/2011/12/23/
> backbone-js-is-not-an-mvc-framework/

Many other people share this same viewpoint about the fruitlessness of trying to one-for-one match today's MV* with a traditional design pattern. The idea of the usefulness of the framework taking priority over its categorization gained even more steam when the AngularJS team weighed in with a similar conclusion about their framework. Igor Minar (from the AngularJS team) famously blogged that developers will argue endlessly about how to categorize a particular MV* framework. He went on to state that AngularJS started out more like MVC, but over time it has become a little more like MVVM. In truth, it's a little like both. In this same blog entry, he proposes the term *MVW*, which has since stuck:

> *I'd rather see developers build kick-ass apps that are well-designed and follow separation of concerns than see them waste time arguing about MV* nonsense. And for this reason, I hereby declare AngularJS to be MVW framework—Model-View-Whatever. Where Whatever stands for whatever works for you.*
>
> Source: https://plus.google.com/+IgorMinar/posts/DRUAkZmXjNV

Knowing that most MV* implementations only loosely base their design on the original pattern helps us remember that it's not so important to try to brand the framework as one pattern or another.

2.2 *Common MV* concepts*

Now that you know what MV* is, let's go over a few common concepts that are frequently found, no matter the implementation. In the examples for each concept, you'll quickly begin to see that even though the syntax and approach may vary between frameworks, the ideas are the same. Before we begin, let's take a moment to review at a high level the concepts covered in this section:

- *Models*—Models represent the data of our application. They contain properties and possibly logic to access and manage the data, including validation. The model often contains business logic as well.
- *Views*—Views are what the user sees and interacts with and are where models are visually represented. In some MV* implementations, views may also contain presentation logic.
- *Templates*—Templates are the reusable building blocks for views when dynamic content is needed. They contain placeholders for data, as well as other instructions for how content in the template should be rendered. One or more templates will be used to create a view in an SPA.
- *Binding*—This term describes the process of associating the data from a model with an element in a template. Some MV* implementations also provide other types of binding, such as bindings for events and CSS styles.

Figure 2.6 gives a big-picture view of how these concepts relate to each other in an SPA. These concepts are probably the least common denominator in building SPAs. Other features, such as routing (covered in chapter 4), are also common (and necessary) but may not be provided universally. Not to worry, though. I cover many of the other concepts later in the book. We just need a sound foundation to begin with.

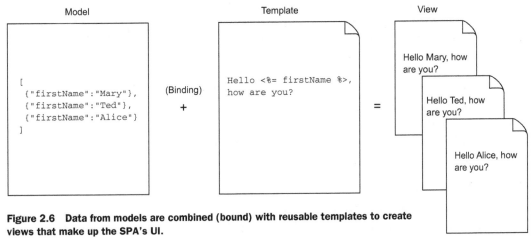

Figure 2.6 Data from models are combined (bound) with reusable templates to create views that make up the SPA's UI.

2.2.1   Meet the frameworks

Because we're using three frameworks for illustration in this section, some introductions are in order. Each represents a slightly different approach to these basic MV* concepts. Seeing the different approaches, though, should give you a broader perspective ultimately. The three frameworks are as follows:

Description: As mentioned before, Backbone.js doesn't perfectly fit a traditional design pattern but could be described as being somewhere between MVC and MVP. Backbone.js is code driven. Models and views are created programmatically, using JavaScript code in this

URL: http://backbonejs.org

framework, by extending Backbone.js objects. By extending core objects, you automatically inherit a lot of built-in functionality. The framework also provides other out-of-the-box features to make routine tasks easier. Backbone.js doesn't provide everything you'll need in your SPA, though, so you must fill certain gaps using other libraries or frameworks.

Description: Knockout may not perfectly fit with the original MVVM definition, but it's fairly close. In this framework, the model is *any* source of data, not an explicit object structure prescribed by the framework. Views and templates are created with plain HTML. The ViewModels that map model data to UI elements

URL: http://knockoutjs.com

and provide views with behavior are created programmatically using JavaScript code, but most everything else is done *declaratively* by adding custom attributes to the HTML. Knockout is mainly concerned with making the binding process clean and easy. Though this makes the framework small and superbly focused, it leaves you to look to other frameworks and libraries for all other SPA requirements.

Description: AngularJS humbly describes itself as the "Superheroic JavaScript MVW Framework." The creators of AngularJS designed it to be a one-stop-shopping kind of framework. Most, if not all, of your SPA needs are covered by this framework. AngularJS mixes and matches concepts that its creators liked

URL: https://angularjs.org

from traditional patterns, as well as from other popular frameworks, to come up with a nicely balanced palette of out-of-the-box features. Part of your work in this framework will be done programmatically via JavaScript code, and part will be done declaratively using custom HTML attributes.

2.2.2   Meet our MV* project

To help illustrate our list of common concepts, you'll create a simple online employee directory. You'll create it three ways, using each of the frameworks previously described. Later in the book, you'll learn about more-advanced topics, such as routing and server transactions. For now, you'll stick to the basics for this project. Our example, though somewhat contrived, still covers basic CRUD operations over a list. That should be sufficiently challenging for an introduction.

Let's go over our objectives for this example:

- Create a simple SPA to enter employee information.
- Build an easy-to-use UI for entering each employee's first name, last name, title, email, and phone.
- Keep track of each entry as part of a list, with the screen split between the entry form on the left and the directory's entry list on the right.
- Have two buttons on the entry side of the SPA: one to add a new entry and one to clear the form.
- Have one button next to each entry to remove the entry from the list.
- Have indicators next to each entry field to denote whether the field's entry requirement has been met. (Each indicator should update as the user types.)

Now that you've reviewed the objectives, take a look at the screenshot of the final product (see figure 2.7). The application will look and behave the same for each MV* framework used.

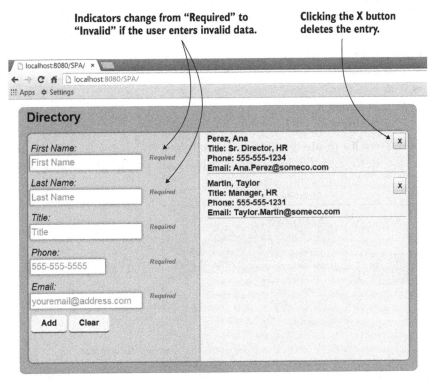

Figure 2.7 Screen capture of the online directory. The user enters information in the form on the left. Valid entries appear in a list on the right.

Throughout our discussion of MV* concepts, I'll refer to this example. I'll also talk about how different philosophies by the framework creators affect the type of code you'll create. Although only certain parts of the code will be used for illustration, all of the code for each MV* version is in appendix A and available for download.

2.2.3 Models

You know from our discussion of patterns that models often contain business logic and validation. They also represent the data in your application. The data they contain shouldn't be a motley crew of unrelated information, though. They're called *models* because they model a real-life entity that's important to the application's logic.

For example, if you were building an online reservation system for a hotel, your models might include the hotel, a room, an agent, a customer, the reservation, amenities, notes, invoices, receipts, and payments. What about a web-based application for teachers? You'd need to have data representing the school, its teachers, the students, courses, and grades, at a minimum. Each model in the application would represent a real-world object. Consequently, the larger and more complex the system, the more types of models you'll have.

Let's see what a model's data would look like for our online employee directory. Remember that models mirror things in the real world. They contain not only data but behavior as well. In this case, you're going to model a directory listing. I'll keep it extremely simple to make sure the concept doesn't get buried in too much code. Here's the information we're going to keep track of in each model:

- First name
- Last name
- Title
- Email address
- Phone number

The employee list inside the directory would be a collection (array) of these models. Figure 2.8 illustrates what this would look like from a conceptual standpoint.

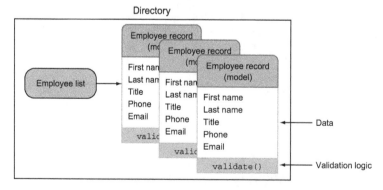

Figure 2.8   The application's data in our online directory project is just an array of employee models. Each model is an object that contains the employee information we'll see onscreen.

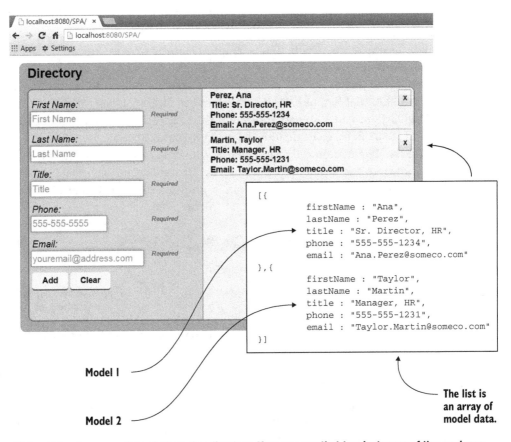

Figure 2.9   Screen capture of the online directory. Here you see that two instances of the employee model have been added to the list.

To help you visualize what the models will look like when they're added to the collection and rendered in the view, you can look at the screenshot of the employee directory application again (see figure 2.9). Remember, each model in the list is an object in an array. In this version of the screenshot, I've superimposed a snapshot of the data inside each model that has been added to our list. This will help you see the models in action.

Now that you have a mental picture of how the employee models will be used, let's talk about how a model is defined in each type of framework. How you create a model in an MV* application varies, depending on the framework you're using. As I mentioned, the framework might not be an exact match for one of the traditional design patterns, but the implementation will certainly be influenced by the pattern.

IMPLIED MODELS

In some MV* implementations, the model is just the data itself, not an explicit structure prescribed by the framework. This data can be from any source, including POJOs and HTML form controls in the UI itself. There are no restrictions on what you can use for the source data when the model is implicit. This is the case for both Knockout and AngularJS.

For example, in our fictitious employee directory, we need the data for the employee model to come from the entry form the user fills out. So instead of creating a JavaScript object or getting JSON from the server, we need to capture data directly from the INPUT fields of our HTML form when creating each entry in the directory's list.

AngularJS provides an easy shortcut for this. If you need your model data to come from an INPUT field, you can add a custom attribute called ng-model to *each* field (see listing 2.1). The attribute declares that model data is sourced from the HTML form element where the attribute is placed. The attribute magically establishes the form-Entry model if it doesn't already exist and gives it a property called firstName. Then it ties formEntry.firstName to this INPUT field.

Listing 2.1   AngularJS model

```
<input id="firstName" name="firstName" type="text"
ng-model="formEntry.firstName"
required                                    ◄── ng-model is AngularJS's
placeholder="First Name"/>                       custom attribute
```

Once established, the model is readily available in your JavaScript code. One of the many benefits of using an MV* framework is keeping the complex, boilerplate code that marries the data and UI external to our application's logic. This one attribute is a great example.

In Knockout, the model is again implied, not explicitly declared (see listing 2.2). In this framework, you add custom attributes to *each* INPUT field just as we did in the AngularJS version. This time, the attribute is called data-bind.

With Knockout (in true MVVM fashion), the attribute ties the INPUT field with a matching property in the ViewModel. In turn, our JavaScript code gains access to the field through the ViewModel.

Listing 2.2   Knockout model

```
                                                  data-bind is Knockout's
                                                  custom attribute
<input id="firstName" name="firstName" type="text"
data-bind="hasFocus: isFocused,
value: entry.firstName,
valueUpdate: 'afterkeydown'"                   ◄── A matching property from
placeholder="First Name" />                        a ViewModel you'll define in code
```

With both AngularJS and Knockout, your model could have been any data source. Because you're working from an entry form, that's where you needed your model's data to come from. In both cases, no model object was explicitly defined. Instead, each framework provided a custom attribute you could add to the HTML to establish the entry form as the source of the model's data. Now let's see how to create a model in Backbone.js, where models are explicitly defined in code.

EXPLICIT MODELS

In MV* implementations where an explicitly declared model is required by the framework, the model is created as a JavaScript object. Backbone.js is a prime example of this. Backbone.js models can have logic in addition to data, such as validation, default data, and custom functions. You also inherit a lot of functionality. Just by extending the framework's model to create your own, you automatically receive a wide variety of base functionality without even writing code.

The ability to immediately inherit a lot of functionality makes creating a model in these types of frameworks powerful and flexible. For example, in Backbone.js you can create a bare-bones model in a single line of code:

```
var EmployeeRecord = Backbone.Model.extend({});
```

To use the object, you create a new instance of it and call any functions it has available out of the box. With this single declaration, your model right away has a variety of built-in behaviors such as validation, functions to execute RESTful services, and much more. See the online documentation for the full list (http://backbonejs.org).

It's equally as easy to assign properties to a Backbone.js model. To create a new property called `firstName` and set its value to `Emmit`, you can either pass in `{firstName : "Emmit"}` to the object's constructor or use the model's built-in set method:

```
var employee = new EmployeeRecord({});
employee.set({firstName : "Emmit"});
```

The following listing illustrates the Backbone.js version of the employee model for our online directory. The validation needed for the directory example makes the source for the model quite verbose.

Listing 2.3 Backbone.js model

```
var validators = {                          ◄──  Define validation for data being
    "*": [ {                                      set on the model's properties
        expr: /\S/,
        message: "Required"
    } ],
    "phone": [ {
        expr: /^[0-9]{3}-[0-9]{3}-[0-9]{4}$/,
        message: "Invalid"
    } ],
    "email": [ {
        expr: /^[a-z0-9!#$%&'*+\/=?^_`{|}~-]+(?:\.
        [a-z0-9!#$%&'*+\/=?^_`{|}~-]+)*@
        (?:[a-z0-9](?:[a-z0-9-]*[a-z0-9])?\.)+[a-z0-9]
        (?:[a-z0-9-]*[a-z0-9])?$/i,
        message: "Invalid"
    } ]
};
                                             Keep track of
                                          ╱  specific errors
function validateField(value, key) {      ◄
    var rules = validators["*"].concat(validators[key] || []);
```

```
        var broken =
        _.find(rules,function(rule) {return !rule.expr.test(value);});

        return broken ? {"attr":key,"error":broken.message} : null;
}

var EmployeeRecord = Backbone.Model.extend({                    ◄──┐ Create the model
    validate: function(attrs) {                                     ┘
        var validated = _.mapObject(attrs, validateField);
        var attrsInError = _.compact(_.values(validated));
        return attrsInError.length ? attrsInError : null;
    },
    sync: function(method, model, options) {
        options.success();
    }
});
```

There seems to be a lot more going on than there is. We inherit the power of the Backbone.js model just by extending its base object. But the framework leaves it up to you as to how you want to validate the data. It gives you a couple of hooks with `validate(attrs, options)`, and you can fill in the rest however you want.

2.2.4 Bindings

The term *binding* is another concept you should understand if you plan on using an MV* framework. This term is used frequently when talking about UI development. In plain English, it means to tie or connect two things together. In UI development, whether we're talking about desktop programming with a language like .NET or web development with MV*, we mean linking a UI element in the view (such as a user input control) to something in our code (for example, a model's data).

It doesn't have to be just data, though. Different libraries and frameworks offer different types of bindings. Styles, attributes, and events such as `click` are just a sampling of what can be bound to the UI. The binding types that are available vary, depending on the framework. You'll look at the code for a few approaches in this section, just to illustrate.

How exactly do we declare a binding in our application? MV* frameworks make binding something in our code to an element in the UI simple. Understanding how to declare a binding starts with getting to know the syntax.

BINDING SYNTAX

Binding syntax comes in two flavors:

- *Expressions*, which are special characters that wrap/delimit the bound item
- HTML *attributes* (called *directives* in AngularJS or *bindings* in Knockout)

With both types, the binding syntax is freely mixed with the HTML of the template. Table 2.1 lists a few examples of the binding syntax used by some popular libraries/ frameworks. This is by no means an exhaustive list, but it should give you a general idea.

Keep in mind, also, that the table is using simple text bindings to illustrate syntax styles. As noted previously, things other than data, such as events and CSS styles, may also be supported. See the documentation for each library/framework to see the complete list of bindings supported and additional usage instructions.

Table 2.1 Binding is in the form of either an attribute or an expression. AngularJS supports both styles to some extent.

Framework/library	Type	Example
Knockout http://knockout.com	Attribute	`data-bind="text: firstName"`
AngularJS (type 1) https://angularjs.org	Attribute	`ng-bind="firstName"`
AngularJS (type 2)	Expression	`{{ firstName }}`
Mustache http://mustache.github.io	Expression	`{{ firstName }}`
Handlebars http://handlebarsjs.com	Expression	`{{ firstName }}`
Underscore.js (default) http://underscorejs.org	Expression	`<%= firstName %>`

After you look at the documentation of the framework or library to get a feel for the syntax, the next thing to understand about binding is the directional flow of data in the binding.

BINDING DIRECTION

Binding something in our code to a visual element in the view can be bidirectional, single-directional, or a one-time binding. The type of binding relationship is also established via the MV* framework.

TWO-WAY BINDING

In bidirectional, or two-way, binding, after the binding link is established, changes on either end cause updates on the opposite side. This keeps the two sides in sync. In a web application, two-way binding is associated with UI controls, like those in a form, that support user input.

Knockout is a great library to illustrate the concept of two-way binding. Binding is, after all, this library's main purpose. As you saw previously, creating a binding is as easy as typing a custom attribute called `data-bind` right in the HTML. The `data-bind` attribute tells Knockout that something in the UI is going to be bound to a property in a ViewModel. In the following example, we're binding the *value* of an INPUT control to a ViewModel property called `firstName`:

```
<input data-bind="value: firstName" />
```

For the other half of the two-way binding relationship, you tell Knockout you want the property to be observed for any changes by wrapping its data in a Knockout observable object. (Remember observables from the Observer pattern?)

```
var myViewModelObject = {
   firstName : ko.observable("Emmit")
};
```

Because of the two-way binding established by this small amount of code, these two items will stay in sync automatically.

Binding is just as easy, or more so, with AngularJS. You already saw AngularJS's two-way binding in action during our discussion of models. You add the attribute ng-model to the HTML of the INPUT tag:

```
<input ng-model="firstName" />
```

On the JavaScript code side, you have a $scope object instead of a ViewModel. Scopes are similar in that they sit between the view and our JavaScript code and give us access to the model.

One nice thing about this framework is that AngularJS's magic automates a lot of the two-way setup. First, the $scope object automatically monitors models for changes. Second, you don't even have to create the $scope object; AngularJS will hand it to you, if you ask for it. Then, in your code, you can refer to the property via the $scope object like this:

```
$scope.firstName
```

That's it. Now both the INPUT field and the property are bidirectionally bound. Changes on either side affect the other. Pretty easy, huh?

You've seen the approaches to two-way binding from two different frameworks. Even so, the concept remains the same in both. Now let's take a quick look at binding in a single direction.

ONE-WAY BINDING

When binding is single-directional, or one-way, changes in the state of the source affect the target but not the other way around. This type of binding is normally associated with HTML elements that don't require any input from the user, such as a DIV or SPAN tag. With these types of elements, you're interested in its text, not its value. You still access the data on the JavaScript side in the same manner, but in the template you choose the attribute specifically for one-way text binding.

With Knockout, you change the word *value* to *text*:

```
<span data-bind="text: firstName"></span>
```

In AngularJS, the attribute itself changes from ng-model to ng-bind:

```
<span ng-bind="firstName"></span>
```

Once again, you can see that the binding concept remains the same even though you're looking at different MV* frameworks.

TIP Knockout provides an additional way to make even bindings for user input one-way, in case you need that behavior. You just remove the observable "wrapper" from the ViewModel property like this: `firstName : "Emmit"`.

You might be wondering at this point, why bother with the one-way types? Why not use two-way binding always? Well, usually something as magical as automatic, two-way binding comes at a cost. Two-way binding has slightly more overhead. No need to panic and avoid it, though. For most views, this overhead is negligible. But if you have a ton of bindings throughout your application, you should use any means to save on overhead.

If your view receives input from the user, and you need the data and view to stay constantly in sync, use two-way binding. When you have read-only UI elements, use one-way binding. One-way will keep the view updated when the model changes but doesn't bother with trying to monitor the view side, because the element is read-only.

ONE-TIME BINDING

One-time binding is a type of one-way binding that happens only once. Nothing is automatically observed for changes. No subsequent updates occur if the source changes or the target changes.

With one-time binding, after the template and the data are combined and rendered as the view, the process is done. If new changes need to be applied to the view, the entire process starts over. The previous view is destroyed, and the new data is combined with the same template to generate the view anew.

I've saved Backbone.js for this section. The typical approach for rendering templates when using Backbone.js is through one-time binding (though some Backbone-compatible libraries and plugins offer the other two types). With AngularJS and Knockout, after the bindings are established, they're reused. In Backbone.js, the general idea is that when new data is needed, the view is destroyed (with the bindings) and re-created. I'll talk more specifically about templates in the next section.

NOTE Backbone.js doesn't have templating/binding capabilities built in but instead lets you pick the outside library of your choice for the task. Its default is the utility library Underscore.js.

To recap the types of bindings we discussed, consider table 2.2.

Table 2.2 Bindings can be two-way, one-way, or one-time.

Binding type	Behavior
Two-way	Bidirectional—keeps data and view constantly in sync.
One-way	Single-directional, or one-way—changes in the state of the source affect the target, but not the other way around.
One-time	One-way—occurs only once at render time, from model to view.

In the next section, you'll see binding in action with template examples from our online employee directory.

2.2.5   *Templates*

A *template* is a section of HTML that acts as a pattern for how our view is rendered. This pattern can additionally contain various types of bindings and other instructions that dictate how the template and its model data get processed. A template is also reusable, like a stencil.

One or more templates are used to create a view, with complex views often having multiple rendered templates on the screen at the same time. The part of the MV* framework, whether built in or via an outside library, that marries the template and the model's data is generally referred to as a *template engine*. Figure 2.10 illustrates the marriage of data from the employee directory form (our model) and a template to arrive at what the user sees onscreen.

You should now be able to recognize bindings when you see them, so let's take a look at some real examples of templates and their bindings taken from our MV* project. I've highlighted the bindings so you can easily see which part of the template is the binding and which part is just the HTML.

WHAT TEMPLATES LOOK LIKE

One thing all templates have in common is that they represent some part of our view. What this means for you as a developer is that, apart from the binding syntax, views

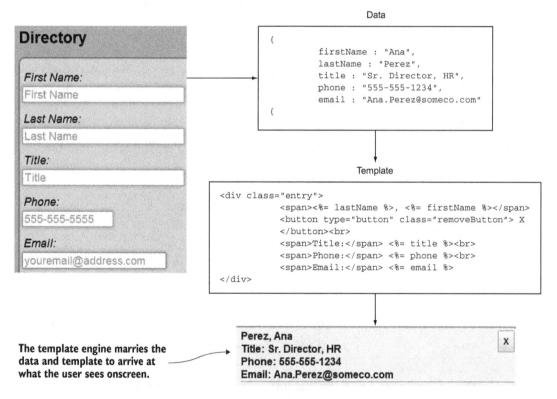

Figure 2.10   The fully rendered template, created by a template engine

are just HTML. This also means that if you have a web designer on the team, views can be constructed by the designer as well.

The following listing shows our Knockout template. Notice that it has custom attributes, but apart from that it's normal HTML.

Listing 2.4   Knockout template

```
<li class="entry">
   <button type="button" class="remove-entry"
      data-bind="click: removeEntry">&#9587;</button>

   <span data-bind="text: $data.lastName"></span>,
   <span data-bind="text: $data.firstName"></span>
   <br />

   <span>Title:</span>
   <span data-bind="text: $data.title"></span>
   <br />

   <span>Phone:</span>
   <span data-bind="text: $data.phone"></span>
   <br />

   <span>Email:</span>
   <span data-bind="text: $data.email"></span>
</li>
```

This click binding removes the entry

Data bindings link our form fields to the ViewModel's data

Do you remember from our discussion of binding syntax that with AngularJS we could use either expressions or attributes? For the online directory project, we're using expressions just to demonstrate those (see the following listing). You can use ng-bind if you prefer the attribute style.

Listing 2.5   AngularJS template

```
<li class="entry"  ng-repeat="entry in entries">

   <button type="button" class="remove-entry"
   ng-click="removeEntry(entry)">&#9587;</button>

   {{entry.lastName}}, {{entry.firstName}}<br />

   Title: {{entry.title}}<br />
   Phone: {{entry.phone}}<br />
   Email: {{entry.email}}

</li>
```

Stamps out this template for every entry object in the list of entries

Calls a function, passing the current entry object

What's neat about templates in Backbone.js is that you aren't confined to a particular template syntax, because there's no built-in template library. Backbone.js allows you to use the template engine of your choice. In our directory project, we're using the default, which is Underscore.js (see the following listing). Underscore.js has a default delimiter of `<%= %>` for its expressions, but the delimiters can be anything you want (including `{{ }}`).

Listing 2.6   Backbone.js template using the Underscore.js template library

```
<button type="button" class="remove-entry">&#9587;</button>
<%= lastName %>, <%= firstName %><br />          We're sticking with the default
Title: <%= title %><br />                        Underscore.js as the template engine,
Phone: <%= phone %><br />                         but we could substitute a different one
Email: <%= email %>
```

These examples provide a good introduction to templates and the various binding styles that are used. One thing we haven't talked about yet, though, is how the process gets triggered.

TEMPLATE RENDERING

In AngularJS, the rendering of a template happens automatically, as soon as the application starts. AngularJS searches through the DOM for its custom attributes, including those for binding templates.

In other frameworks, this step isn't difficult but may be a little more explicit. Knockout, for example, requires a one-liner in your JavaScript code for each View-Model to activate the bindings:

```
knockout.applyBindings(myViewModel, $("#someElement")[0])
```

Knockout has a special function you call, `applyBindings`, which renders the template with the model data supplied by the ViewModel. The first parameter is the ViewModel itself. The second is the place in the DOM you want Knockout to start looking for bindings for the given ViewModel. The second parameter is optional, but for efficiency you should use it in order to confine the binding process to a particular parent element.

> **TIP** `$("#someElement")[0]` is the way in jQuery to access the underlying DOM object referenced in its selector, because jQuery doesn't know how many elements will be a match for a given selector. You can also use the Java-Script `document.getElementById("someElement")` method as the second parameter.

In Backbone.js, rendering the template is a bit more of a manual process. The framework provides `template` and `render` as hooks for the external template engine of your choice. To render the template to the screen, you have to run it through the compile-and-render process. You'll see the view in its entirety in the next section, but for now let's focus on the rendering of the template, as shown in the following listing.

Listing 2.7   Backbone.js template compile and render

```
template : _.template(templateHTML),          Compiles the template
render : function() {                          into a reusable function
    var modelAsJSON = this.model.toJSON();
```
Translates the model data to a JSON string

Marries the
data and HTML

```
var renderedHTML = this.template(modelDataAsJSON);
this.$el.html(renderedHTML);
return this;
}
```

Replaces the element's content
with the rendered HTML

The preceding code seems quite verbose when compared to the other two frameworks. The ability to choose whichever template engine you want is a great trade-off, though.

You now know what templates are and how to create them. The lingering question you might have is where do you keep their source code?

WHERE TO KEEP TEMPLATES

Templates can either be included in the initial download of your SPA (*inline*) or downloaded on demand as external *partials* (or *fragments*).

INLINE TEMPLATES

If your template uses the expression style of binding syntax and isn't downloaded on demand, you'll need to place it inside SCRIPT tags. You use SCRIPT tags to avoid accidentally showing the user the binding code before the render process happens. The browser won't try to display code within the SCRIPT tags.

To prevent the browser from trying to execute the script as JavaScript code, you'll need to give the SCRIPT tag's Multipurpose Internet Mail Extensions (MIME) type something other than text/javascript or application/javascript, as shown in the following listing.

Listing 2.8 Inline template

```
<script type="text/template" id="myTemplate">
    Hello, <%= firstName %>, how are you?
</script>
```

Wrapping a template in SCRIPT tags
hides its source. Non-JavaScript MIME
types aren't treated as JavaScript code.

If your inline template uses attributes for its binding syntax, there's nothing else special you need to do. SCRIPT tags aren't needed. Also, because attributes aren't displayed anyway, there's no chance the user will accidently see the bindings before the view is rendered.

TEMPLATE PARTIALS

If you download the template on demand, there's no need for SCRIPT tags, even if you're using expressions. The dynamically fetched template can be used directly by the template engine, which avoids the issue altogether.

As noted previously, these on-demand templates are sometimes referred to as *partials* or *fragments*. They're not part of the initial HTML document that's loaded with your application. Instead, they're fetched as snippets of source code directly from the server at runtime.

Now that you have a good idea about models, binding, and templates, you need to finally see how they culminate into the view the user sees and interacts with. In the next section, you'll look at how MV* frameworks approach views.

2.2.6   *Views*

As you saw during our discussion of templates, frameworks such as Knockout and AngularJS use declarative bindings in their templates, usually in the form of special attributes added to HTML elements. In these frameworks, the templates and views are pretty much the same thing. Thus, when composing views in these frameworks, you need to decide only whether the templates will be kept inline or downloaded on demand. This is more of a design issue.

In a code-driven framework like Backbone.js, the approach is to programmatically create the view. The following listing is an example from our directory application of a Backbone.js view. Don't worry if you don't understand everything in the example right now. When you're ready, appendix A contains a complete walk-through of the code.

Listing 2.9   Backbone.js view example

```
var Employee = Backbone.View.extend({
    tagName: "li",
    template: _.template(templateHTML),
    render: function() {
        this.$el.html(this.template(this.model.toJSON()));
        return this;
    },
    events: {
        "click .remove-entry": "removeEntry"
    },
    removeEntry: function() {
        this.model.destroy();
        this.remove();
    }
});
```

Define the element type — *tagName: "li"*

Compile the template — *template: _.template(templateHTML)*

Extend the built-in Backbone.js view object

Render the view and attach it to the DOM

Define the behavior for the click event

Perform some cleanup anytime the view is removed

Backbone.js allows you to define traits for your view, such as its CSS class name and the type of element it will be. Additionally, you're given the freedom to define key milestones in the life of the view, such as its rendering and removal, in any manner you wish.

The discussion on views rounds out our conversation of basic MV* concepts. It's great to understand the concepts, but what does an MV* framework do for us? In the next section, I'll discuss how using an MV* framework can make our lives as SPA developers much easier and our code much cleaner.

2.3   *Why use an MV* framework?*

Deciding to use any external software in your project shouldn't be taken lightly. You are, after all, introducing a dependency. That being said, however, when its benefits exceed the costs, a new dependency is worth considering. This section presents some of the key benefits of using MV* frameworks.

2.3.1 Separation of concerns

As mentioned previously, MV* frameworks provide a means to segregate JavaScript objects into their basic roles based on their underlying design pattern or patterns. Each part of the code can be focused on a particular responsibility to the application.

This overarching concept of separation of concerns helps us design objects with a particular purpose. Models can be dedicated to data, views can be dedicated to the presentation of data, and components such as controllers, presenters, and ViewModels can keep these two parts communicating with one another without being joined at the hip. The more dedicated an object is to a singular purpose, the easier it is to code, test, and update after it's in production.

MV* frameworks also reduce the tendency to write spaghetti code by providing framework elements that require us to write code in a particular way to facilitate loose coupling. This keeps our HTML as clean as possible by removing embedded JavaScript and CSS code. It also keeps our JavaScript free from deep coupling with DOM elements.

Here's a classic AngularJS example demonstrating how MV* can make our code cleaner. Figure 2.11 shows a SPAN tag (right) mirroring what's being typed into an INPUT field (left).

Figure 2.11 In this example, a SPAN tag's contents are being updated dynamically as the user types into an INPUT field.

Let's create the example from figure 2.11, first written as spaghetti code and then with AngularJS. Listing 2.10 is the source code, written as tightly coupled HTML and JavaScript. *Tightly coupling* means making direct references or calls from one function or component to another. This joins them at the hip, so to speak.

Writing code this way works, but it can prove to be difficult to read and a pain to update later. If an entire single-page application were written like this, you can imagine how monumentally difficult it would be to maintain.

Listing 2.10   Tightly coupled HTML and JavaScript

```
<html>
<body>
    <input id="name"
    onKeyUp="document.getElementById('output').innerHTML
    = document.getElementById('name').value">
    <span id="output"></span>
</body>
</html>
```

Don't do this!

> **WARNING** The code in listing 2.10 dynamically updates the SPAN as you type but is hard to read and difficult to maintain.

Now, in the following listing, we use the AngularJS framework's ability to abstract away much of the boilerplate code needed to achieve the same results.

Listing 2.11 AngularJS example

```html
<html>
<body ng-app>
    <input ng-model="name">
    <span>{{name}}</span>
    <script src="js/thirdParty/angular.min.js"></script>
</body>
</html>
```

> The AngularJS framework marries the **INPUT** field with the **SPAN** tag, removing the need to put JavaScript code in your HTML

Believe it or not, that small bit of code is all that's needed. Of course, this is a contrived example. Even using a framework as powerful as AngularJS, complicated applications will have complicated logic. For all the reasons I just mentioned, though, you'll spend more of your time writing business logic, not the low-level, routine plumbing.

2.3.2 Routine tasks simplified

MV* frameworks also simplify some of the tasks we as developers deal with on a regular basis. Take, for instance, repetitively printing out the data from a list, complete with HTML markup, to the screen. That's a run-of-the-mill task, but the mechanics involved take a good deal of code to pull it off. Moreover, we find ourselves repeating the same code over and over every time we need to do this.

Let's consider the employee directory from the beginning of the chapter. One of the requirements is to be able to add an employee's data as an entry to a list. If you had to code all the mechanics by hand, you'd find yourself manually creating DOM elements for each entry in a JavaScript loop. The code wouldn't be pretty, and chances are it wouldn't be reusable for other tasks.

MV* frameworks take the drudge work out of tasks like this. Take the code in listings 2.12 and 2.13. This is how we're adding entries to our list using Knockout. Listing 2.12 is from the HTML side of things. For brevity, this isn't the entire source code, only the portion to add to the directory's employee listing. The complete source code can be found in appendix A.

Listing 2.12 Employee list HTML

```html
<ul class="entry-list" id="entryList"
    data-bind="foreach: entries">
</ul>
```

> An empty UL and a foreach binding to iteratively build our list

Notice that we don't have any JavaScript code in our HTML. The following listing shows the ViewModel backing this section of the template.

Listing 2.13   Employee list JavaScript

```
self.entries = ko.observableArray();
self.addEntry = function(e) {
    var newEntry = {
        firstName : self.entry.firstName(),
        lastName : self.entry.lastName(),
        title : self.entry.title(),
        phone : self.entry.phone(),
        email : self.entry.email()
    };
    self.entries.push(newEntry);
};
```

Special Knockout array that keeps the array data in sync with the HTML

Create a new entry whenever the Add button is clicked

Add the entry to the array, and Knockout takes care of the rest

With a few subtle attributes and a minimal amount of code, we were able to accomplish our list of management needs. Taking the grunt work out of routine tasks like this greatly simplifies life as a programmer.

2.3.3 *Productivity gains*

From a development standpoint, being able to devote your time and energy to your business logic is a definite boost to productivity. When we do decide to use an external library or framework, we're removing the burdens of having to maintain that part of the code base ourselves. We also use the expertise of their authors in the areas that the particular framework covers. Sure, you could create your own routines to do the same thing, but it would take an enormous effort to get it to the level of the MV* implementations out there.

You also have an incredible amount of community-based knowledge on the web for most libraries/frameworks, should you run into problems. Most authors of MV* have mechanisms for reporting bugs too. This means that periodically code fixes are tested and released, without you having to spend your time on the issue.

If you're doing everything yourself, you're maintaining your own business logic, *plus* the extra bug fixes and testing for all of the structural code provided from external libraries/frameworks.

2.3.4 *Standardization*

As you'll hear me repeat throughout this book, writing a robust web application with a clean, scalable code base is already difficult. This difficulty can be compounded in a single-page app. So the last thing you need is to have everyone on the development team writing code in completely different styles.

You want to be able to read your teammate's code as if it were your own. Otherwise, you'll continuously waste time deciphering some "foreign" style of coding before you can get around to updating it. Even if you're alone, not working with a team, having uniform code standards will help you when it's time to revisit something you wrote to make changes.

MV* libraries and frameworks have certain conventions that must be followed in order to use the software. This will compel you to write your application's code in a more formal, standardized way.

2.3.5 *Scalability*

As discussed previously, MV* frameworks inherently promote the separation-of-concerns concept. This, in turn, also makes a project more scalable, because loosely coupled objects can be reworked with minimal effect on other objects.

Objects can also be swapped out entirely to make room for new functionality without causing a huge ripple effect throughout the project. This allows the project to grow more gracefully, because code changes tend to have much less negative impact.

Now that you've seen some of the core MV* features, which style seems easier? Which is more difficult to use? You'll have to be the judge. Some people don't like having the declarative style of bindings freely mixed with the HTML page itself as you see with MVVM. Others prefer it over having to use so much boilerplate code to create the view.

Although you'll ultimately have to decide which framework is right for you and your project, section 2.4 will give you a few things to think about as you're making your decision.

2.4 *Choosing a framework*

After you've decided you do want to use an MV* library or framework, you have a lot to choose from. Even if you decide on a particular style you like better, you'll still have a lot of candidates to weed through. Just to give you an idea, here are some popular client-side MV* options available at the time of this writing:

- AngularJS (https://angularjs.org)
- Agility.js (http://agilityjs.com)
- Backbone.js (http://backbonejs.org)
- CanJS (http://canjs.com)
- Choco (https://github.com/ahe/choco)
- Dojo Toolkit (http://dojotoolkit.org)
- Ember.js (http://emberjs.com)
- Ext JS (www.sencha.com/products/extjs)
- Jamal (https://github.com/adcloud/jamal)
- JavaScriptMVC (http://javascriptmvc.com)
- Kendo UI (www.telerik.com/kendo-ui)
- Knockout (http://knockoutjs.com)
- Spine (http://spinejs.com)

As you can see, you have quite a few choices. And those are the libraries/frameworks themselves. If you decide to choose a framework that's not all-inclusive, the lists of libraries and frameworks to handle the other features, such as routing and view management, are nearly as long. In a few years, we went from relatively few choices to an overwhelming number of them.

It's rather unproductive to try to point out which ones are "better" than others. It's all a matter of opinion. Also, because they're all different and have a different number of features and styles, it's hard to make an apples-to-apples comparison. But I can offer a list of things to keep in mind as you're making your decision:

- *A la carte or one-stop shopping*—This is completely subjective, but do you want a framework that has everything built in? Or do you prefer something that's as small as possible and focused on a few core features? There are arguments for both. Some people would rather not have to worry about finding other libraries for missing features. That's just more dependencies to worry about and more potential points of failure. You'd also have to be versed in software from various providers instead of just one. But some people point out the other side of the coin: by going with an all-inclusive solution, you're "putting all your eggs in one basket." If the framework ever stops being supported, it'll be tougher to replace everything than a single supporting library. Smaller offerings, such as Knockout and Backbone.js, are great if you want to go minimal, but you'll have to look elsewhere to fill in any gaps when writing your SPA. Frameworks such as Ember.js, Kendo UI, and AngularJS plug most gaps but hide a lot of what's going on with their framework magic. This is a negative for some people who want more control.

- *Licensing and support*—Budget is always a factor. For your project, do you have money to spend on a framework, or do you need something that's free? Are you required by your company to purchase a commercial product? Does your company require you to be able to purchase a certain level of support for any software used in its projects? Is your project mission critical? Is a minimum turnaround required for bug fixes and updates?

- *Programming style preference*—Knockout and Kendo UI fall squarely in the MVVM camp. Others, including Backbone.js and Ember.js, are more MVC and/or MVP. AngularJS is a little more MVVM but still retains some MVC-like features. Any of these can be used to create large, robust applications. Your selection boils down to your personal preference after you've tried a few of them.

- *Learning curve*—This might be a minor point to some, because given enough time you can learn to use any framework. Some are definitely more difficult to wrap your head around than others. You might not have months to get up to speed.

- *Number of bugs and fix rate*—All software has a certain number of bugs at any given time. That's just the way things are. But what you can factor into your decision is the percentage of high and critical bugs the software experiences over time. Also, how fast are they being fixed? If a large number of important bugs have been sitting there for a long time, that's probably a red flag.

- *Documentation*—How good is their documentation? How up to date is it? Some MV* providers offer free online videos and interactive training. Are there code examples to go along with the API documentation?
- *Maturity*—We can't judge how good the framework is by how mature it is. We can, however, get a warm and fuzzy that it's here for the foreseeable future if it's pretty mature. If software is fairly new, it's probably still going through "growing pains." That might be tolerable for applications that aren't a high priority. If the software is constantly changing, though, it would be nearly impossible to create a mission-critical application with it.
- *Community*—This aspect is sometimes overlooked, but if you plan on including third-party software as a dependency, it's nice if it has a large community following. There's strength in numbers. Sooner or later, you'll run into situations that aren't covered in the documentation. Finding help in online forums and blogs can be a lifesaver.
- *How opinionated is it?*—For routine tasks, such as creating objects and lists or sending, receiving, and processing server requests, how flexible is it? Does it limit you by imposing strict guidelines (and are you OK with that)? How well does it play with any other libraries/frameworks in your arsenal?
- *POC (proof of concept)*—Once you've narrowed down your choices to a select few, do a POC for each to get a feel for it in practice. You'll always encounter situations in your real project that you didn't anticipate and be forced to search for workarounds. That's just the nature of the beast. But by doing a simple POC with at least basic CRUD functionality, you'll be able to make a decision. Preferably, your CRUD operations will include a list of objects so you can get a feel for how easy it is to manage a collection as well.

As you can see, you have many factors to think about when choosing an MV* framework. But you're now acquainted with the traditional design patterns and the basic core concepts. You've also been exposed to some of the design differences of MV* libraries/frameworks. With that and this list of points to consider, you'll be able to make a more informed choice when the time comes.

2.5   *Chapter challenge*

Now here's a challenge for you, to see what you've learned in this chapter. Let's see if you, on your own, can use one-way bindings to create a simple view. Let's pretend that your local library wants to begin offering e-books online and has reached out to the community for help. The library already has converted its first set of books to e-books but needs someone with web development skills to set up the e-book site. Pick any one of the three MV* frameworks from this chapter (or a different one if you prefer) and create a view that's contains a list of a few books. The view should have the following format:

- *Header*—The header should contain the library name, address, and phone number. It should also display the name of the user logged in. For the user, create a JavaScript variable and use your name as its value. Then create a simple binding to display this value in the view's header.

- *Body*—Create a list of book objects (book title, author, and simple description) in JavaScript. In the body, choose a binding that prints each book in the list iteratively.

2.6 Summary

Understanding the information in this chapter will help you going forward. Let's review:

- The traditional design patterns that had a major influence on MV* libraries/ frameworks are MVC (Model-View-Controller), MVP (Model-View-Presenter), and MVVM (Model-View-ViewModel).
- The model represents your data. In MVVM, this object is mainly just data. In the other two patterns, the model also contains other kinds of logic, including logic to manage the data.
- The view represents the part of the application that the user sees and interacts with.
- The third object, the controller or presenter or ViewModel, is an intermediary object of one degree or another, keeping the model and the view decoupled but interactive.
- Each pattern must be adaptable to its environment. The authors of MV* libraries/frameworks have had to take various liberties with traditional patterns in order to create solutions that work in a browser setting.
- Some basic MV* concepts to know are models, bindings, templates, and views.
- You should keep a variety of considerations in mind when choosing an MV* framework: a la carte or one-stop shopping, licensing and support, programming style preference, learning curve, bugs and fix rate, documentation, maturity, community support, and how opinionated it is.
- When you narrow your choices to two or three, try doing a proof of concept with each to get a feel for its use in your project.

Modular JavaScript

JavaScript is a powerful yet extremely flexible language that has become the de facto standard for adding interactivity to web applications. Even large companies such as Amazon.com, Google, and Walmart rely on it. It's remarkably easy to learn and even easier to add working code to a web page. So it's no wonder that the freedom it offers and its ease of use have contributed to its popularity.

The friendliness of the language is a double-edged sword, though. In any language as dynamic as JavaScript, it can be easy to find yourself with a chaotic code base if you're not careful. In a presentation for Google Tech Talks, renowned developer, architect, author, and speaker Douglas Crockford stated that JavaScript has "some of the best ideas ever put into a programming language" (see http://google code.blogspot.com/2009/03/doug-crockford-javascript-good-parts.html). He added, however, that it also has "some of the worst ideas ever put into a programming language."

Fortunately, following best practices and proven design patterns goes a long way toward keeping your project under control. One such pattern that's particularly useful in the development of modern web applications is the module pattern. Modules provide an elegant way to structure your code. They also help avoid many issues that would otherwise arise from having your entire application in a single page. This chapter provides an in-depth look at modules and why you should consider using them in an SPA.

3.1 What is a module?

In general, a *module* can be defined as a part, or component, of a larger structure. The term *module*, however, can have a variety of meanings depending on the context, even within the category of software development. Sometimes you'll hear people talking about a module in a more general sense. They might say, for example, "the payments module" or "the trip planner module." In these cases, it would be perfectly legitimate for them to be referring to the feature as a whole. When we're specifically referring to a JavaScript code module, we mean a single function—a special function created by using the module pattern.

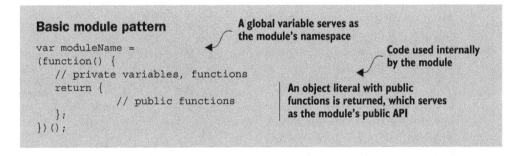

Don't worry about the strange syntax at this point. Section 3.3 provides greater detail. For now, you'll continue learning the basics of modular programming by reviewing a few concepts.

3.1.1 Module pattern concepts

Before moving forward, let's take a moment to get acquainted with a few module pattern concepts:

- *Namespace*—A namespace is a way to provide a particular scope for a group of related members. Though namespaces aren't part of the JavaScript language currently, you can still achieve the same effect by assigning your module function to any variable with a wider scope (a global variable, for example).

- *Anonymous function expression*—An expression exists if your code is part of an expression and doesn't start with the `function` keyword. If the function expression being assigned is unnamed, it's called an anonymous function expression. The module's body is contained within an anonymous function expression.
- *Object literal*—JavaScript provides a sort of shorthand for creating objects known as *literal notation*, which declares an object by using curly braces, with its properties defined as key-value pairs. Object literals are described in more detail in section 3.3.2.
- *Closures*—Normally when a function finishes executing, the life of any local variables created within it comes to an end as well. An exception to this is a closure, which occurs when a function contains variable references outside its own scope. In JavaScript, each function has its own scope property, which references the variables of its outer scope. Every function always has an outer scope, even if that outer scope is just the global scope (so technically all functions are closures). Closures are important to our discussion because even though the module pattern's outer function executes immediately, any objects or values up the scope chain referenced in the return statement can't be garbage collected while the module is still in use.

3.1.2 The module's structure

A module's structure cleverly uses a function as a container to encapsulate its logic. This is possible because variables and functions declared locally inside the module aren't directly accessible from outside its outer function. Access to the module's internal functionality is regulated by what's exposed in the return statement (see figure 3.1).

To see how to use such an odd-looking construct, let's take a simple function and rewrite it by using the module pattern. The following function adds two numbers and returns the result:

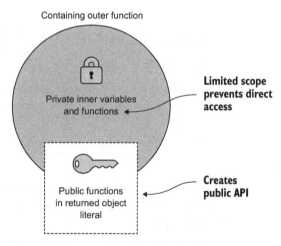

Containing outer function

Private inner variables and functions

Limited scope prevents direct access

Public functions in returned object literal

Creates public API

Figure 3.1   In a module, the outer function encapsulates its functionality. There's no direct access to internal variables and functions. Access is regulated via functions in the object literal it returns.

```
var num1 = 2;
function addTwoNumbers(num2) {
    return num1 + num2;
}

alert( addTwoNumbers(2) );
```

Alerts "4"

Listing 3.1 shows the same functionality, now written as a reusable module. Notice how the pattern has abstracted away the internal details of the module. Users of the function don't have to worry about how the module does what it does. They know that calling the function addTwoNumbers() in the public interface will alert the correct result. Again, in section 3.3 you'll see exactly how this is made possible.

Listing 3.1   Function to add two numbers rewritten as a module

```
var numberModule = (function() {
    var num1 = 2;

    function addNumbersInternally(num2) {
        return num1 + num2;
    }

    return {
        addTwoNumbers : function(num2) {
            alert(addNumbersInternally(num2));
        }
    };

})();

numberModule.addTwoNumbers(2);
```

Private variable num1 contains initial state

Private function addNumbersInternally() does the work

Alerts the result from the call to addTwoNumbersInternally()

Call the module's public functions like this

3.1.3   The revealing module pattern

Part of the appeal of the module pattern is that a clear division is created between the internal workings of the module and its publically available functions. A heavily used variation of the module pattern that makes this division even clearer is called the *revealing module pattern*.

Proposed by Christian Heilmann, this slightly improved version seeks to make the public interface's use self-evident. To do this, it moves any code needed by the API internally as well, leaving the public functions as mere pointers to the internal code. The following listing demonstrates the same module from listing 3.1, written using the revealing module pattern.

Listing 3.2   Revealing module pattern

```
var numberModule = (function() {
    var num1 = 2;

    function addTwoNumbers(num2) {
        alert(num1 + num2);
    }

    return {
        addTwoNumbers : addTwoNumbers
    };

})();

numberModule.addTwoNumbers(2);
```

Public addTwoNumbers() function is a pointer to the private addTwoNumbers() function

Use the module in the same way

As you can see, the public API is much cleaner and more readable. You'll use this version of the module pattern for the examples in the rest of this chapter. Now that you have a basic understanding of a module, let's talk about the reasons why you should consider modular programming.

3.2 *Why modular programming?*

The module pattern was created in 2003 and popularized by Douglas Crockford through his lectures. The structure does the following:

- Keeps parts of our code private, only for use within the module
- Creates a public API to regulate access to the module's functionality

We can also assign a single namespace for the module and its related submodules to reduce the pollution of the global namespace. Why are these things important, though? Just looking at the module pattern's syntax for the first time can be off-putting, maybe even a little intimidating. If you can get past the unusual syntax, however, there are good reasons to consider using the module pattern in an SPA.

3.2.1 *Avoiding name collisions*

Name collisions for variables and functions can happen, even for small applications. The likelihood magnifies exponentially the larger your application gets, because in JavaScript all your variables and functions get thrown into a global namespace. Going back to Douglas Crockford's presentation, he says, "The worst part [of the JavaScript language is] by far—global variables." He says this to specifically point out the problem of name collisions for globally defined code. When all your objects are in the global namespace, they all share the same scope. When you have variable or function declarations in the same scope, with the same name, no error is generated. The last declaration overrides any prior declarations. This can lead to unexpected results, which are difficult to troubleshoot. Let's consider the following example.

Pretend you have a new startup company called The Simpler Times Gourmet and you're creating a single-page application for it to sell your gourmet wares. (Chapter 4 covers the creation of views, so for now you'll confine the UI to a couple of DIV tags to stay focused on the code.) You want to entice new customers to order something by offering a generous 25% discount on their first order. You'd also like to reward returning customers, but allowing everyone to take 25% off doesn't provide the profit you'll need to make your first year's earnings goal. So for now, you'll offer discounts only to new customers.

At first, everything's going swimmingly. Your code correctly greets existing customers with a simple welcome message. Only new customers are greeted with a message about a 25% discount. I've hardcoded this example so it's sure to trigger the message for *returning* customers. Figure 3.2 shows the output in the browser.

Listings 3.2 and 3.3 show the working code. This design doesn't use modules. When the DOM is ready, you call getWelcomeMessage() (defined in welcomeMessage.js) to return the appropriate greeting. The greeting is then inserted into the

Figure 3.2   Returning customers correctly greeted with a simple message and no mention of a discount

content DIV via jQuery's html() function so the message can greet arriving customers, as shown in the following listing.

Listing 3.3   index.html

```
<!DOCTYPE html>
<html>
<head>
<link rel="stylesheet" href="css/default.css">
</head>
<body>
    <div class="siteMain" id="container">
            <div id="header" class="header">The Simpler Times Gourmet</div>
            <div id="content" class="content"></div>
    </div>
    <script src="js/thirdParty/jquery.min.js"></script>
    <script src="js/welcomeMessage.js"></script>
    <script>
            $(document).ready(function() {
                    $("#content").html(getWelcomeMessage())
            });
    </script>
</body>
</html>
```

getWelcomeMessage() returns the appropriate greeting

Pay particular attention to the way the result of the getStatus() function in listing 3.4 is used. Whether the correct message displays depends on whether getStatus() returns existing or not.

NOTE   The jQuery .ready() function guarantees that the DOM will be ready before the function defined inside executes.

Listing 3.4   welcomeMessage.js

```
var customerLoggedIn = true;
var customerName = "Emmit";
var isNewCustomer = false;
```

```
function getStatus(){
    if(customerLoggedIn){
        if(isNewCustomer){
                return "new";
        } else {
                return "existing";
        }
    } else {
        return "unknown";
    }
}
```

getStatus() checks whether the customer is new or existing

```
function getWelcomeMessage(){
    if(getStatus() !== "unknown" ) {
        if(getStatus() === "existing" ) {
                return "Hi again " + customerName
                + ", glad to see you back!";
        } else {
                return "Welcome " + customerName
                + " - 25% off entire purchase!";
        }
    } else {
        return "Sign up for some great gourmet deals!";
    }
}
```

getWelcomeMessage() depends on getStatus() in determining the message to return

Everything works as expected until an enhancement is added to the application. It seems pretty benign, just an additional JavaScript file with code to display a message about the current status of the shopping cart. But after adding the code, functional tests fail. The cart status message is correct, but returning customers suddenly get an erroneous message offering them the 25% discount also. Now everyone, regardless of customer status, is offered the new customer discount. Figure 3.3 shows the welcome screen after the new file is added.

When the new file was unit tested in isolation, it seemed to work fine. Why did it cause issues when added to the site? As you'll see in listing 3.5, a name conflict is to blame. The developer who created the new file inadvertently included a function called getStatus(). Because both the original getStatus() and the new get-Status() are defined in the global namespace, a name conflict arises.

Figure 3.3 Suddenly everyone's being told they're in for a big discount!

Listing 3.5 shoppingCartStatus.js

```
var cartActiveItems = [];

function getStatus(){
    if(cartActiveItems.length > 0){
        return "pending";
    } else {
        return "empty";
    }
}

function getStatusMessage(){
    if(getStatus() === "empty" ) {
        return "Cart is empty";
    } else {
        return "Cart (" + cartActiveItems.length + " items)";
    }
}
```

> Added function getStatus() creates a name conflict

Unfortunately, you get no error messages in the browser. Because the new file was included last (see listing 3.6), the new getStatus() function merely overrides the first one (see figure 3.4). It's as if the first one never existed.

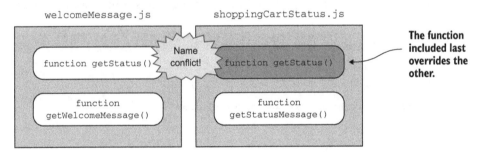

Figure 3.4 Without a module to limit the scope of each function, both are added to the same global scope, causing a name conflict.

Now the wrong getStatus() function is used by the getWelcomeMessage() function to create the greeting. What's interesting about this example is that the getStatus() function in the new file has nothing whatsoever to do with the welcome message, yet it still has a profound effect on the result.

Listing 3.6 index.html

```
<!DOCTYPE html>
<html>
<head>
<link rel="stylesheet" href="css/default.css">
</head>
```

```
<body>
    <div class="siteMain" id="container">
        <div class="header" id="header">
            <div id="banner" class="banner">
            The Simpler Times Gourmet
            </div>
            <div id="cart" class="cart"></div>
        </div>
        <div id="content" class="content"></div>
    </div>
    <script src="js/thirdParty/jquery.min.js"></script>
    <script src="js/welcomeMessage.js"></script>
    <script src="js/shoppingCartStatus.js"></script>
    <script>
        $(document).ready(function() {
            $("#content").html(getWelcomeMessage());
            $("#cart").html(getStatusMessage());
        });
    </script>
</body>
</html>
```

> **Header now includes area for shopping cart status**

> **Second getStatus() function overrides the first**

> **getWelcomeMessage() uses the wrong getStatus(), creating the wrong message**

Now let's see if we can fix this mistake. Let's try recoding the application's logic by using modules. I've tried to keep the logic of each function as close to the original as possible, so it's easier to follow along. The following listing shows your new index page.

Listing 3.7 index.html

```
<!DOCTYPE html>
<html>
<head>
<link rel="stylesheet" href="css/default.css">
</head>
<body>
<div class="siteMain" id="container">
        <div class="header" id="header">
            <div id="banner" class="banner">
            The Simpler Times Gourmet
            </div>
            <div id="cart" class="cart"></div>
        </div>
        <div id="content" class="content"></div>
    </div>
    <script src="js/thirdParty/jquery.min.js"></script>
    <script src="js/STGourmet.js"></script>
    <script src="js/customer.js"></script>
    <script src="js/welcomeMessage.js"></script>
    <script src="js/shoppingCart.js"></script>
    <script>
        STGourmet.init();
    </script>
</body>
</html>
```

> **Two new files added**

> **STGourmet.init() is the single kickoff point for the entire application**

You'll immediately notice a few changes, including the addition of a couple of new JavaScript modules. First, your call to jQuery to update the DIV content has been replaced with a call to your first module. The application now starts with a single call to the STGourmet module's only public function, init().

Second, you now have a total of four includes, not counting jQuery. The existing JavaScript files have been recoded in module format but kept in their original include files. You also have a couple of new modules. Pay attention to the load order. If you're using standard SCRIPT tags to load the files, modules must be ordered so that any variables or functions needed later are already loaded when needed. STGourmet is your main module, so it must be first in the list. Customer has functions that are used later, so it will come second.

Chapter 9 presents ways to combine and minify your code for better performance. Section 3.4 also covers using a third-party library called RequireJS to load modules asynchronously. For now, you'll leave them as normal file includes, which get loaded synchronously. Therefore, load order is important.

NOTE When modules are included using the SCRIPT tag, load order is important! Modules should be loaded in the order in which they're needed.

Listing 3.8 shows your first module. In it, you define STGourmet as the single global variable in the whole application. This carves out a single namespace where your entire application will live. Again, don't worry about the syntax for the module pattern itself right now. Section 3.3 covers that thoroughly. For now, let's continue to focus on how the modules are used to solve the name conflict problems.

Listing 3.8   STGourmet.js

```
var STGourmet = (function($) {                      STGourmet becomes the
                                                    application's namespace
    function init() {
        $(document).ready(function() {
            STGourmet.shoppingCart.displayStatus();
            STGourmet.welcomeMessage.showGreeting();
        });
    }
                                            Anything in the return is public,
    return {                                so init() is our only public function
        init : init
    };                                              jQuery is imported into the module at
                                                    the bottom and aliased as "$" at the top
}) (jQuery);
```

STGourmet's two submodules, shoppingCart and welcomeMessage

Because only functions declared in the return statement are public, this module's init() is its only public function. In index.html, we started the application by calling STGourmet.init(). This, in turn, calls the displayStatus() function of the shoppingCart submodule and the showGreeting() function of the welcomeMessage submodule.

The following listing contains your customer module. Because our three private hardcoded variables aren't part of the shopping cart or the greeting, this code was pulled out into a module of its own.

Listing 3.9   customer.js

```
STGourmet.customer = (function() {

    var customerLoggedIn = true;
    var customerName = "Emmit";
    var isNewCustomer = false;

    function isLoggedIn() {
            return customerLoggedIn;
    }

    function getName() {
            return customerName;
    }

    function isNew() {
            return isNewCustomer;
    }

    return {
            isLoggedIn : isLoggedIn,
            getName : getName,
            isNew : isNew
    };

})();
```

> Adding .customer to STGourmet creates a new submodule

> Code not in the return statement is private and can't be accessed outside the module

> Anything declared in the return statement is public

SUBMODULES

One unique thing you did in this file was to create a submodule. It's a common practice when creating an application using the module pattern to create submodules. This allows you to break the code into separate modules, yet still have it be part of the same namespace.

You'll notice you didn't start the submodule declaration with var. This was no accident. In reality, you're using dot notation to add a new property to the previously defined function object called STGourmet. By adding .customer to your STGourmet object, you create a submodule named customer (see figure 3.5).

Initial module

STGourmet.customer

Submodule

Figure 3.5   You use dot notation, *without* a var, to declare a submodule. What you're really doing is adding a property called customer, which itself contains a module.

The following listing contains your `welcomeMessage` submodule. As you can see, it contains the same logic as before, only wrapped in the module pattern.

Listing 3.10 welcomeMessage.js

```
STGourmet.welcomeMessage = (function() {                    ◄── Submodule called
                                                               welcomeMessage
    function getStatus(){
            if(STGourmet.customer.isLoggedIn()){
                    if(STGourmet.customer.isNew()){
                            return "new";
                    } else {
                            return "existing";
                    }
            } else {
                    return "unknown";
            }
    }

    function getWelcomeMessage() {
            if(getStatus() !== "unknown" ) {
                    if(getStatus() === "existing" ) {
                            return "Hi again " + STGourmet.customer.getName()
                            + ", glad to see you back!";
                    } else {
                            return "Welcome "
                            + STGourmet.customer.getName()
                            + " - 25% off entire purchase!";
                    }
            } else {
                    return "Sign up for some great gourmet deals!";
            }
    }

    function showGreeting(){
            $("#content").html(getWelcomeMessage());
    }

    return {
            showGreeting : showGreeting
    };

})();
```

Finally, the following listing contains your `shoppingCart` submodule.

Listing 3.11 shoppingCartStatus.js

```
STGourmet.shoppingCart = (function() {                      ◄── Submodule called
    var cartActiveItems = [];                                   shoppingCart

    function getStatus(){
            if(cartActiveItems.length > 0){
```

```
                        return "pending";
                } else {
                        return "empty";
                }
        }

        function getStatusMessage(){
                if(STGourmet.customer.isLoggedIn()
                && getStatus() === "empty" ) {
                        return "Cart is empty";
                } else {
                        return "Cart ("
                        + cartActiveItems.length
                        + " items)";
                }
        }

        function displayStatus(){
                $("#cart").html(getStatusMessage());
        }

        return {
                displayStatus : displayStatus
        };

})();
```

Now that you have all of your code in modules, avoiding any name conflicts, let's see what the application looks like (see figure 3.6).

Figure 3.6   Using modules, our welcome message is once again correct!

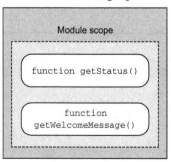

welcomeMessage.js

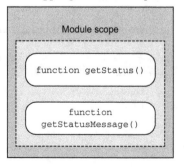

shoppingCartStatus.js

Using the module pattern, you can easily write code without fear of name conflicts. Now both getStatus() functions can coexist, with each functioning as expected (see figure 3.7).

Figure 3.7   Now that each getStatus() function lives in its own module, there are no more name conflicts.

As you've seen, the module pattern gives you the freedom to name your variables and functions any way you want, without worrying about name conflicts from code inside other modules. This small detail becomes crucial as your project grows in size and complexity.

3.2.2 *Protecting your code's integrity*

In some languages, access to certain parts of an application's code can be controlled through access-level modifiers, such as `public` or `private`. In JavaScript, the keyword `private` is reserved but not available as of this writing. So you can't explicitly declare an attribute of an object to be private. But as you've already seen, you can still limit the accessibility of variables and functions with the module pattern. This is possible because variables and functions declared inside a function are private in the sense that they're scoped to the containing function. The ability to restrict access to certain parts of a module's code prevents other code from directly changing its internal state. This keeps the internals of the module working as expected and its data from being set to something that's invalid for the module's intended purpose.

Let's illustrate with a basic counter. A simple function to increment a value every time it's invoked is pretty innocuous:

```
var count = 0;

function incrementCount() {
    ++count;
}

function printCount() {
    console.log("Count incremented: " + count + " times");
}

function displayNewCount() {
    incrementCount();
    printCount();
}
```

> Correctly increments the count and prints "Count incremented: I times"

The code as it's currently written works correctly. But there's nothing to prevent the author of `displayNewCount()` from updating the count variable directly, even though it's vital for `incrementCount()` to work properly. Let's imagine the programmer wants to change `displayNewCount()` so it prints the word *time* at the end if the count is 1; otherwise, it ends the sentence with the word *times*. Let's see what happens if the function is allowed to update the count variable itself:

```
var count = 0;

function incrementCount() {
    ++count;
}

function printCount() {
```

```
        if(count === 1) {
                count = count + " time";
        } else {
                count = count + " times";
        }
        console.log("Count incremented: " + count);
}
```

> Variable count is put into an invalid state when it's concatenated with a string

```
function displayNewCount(){
    incrementCount();
    printCount();
}
```

> Prints "Count incremented: I time" the first time but "Count incremented: NaN times" thereafter

By being allowed to directly manipulate the data used by the incrementCount() function, the printCount() function causes the value of the count variable to be NaN (not a number), which is invalid for our business logic.

Now let's rewrite the code by using the module pattern. In the next listing, we're providing only the consumer of incrementCount() access to the current count via its public interface. This effectively blocks the direct manipulation of the variable.

Listing 3.12 Code rewritten using a modular design

```
var Counter = (function() {
    var count = 0;

    function incrementCount(){
            ++count;
    }

    function getCount(){
            return count;
    }

    return {
            incrementCount : incrementCount,
            getCount : getCount
    };

})();

Counter.displayUtil = (function() {

    function printCount(){
            var count = Counter.getCount();
            if(count === 1) {
                    count = count + " time";
            } else {
                    count = count + " times";
            }
            console.log("Count incremented: " + count);
    }

    function displayNewCount(){
```

> The count variable is private and no longer directly accessible

> Access to the count variable controlled by the module's public API

> printCount() function must get the count from the main module's getCount()

```
            Counter.incrementCount();
            printCount();
    }

    return {
            printCount : printCount,
            displayNewCount : displayNewCount
    };

})();
```

Calling displayNewCount() via the public API correctly increments and prints the statement

Bulletproofing code that will be used correctly is difficult enough. This task becomes almost impossible if you can't prevent the internal workings of your code from being misused. The module pattern offers a way to manage access to internal code.

3.2.3 Hiding complexity

When we talk about hiding complexity in programming, it's not because we're trying to keep secrets. We're also not talking about security. We're referring to the difference between having complicated logic for a particular feature strewn across a multitude of global functions versus internalizing the complex logic and putting only what other developers need to use in a public interface. It reduces clutter and makes it clear which functions to call in order to correctly use the functionality. Figure 3.8 illustrates

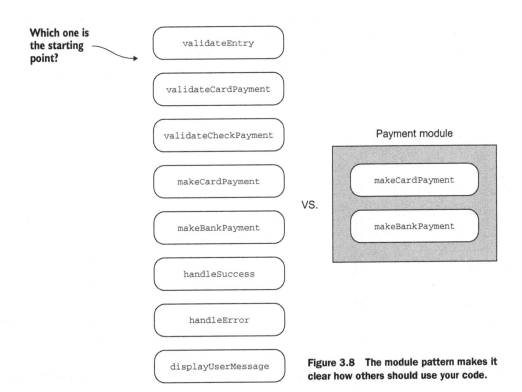

Figure 3.8 The module pattern makes it clear how others should use your code.

how a module with a public API can make it easier for other developers to know how to use your code.

By hiding the complexity of your module, you're enabling others on your team to use it without having to understand all the nuts and bolts of its internal code.

3.2.4 *Reducing the impact of code changes*

Internalizing how your code works also means that other programmers will be coding to only your public interface. As long as the behavior is the same when using the module's API, the internal code can change without forcing other parts of the application to change in turn. Reducing the amount of change to other parts of the system reduces the amount of effort and time that goes into code maintenance.

You, as the programmer of the module, can more freely make changes to your code. If the contract of your API remains intact, the chance of inadvertently introducing unrelated code bugs is greatly lessened.

3.2.5 *Organizing your code*

Staying organized makes our lives easier and more efficient. This is true in programming as well. Unless you're using the ECMAScript 6 version of JavaScript, you can't formally declare your code as part of a class or module or subroutine. Nevertheless, the ability to define a group of variables and functions as part of a unit of functionality is a good practice.

The module pattern gives you a way to take your code out of the global namespace and organize it in a more meaningful way. You can start to think of the code in terms of its overall functionality rather than individual functions (see figure 3.9).

Ultimately, refactoring your code into well-organized units will lead to greater efficiencies in terms of reuse, maintenance, and future updates.

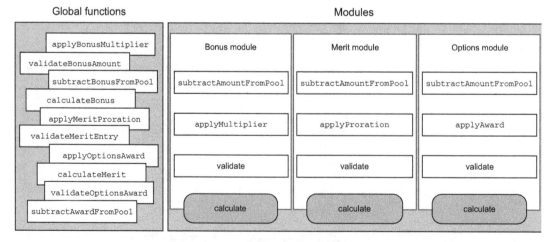

Figure 3.9 The module pattern helps organize code into units of functionality rather than individual functions.

3.2.6 *Understanding disadvantages of the module pattern*

Unfortunately, there's no silver bullet when creating complex code. This is especially true of modern web applications. For all the benefits offered by the module pattern, you should be aware of some of its disadvantages:

- *When testing*—Some people don't like the inability to unit test private functions inside the module. Others, however, advocate that unit-testing functionality via the module's public API is a more valid way of testing. Therein lies the controversy. Even though the inability to test private code is seen as a disadvantage by some, others feel that if you have to test private functions, then you should consider whether they should be made public. Their argument is that unit tests should be designed to test the interfaces to an object, not the private code within the object.
- *When extending objects*—JavaScript programmers are used to being able to extend any object, at any time, by merely adding to it. This is a testament to the powerful yet flexible nature of the language. But as you've learned, objects that are defined within the module and aren't part of the public API are unreachable outside the module. Therefore, adding a new property or method to a private object inside the module won't work. Then again, seeing this as a disadvantage is all in how you look at it. As you saw previously, this can also protect the integrity of your module's core functionality.

3.3 *The module pattern dissected*

So far you've learned a great deal about the module pattern and how to use it. What you haven't done is take a deep dive into its structure. Understanding *why* its syntax is the way it is will help you feel more comfortable when incorporating the module pattern in your single-page application. In this section, you'll dissect the module pattern to see how it does what it does.

Let's start by revisiting the original boilerplate structure to have it fresh in your mind:

```
var moduleName = (function() {
    return {
    };
})();
```

This formula is the skeleton for the basic module pattern.

3.3.1 *Achieving privacy*

JavaScript has only two types of scope: local and global. Declarations made inside a function are local (private), and those made outside any function are global (public). Because you can't explicitly mark variables and functions as public or private, you're left with only their scope to work with. That narrows things down a great deal.

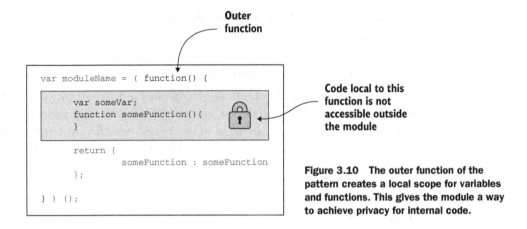

Figure 3.10   **The outer function of the pattern creates a local scope for variables and functions. This gives the module a way to achieve privacy for internal code.**

The only way to achieve privacy in JavaScript is to make your declarations locally within a function. Figure 3.10 highlights the anonymous function of the pattern, which internalizes the module's functionality.

As you may recall from our discussion of the module pattern in the previous section, this ability to internalize code is essential to achieve its benefits, such as avoiding name conflicts, protecting your code's integrity, and providing managed access to the module's functionality.

3.3.2   *Creating the public API*

You create the public API of a module by combining a few techniques. These techniques make for unusual syntax but work perfectly together to give the desired effect.

RETURN AN OBJECT LITERAL

Instead of a simple value, such as `true` or 3, an object is returned in your module pattern (see figure 3.11).

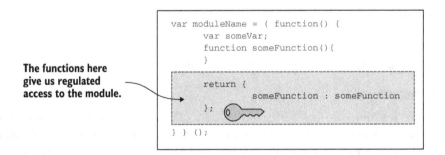

Figure 3.11   **An object literal is returned. Its functions have access to the module's internal variables and functions. This gives calling code regulated access to the module's functionality.**

The returned object can have any assortment of variables and functions, but functions are what allow you to expose behavior. That's why you typically see only functions available in the returned object.

The object literal is favored for the returned object, because its syntax provides a nice facility to define an object in a single, hierarchical fashion without the need for the new keyword. As you saw earlier in the revealing module pattern, the exposed functions are merely pointers to the inner functions.

Refresher on object literals

As a refresher, let's look at object literals. In JavaScript, you can create objects with the new keyword, with the `Object.create()` function (ECMAScript 5), or with literal notation (also referred to as an *object initializer*). With literal notation, the object is defined using curly braces. Its properties and values are in the form of name-value pairs, separated with a colon. You'll also need to put a comma after each pair *except* the last one. Values can contain variables, functions, or other objects. Here's an example:

```
var employee = {              ◄─── Begin object declaration
        firstName : "Bob",         Declare variables
        lastName : "Jones",
        deptInfo : {
                dept : "Accounting",
                bldg : "C Building",       Nest objects
                floor : "1st floor"
        },
        getFullName : function(){
                return this.firstName + " "
                + this.lastName;
        },
        getDeptInfo : function(){          Declare functions
                return this.deptInfo.dept + ", "
                + this.deptInfo.bldg + ", "
                + this.deptInfo.floor;
        }
}                             ◄─── End object declaration
console.log(employee.getFullName()        Prints "Bob Jones: Accounting,
+ ": " + employee.getDeptInfo());         C Building, 1st floor"
```

CAUSE THE FUNCTION TO RETURN IMMEDIATELY

Normally when a function is declared, it doesn't return until it's invoked by other code calling it. In the case of the module pattern, you need the variable you're using for the module's namespace to point to the returned object literal, not the function itself. This is accomplished by adding the trailing set of parentheses to the structure (see figure 3.12).

Without the trailing parentheses, the variable will be assigned the entire function, not the object being returned. With them, however, the anonymous function is

```
var moduleName = ( function() {
      var someVar;
      function someFunction(){
      }

      return {
              someFunction : someFunction
      };

} ) ();
```

Figure 3.12   The trailing parentheses cause the anonymous function of the module pattern to be invoked immediately, returning the object literal.

This causes immediate invocation.

invoked immediately, returning the object literal to the assigned variable. This is referred to as an *immediately invoked function expression,* or IIFE.

A CLOSURE IS FORMED

In order for this entire collection of techniques that are used to form this pattern to work, any private variables or functions referenced/in scope by the returned object literal can't be garbage collected. If they were, you'd get errors when trying to use the API. But a special situation occurs when your object literal is assigned to the module-Name variable. The object literal functions are now available for use, so they can't be garbage collected. Because these functions in the object literal also have references to internal private objects, those objects can't be garbage collected either. As you learned in our definition of a closure, this is possible because all functions have a scope that references an outer lexical scope. It's the closure that keeps the internal functionality alive long after the IIFE has finished executing (see figure 3.13).

In holding onto their references, the module's inner functions can continue to safely operate without becoming undefined when the outer function finishes executing.

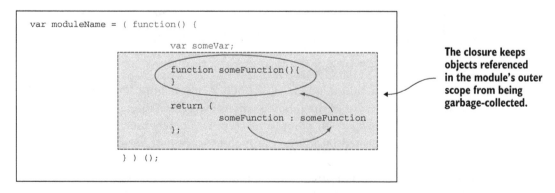

Figure 3.13   A closure keeps any variables or functions referenced in the IIFE alive, even after execution.

3.3.3 Allowing for global imports

The trailing parentheses also give you a way to declare items you want passed into the anonymous function via its parameters. In module terms, these external objects you're bringing inside for internal use are called *imports*.

Using this facility to import global variables into the module is a common practice. It not only makes it clearer to someone reading the code what's being used but also helps speed up the variable resolution process for the interpreter. Finally, it allows you to alias a global variable, if desired, within the scope of the function. Take, for example, jQuery:

```
var moduleName = (function($) {

    function init() {
            $("#div-name").html("Hello World");
    }

    return {
            init : init
    };
}) (jQuery);
```

jQuery aliased as $ via the function parameters

jQuery imported

The $ is the way most of us like to reference jQuery. It's much easier than typing out *jQuery* all the time. But many libraries out there also want to use $ in their code. Because you're specifically aliasing jQuery locally within this module, there's no chance for the $ in this instance to conflict with the $ from another library.

3.3.4 Creating the module's namespace

The final part of the module pattern is the establishment of its namespace. This namespace gives you a way to call the module's public API, as well as somewhere to assign any submodules that may be desired.

In JavaScript, a function can be declared or assigned as an expression. You just read that the outer function of the module pattern is an IIFE. The assignment of the immediately invoked anonymous function to a variable not only gives you a pointer to the returned object literal but also creates the module's name. It also defines the module's namespace if submodules are attached (see figure 3.14).

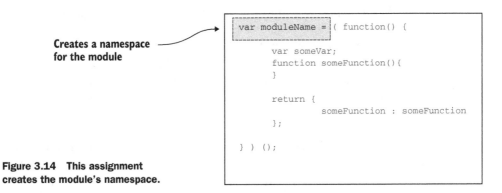

Creates a namespace for the module

```
var moduleName = ( function() {

        var someVar;
        function someFunction(){
        }

        return {
                someFunction : someFunction
        };

} ) ();
```

Figure 3.14   This assignment creates the module's namespace.

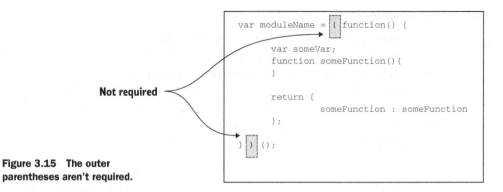

```
var moduleName = ( function() {

        var someVar;
        function someFunction(){
        }

        return {
                someFunction : someFunction
        };

} ) ();
```

Not required

**Figure 3.15 The outer
parentheses aren't required.**

> **TIP** The parentheses around the IIFE aren't required because this is a func-
> tion expression. This visually establishes a boundary for the module (see fig-
> ure 3.15).

And with that final note, your dissection of the module pattern is complete. As you
can see, each part of the pattern has a purpose. The end result from incorporating
this pattern is that your code base can remain clean, purposeful, and able to grow with
your project.

3.4   *Module loading and dependency management*

In most browsers, the SCRIPT tag used in your module's source file creates a blocking
condition. The application pauses while scripts are loading. So the more module files
you have, the more lag your users will experience while waiting for the application to
load. A deluge of HTTP requests can also tax your network.

To help alleviate this issue, you can concatenate the modules into as few files as
possible and optimize the final files. Chapter 9 covers tools for these two techniques.
But in spite of the gains from using these two techniques, you still have the SCRIPT
tag's synchronous nature to contend with. To tackle this problem, you can also look at
libraries that load your modules asynchronously.

3.4.1   *Script loaders*

Being able to bypass the blocking condition of the SCRIPT tag gives a tremendous
boost to your application's load time. HTML introduced native nonblocking support
for loading and executing JavaScript code through its defer and async attributes for
the SCRIPT tag. The defer attribute specifies that a script is executed only after the
page has finished parsing. The async attribute, on the other hand, asynchronously
executes the script as soon as it's available. When using the SCRIPT tag, it's up to you
to make sure scripts are correctly ordered so that dependencies are available when
needed. An alternative approach is to use AMD script-loading libraries.

AMD script loaders handle the low-level, boilerplate code to manage the asynchronous download process. They also allow you to specify dependencies that must be
present for a module to function. If the dependent modules aren't there, the

framework will go get them for you and make sure they're downloaded and ready before proceeding. You have a multitude of script loaders to choose from—LABjs, HeadJS, curl.js, and RequireJS, to name a few. Each one is slightly different but serves to tackle loading and management issues. It's also worth mentioning that, though not ratified as of this writing, the ability to asynchronously load scripts is a proposal for CommonJS-style script loaders.

Nothing is ever perfect, though. Asynchronously loading scripts speeds things up but introduces another problem: unpredictable resource availability. When scripts are loaded asynchronously, there's no way to precisely know which one will be first. It's entirely possible for a file to download and start executing before all necessary dependencies are in place. Creating the fastest load time possible is for naught if your scripts fail because their dependencies aren't yet loaded. Good news, though. Most script-loading libraries take care of this issue as well.

Script loaders defer script execution until the file and any required dependencies needed by the module are loaded. Most cache the module as well, so it's loaded only once, no matter how many times it's requested.

To illustrate some basic loading and management concepts, I have to choose a library to use. We'll use RequireJS because it's currently a heavily used script-loading library. RequireJS will also give you a chance to become acquainted with a popular module format that differs slightly from the traditional module pattern you've already seen. It's called the Asynchronous Module Definition (AMD) API. The next sections define AMD and walk you through script-loading basics with RequireJS.

3.4.2 *Asynchronous Module Definition*

AMD started as the draft of the module format for a larger project called CommonJS. CommonJS was an attempt to not only solve the issue of a missing standard module definition in the JavaScript language but also make this single format work for a variety of environments, including the server. But among the CommonJS group, full consensus wasn't reached on the module specification (as of this writing), and AMD was moved to its own group, the AMD JS group (https://github.com/amdjs).

AMD has largely been adopted for use within web browsers. This specification defines not only a standard module format but also how to asynchronously load it and its dependencies. The specification defines two structures: `define` and `require`. I'll talk about both before diving into an example using RequireJS.

DEFINE

Use `define` to declare a module, as you did using the module pattern previously. Like the module pattern, the AMD module allows for imports, which can be accessed via matching function parameters. The body of the AMD module is also nested inside an outer containing function, just like the module pattern. Another similarity is that the AMD module's body contains private functionality that can be exposed via its return statement.

At this point, you're probably asking yourself why AMD exists, if you already had a perfectly good way to create modules using the module pattern. The main reason is that AMD represents a formal specification for defining modules, absent having one in the language. But more specifically, it's a specification for defining modules and their dependencies that are to be loaded asynchronously.

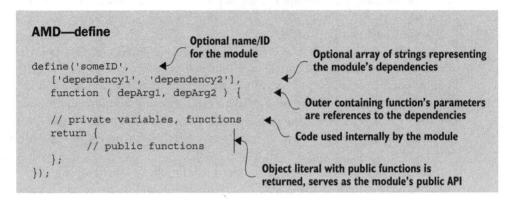

TIP Even though the specification allows for a module ID, it's normally omitted. If the ID is left out, it's generated internally by the script loader. In turn, the module is managed internally via the generated ID. Unnamed AMD modules are more portable, allowing you to freely move the module to new directories without code updates.

Notice that a namespace isn't defined as with the module pattern. Another one of the perks of using AMD and script loaders is that namespaces are no longer needed. Modules are managed by the library. You also don't have to worry about the order of the dependencies. They'll be loaded and available by the time the module's function executes.

REQUIRE

The `require` syntax is used to asynchronously load/fetch a particular module. In this structure, you define the modules to be loaded in the same way that dependencies are declared using the `define` syntax. A callback function is executed when the required modules are fetched and ready.

The `require` structure is a directive, not a module declaration. So whereas module definitions are usually one per physical file, `require` should be used anytime you need it. It can be used by itself or from within a module.

3.4.3 *Using AMD modules with RequireJS*

Quite often concepts are easier to understand after seeing them in action. So let's take one of the earlier examples and convert the modules into AMD-style modules. You'll use RequireJS as the module-loading library to implement AMD.

Before you begin the example, let's go over some RequireJS concepts. Even though you'll focus on module loader concepts, you still have to get some of the RequireJS basics under your belt to be able to complete the example:

- `data-main`—Everything has to start somewhere. Just as a basic Java or C# application has a "main" method, RequireJS similarly has a point of origin. When you add a `SCRIPT` tag to your SPA to include the RequireJS library, you'll add a `data-main` attribute to it. This is the starting point of a RequireJS-loaded application. Normally your main JavaScript file will contain the RequireJS configuration and a `require` directive to execute the initial AMD module.
- `requirejs.config()`—This function establishes the RequireJS configuration options. Its only input is an object literal that will contain all configuration properties and their values.
- `baseUrl`—This is a path relative to your web application's root directory. Any other paths in the configuration object will be relative, in turn, to this path.
- `path`—You have to tell RequireJS where to find your modules. A `path` maps a module name (which you invent) to a path on the web server, relative to the `baseURL` (and the application's root directory). It can be the full path to the module's source file (minus the extension) or a partial path. If a partial directory path is used, the rest of the path to the file must be included anywhere the object is listed as a dependency.

You have many more configuration options, but we'll stick to the basics to keep the emphasis on learning AMD, not RequireJS specifically. If you want to learn more about RequireJS-specific options, the documentation can be found at http://requirejs.org.

Now that you've been introduced to a few basic concepts, let's try converting an example's modules to AMD modules. You'll use the example from section 3.2.2, because it's a small example and will be easy to compare against the original version.

First, you'll need to download the RequireJS library from http://requirejs.org. Figure 3.16 has the correct download option circled.

Figure 3.16 RequireJS has no dependencies to download. You need only the require.js file.

With the necessary files in place, the example's directory now looks like the following listing.

Listing 3.13 AMD example directory structure

```
|-- app
|   |-- example
|   |   |-- modules
|   |   |   |-- counter.js
|   |   |   |-- displayUtil.js
|-- thirdParty
|   |-- require.min.js
|-- index.html
|-- main.js
```

RequireJS library

Two example modules

Main file contains the RequireJS configuration and our application's kickoff point

---

When you open your default URL in the web browser, you'll immediately get the index.html page, because the server has been configured to use it as your welcome page. All you need to do here is add a single JavaScript include to point to the RequireJS library. Inside the SCRIPT tag, you'll use the data-main attribute to let RequireJS know that your main file is called main.js and can be found at the web application's root (see the following listing).

Listing 3.14 index.html

```html
<!DOCTYPE html>
<html>
<head>
<link rel="stylesheet" href="css/default.css">
</head>
<body>
    <!-- starting point defined in data-main -->
    <script data-main="main.js"
        src="thirdParty/require.min.js">
    </script>
</body>
</html>
```

Tells RequireJS where application's main file is located

RequireJS library

Next, you'll need to add some basic configuration to main.js. This example is simple, so you need to configure only your baseUrl and path properties so RequireJS can find the modules. You'll additionally use the require directive to call displayNewCount() from your displayUtil module twice. Calling the function more than once will let you know that the counter is incremented appropriately (see the following listing).

Listing 3.15 main.js

```javascript
requirejs.config({
    baseUrl : "app/example",
    paths : {
            counter : "modules/counter",
            util : "modules/displayUtil"
    }
});
```

baseUrl relative to the web application's root

Path relative to the baseUrl (entry to the left of the colon is the module's name)

```
require(
    [ "util" ],
    function(utilModule) {
            // increment first time
            utilModule.displayNewCount();
            // increment second time
            utilModule.displayNewCount();
    }
);
```

Use the module's name to declare a resource as a dependency

Function parameter receives the object export of the dependency it matches

Inside our callback function, call displayUtil twice to increment counter

Looking at the code for the require call from listing 3.15, notice that you told RequireJS you wanted to use the displayUtil module in the callback function by including its module name from the paths section. Each module-name string in the dependency list should have a matching function parameter. Inside the callback function, you use this parameter to reference the module.

The following listing shows the module for the display utility. Because this is a module declaration, you'll use the define syntax.

Listing 3.16 displayUtil.js

```
define(["counter"], function(counterModule) {
    function printCount(){
            var count = counterModule.getCount();
            if(count === 1) {
                    count = count + " time";
            } else {
                    count = count + " times";
            }
            console.log("Count incremented: " + count);
    }

    function displayNewCount(){
            counterModule.incrementCount();
            this.printCount();
    }

    return {
            printCount : printCount,
            displayNewCount : displayNewCount
    };
});
```

Counter module is a dependency

Code was modified to use the parameter reference to the counter module

In the displayUtil module, your only dependency is the counter module. The body of the module is nearly a one-to-one match with the original, non-AMD version. Keep in mind that you don't need to assign the module to a namespace, because modules are managed internally by RequireJS.

Finally, the next listing shows the counter module. Because it has no dependencies, you can leave out that part of the structure. With no dependencies, your outer function will have no parameters.

Listing 3.17   counter.js

```
define(function() {
    var count = 0;

    function incrementCount(){
        ++count;
    }

    function getCount(){
        return count;
    }

    return {
        incrementCount : incrementCount,
        getCount : getCount
    };
});
```

◄ Dependency list can be left out; module's outer function has no parameters

With all of the files in place, you can start your server and navigate to the default URL. The application will start after the `require` directive is reached. Figure 3.17 shows the network console from the browser. Now you can see the module loader in action.

From the output in the network console, you can see that all required modules were downloaded automatically by the module loader. All you had to do was to add a dependency to your `require` or `define` declaration. Because each dependency was passed into the module via its corresponding function parameter, you had access to the dependent module's public API. Additionally, because RequireJS manages the modules for you, you didn't need any namespaces. This is a testimony to the power of using AMD modules and the module loaders that implement this module specification.

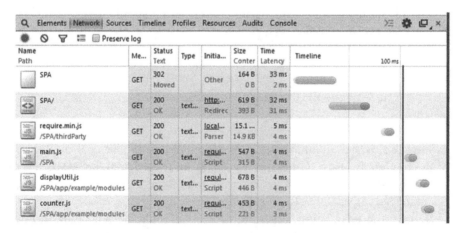

Figure 3.17   The module loader correctly downloads and manages our AMD modules and dependencies. The `require` directive in main.js declares a dependency that instructs RequireJS to fetch the `displayUtil` module. The `displayUtil` module, in turn, has a dependency on the `counter` module that gets dynamically loaded by the module loader.

3.5 *Chapter challenge*

Now here's a challenge for you, to see what you've learned in this chapter. In browsers such as Firefox or Chrome, you can add styles to messages printed to the browser's console by using `%c`, as in this example:

```
console.log("%c" + errorMessage, "color: red");
```

See if you can turn this into a reusable logging module. Expose functions that will print different colors based on these logging modes: debug, info, warning, and error. Internally create variables representing each mode's color: black for debug, green for info, orange for warning, and red for error. You'll also need to define internal functionality that prints in a color that matches the logging mode used.

3.6 *Summary*

This chapter described what a module is and listed what the module pattern does for you:

- Keeps parts of your code private, only for use within the module
- Provides for a public API, which hides complexity and protects the integrity of a component's code by providing regulated access to the internal code
- Prevents name collisions that occur when everything's defined in the global namespace
- Reduces the impact to the project when code changes
- Provides a way to divide areas of concern in your application into manageable, more meaningful units

Nothing's perfect. This chapter also presented some disadvantages of the module pattern:

- Unit testing is limited to a public API.
- Internal objects can't easily be extended.

Finally, you looked at a more formal specification for modules called Asynchronous Module Definition (AMD) and learned how module loaders eliminate the need for namespaces and asynchronously fetch your modules and their dependencies.

In the next chapter, you'll look at another way to separate areas of concern: using MV* libraries to separate your JavaScript code from your HTML.

Part 2

Core concepts

In the second part of the book you'll see how the various pieces of an SPA fit together. You'll also get an introduction to testing an SPA and how client-side automation fits into the picture.

In chapter 4, you'll be introduced to client-side routing. You'll get an overview of router syntax and a comparison of various router styles. Along the way, you'll learn how routers work under the covers and how they affect the state of the application.

Chapter 5 introduces you to design and layout concepts when building an SPA. We'll start with a look at simple designs and then progress into building SPAs with more complex layouts. You'll also see how to incorporate advanced routing and view management into your application.

Chapter 6 gives you a tour of inter-module communication methods, including an introduction to modular design concepts. In this chapter, you'll learn some ways in which modules communicate with each other. I also talk about the pros and cons of each method.

In chapter 7, you'll learn how to communicate with the server and how MV* frameworks can be leveraged to make this process easier. We'll start with the basics of HTTP transactions and then move into more advanced topics such as using promises and consuming RESTful services from your SPA.

Chapter 8 gives you a gentle introduction to unit testing your application. You'll learn basic unit-testing concepts and walk through the testing of the different framework styles talked about in the book.

Finally, in chapter 9, you'll see the role client-side automation plays in both the development and the creation of a build process. This is an advanced topic, so we'll walk through each part of the process, step by step. When you've finished, you'll know not only how to create a client-side build but also some ways to make your development processes faster and more efficient.

Navigating the single page

Part 1 of this book covered views and how they're created. What it didn't cover, though, is client-side routing. This can be used to navigate from one view to the next, but that's only part of the picture. Client-side routing is also about transitioning between different states in the application. This could include modifications to the current view without navigation or other activities that don't include changes in the UI at all.

In this chapter, you'll explore how users navigate in an SPA by using client-side routing. You'll not only learn what client-side routers are but also peek behind the curtain a bit to see how they work.

During our discussion, I'll keep things as framework-agnostic as possible by illustrating with pseudocode. Once you've nailed down the concepts, you'll use what you've learned to create a simple routing example with AngularJS. In the example,

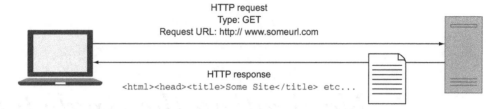

Figure 4.1   In traditional web-page navigation, complete pages are sent back to the browser, triggering a refresh to display the new content.

you'll create a website for a department of a university. Though rudimentary, the example will sufficiently illustrate the basic concepts common to most client-side routers without getting into too many vendor-specific details. You'll also use that same university theme throughout our discussion. This will help you put a real-world face on the pseudocode and illustrations.

4.1   What is a client-side router?

Let's begin this discussion by putting navigation as a whole into context. You'll start with the request and response model used in traditional web application navigation.

4.1.1   Traditional navigation

In a traditional web application, navigation is thought of in terms of complete web pages. When you enter a new URL into the location bar of a browser, usually a request is sent for the page from the browser to a server, which responds by sending you back an entire HTML page (see figure 4.1).

What's actually sent back is the HTML document for the requested page. After the HTML for that page is received, the browser then fetches any other source files referenced by the document, such as any CSS and JavaScript include files. Other assets referenced in the HTML, such as images, also get downloaded as the browser parses the document's HTML and encounters their tags. To display the new content, the browser performs a complete refresh.

4.1.2   SPA navigation

As you already learned, an SPA's DOM typically starts off as a shell in the SPA's index page. That's all that's needed. The SPA's modules and MV* framework, including supporting libraries, are either downloaded with the index page or asynchronously loaded if an AMD script-loading library is used. An SPA also has the ability to asynchronously fetch data and any remote templates (partials) and other resources not already included and to dynamically render views as needed.

As the user navigates, views are seamlessly displayed. This, combined with the asynchronous fetching of data, gives the application a smooth, native-like feel that makes for a great user experience. No more of the jarring interruptions that you usually

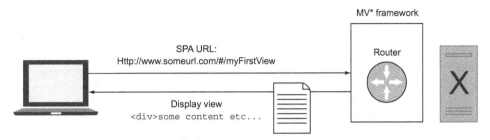

Figure 4.2 In an SPA, the client-side router assumes control of navigation, allowing the SPA to display new views instead of complete pages.

experience when a page is wiped clean and a new page is downloaded and displayed. The SPA does all of this without refreshing the initial page after it's loaded.

After the SPA is loaded, however, users need a way to access additional content within the application. Because an SPA is still a web-based application, your users will expect to be able to use the address bar and the browser's navigation buttons for navigation. But how can navigation in an SPA occur with just one page and no browser refreshes?

As it turns out, it's not only possible, it's easy. The JavaScript component that makes navigation in this single-page environment possible is called a *client-side router* (or just a *router*).

But remember that when I talk about navigation, I'm talking about managing the state of the SPA's views, data, and business transactions as the user navigates. The router manages the application's state by assuming control of the browser's navigation, allowing developers to directly map changes in the URL to client-side functionality (see figure 4.2). I'll get into the details of how it does this later, in section 4.3.

Using this approach, no server round-trips are needed. The router determines when a change in state is needed through various methods of detecting changes in the browser's location, such as listening for particular events. Anytime a URL change occurs, the router tries to match part of the new URL with an entry in its configuration.

Before breaking down the typical parts of a router's configuration, let's look at the big picture. Figure 4.3 provides an overview of the navigation process in an SPA and highlights the role of the client-side router. Notice that at no time does the router interact with the server. All routing is done in the browser.

As you can see in the diagram, when the router matches *paths* from its configuration with real URLs in the browser, it can determine what types of changes in the application's state should occur. Are there any changes in the data of the current view? Is a business process associated with the route? Should the route result in a change in the current view?

Now that you have a mental picture of the basic routing process, let's go over how routes are set up. The next section breaks down the configuration of a router and defines its typical parts.

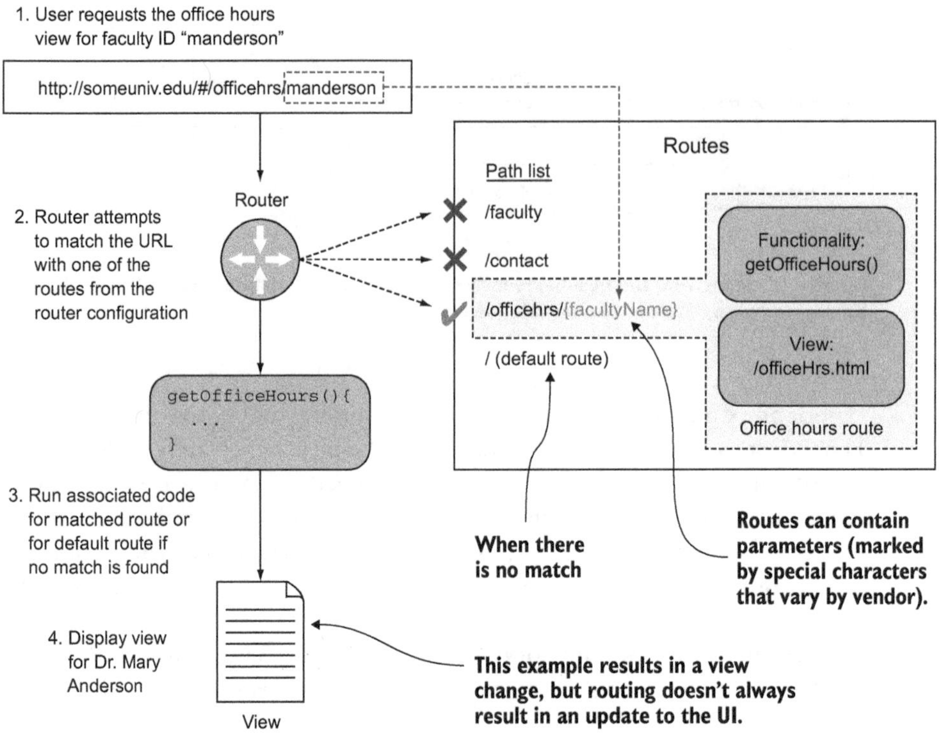

1. User reqeusts the office hours
   view for faculty ID "manderson"

http://someuniv.edu/#/officehrs/manderson

Routes

Path list

2. Router attempts
   to match the URL
   with one of the
   routes from the
   router configuration

Router

✗ /faculty

✗ /contact

✓ /officehrs/{facultyName}

/ (default route)

Functionality:
getOfficeHours()

View:
/officeHrs.html

Office hours route

```
getOfficeHours(){
    ...
}
```

3. Run associated code
   for matched route or
   for default route if
   no match is found

**When there
is no match**

**Routes can contain
parameters (marked
by special characters
that vary by vendor).**

4. Display view
   for Dr. Mary
   Anderson

View

**This example results in a view
change, but routing doesn't always
result in an update to the UI.**

Figure 4.3   **An overview of the SPA navigation process and the role of the router**

4.2   *Routes and their configuration*

No matter which router you use, a certain amount of up-front configuration must be done. You must make entries in the router's configuration file to map out how the router should respond as the user navigates.

Each entry in the router's configuration is called a *route*. Routes are stored in the router's configuration at development time, with each route representing a logical flow within your SPA. You'll typically design your routes as you design the layout for your application. Though router configuration varies from router to router, here are some typical configuration terms:

- *Name*—With some routers, a name is given to the route. In others, the path serves as the route's identifier.
- *Verb*—Routes are sometimes defined with function names that match HTTP verbs—for example, get() or put()—but not always. Some routers use more-generic names such as on() or when() or route().
- *Path*—The path is a part of the URL. The path used to configure the router establishes a link between a URL and a route/route handler. This allows the router to figure out which set of actions to perform. Anytime the URL in the browser changes, the router compares the new URL with all route paths in the configura-

tion file's path list for a match. When one is found, the route is carried out. The path of the route must be a valid part of a URL. Although it's quite common that the path is simple text, some routers allow the use of regular expressions.

- *Functionality*—This is the associated code that may be executed, such as a controller or a callback function. For the route to do anything, you need some associated code to run.

Routers may or may not include a way to define the view via configuration. Remember that routing is about changes in the application's state that don't have to result in a view at all. I include it in the list because the view is a configuration item for some routers:

- *A view*—Most often when a router allows you to include the view as part of the route's configuration, it's the path to an HTML partial. As you may remember from chapter 2, these files are kept separate at development time and include only elements for a particular view. When the view is configured as part of the route, the router typically handles its display and gives the functionality access to the view (or a proxy object for the view, such as a ViewModel).

Figure 4.4 shows an average route in the configuration of some routers, like the one we're using in this chapter. Because each router is different, this figure won't be a

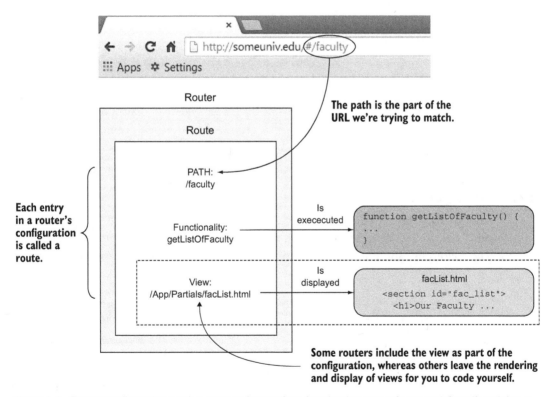

Figure 4.4 Router configuration entries serve as instructions for what happens when a route's path matches a part of the browser's URL.

perfect fit for all routers. You can use it, however, as a general, high-level look at route configuration. Keep in mind that in your SPA, you'll most likely end up with many routes in the router's configuration when your application is completed.

Routers may also provide other, more advanced features. This varies from router to router. Consult the documentation of the router implementation you're using for the full list of available configuration options.

4.2.1   Route syntax

Syntactically, the code for your routes will differ somewhat from router to router. With some router implementations, you configure the route and route handler in separate places, whereas others provide for the configuration of both in the same place. A common theme exists, though, for executing routes. Let's look at some syntax examples.

Table 4.1 is by no means an exhaustive list, but it does give you a few examples. Remember to consult your router's documentation for the exact syntax to be used.

Table 4.1   Examples of client-side router syntax

Framework/library	Path example
Sammy.js http://sammyjs.org	`get('#/routes/faculty', function() {...})`
Kendo UI http://www.telerik.com/kendo-ui	`route("/routes/faculty", function() {...})`
AngularJS https://angularjs.org	`when("/routes/faculty", { ... })`
Backbone.js (2 steps) http://backbonejs.org	1. `routes: {"/routes/faculty": "facultyRoute"}` 2. `on("route:facultyRoute", function () {...})`

Also remember that some MV* frameworks, such as Knockout, don't include a router. In that case, you'll need to find an external router library, such as Sammy.js.

4.2.2   Route entries

Now let's see how a complete route entry might look. Again, we'll use pseudocode right now and wrap things up with a real, working project at the end of the chapter. The following listing illustrates a basic route in which you're able to specify a view in the configuration.

Listing 4.1   Router with view capabilities (pseudocode)

```
ON MATCH OF "/routes/faculty" :                    The functionality that's executed
    FUNCTION NAME : "getListOfFaculty",
    VIEW TO DISPLAY : "App/partials/faclist.html"

                                                   The view that gets displayed
```

The path

This route entry almost reads like a sentence, doesn't it? It's telling the narrative of what needs to happen when the router finds a match to its path in the URL. It's also an easy trail to follow: match the pattern, run the code, and show the result.

Next, let's see the same route, but from the perspective of a router that leaves the view's rendering and display up to you. In the following listing, the router provides only the facility to match the route with a controller or callback function.

Listing 4.2   Router that lets you handle the view (pseudocode)

```
ON MATCH OF "/routes/faculty"
    EXECUTE THIS FUNCTION :
    function() {
        // get faculty list, then call MV*code
        // to render and display view
    }
```

The path →

The functionality that's executed ←

This type of router is handy when you're using a code-driven framework, such as Backbone.js.

TIP   No matter which type of router you use, try to leave your route configuration file devoted to the routes themselves. It's considered a better practice to have the route's callback function use your application's modules to perform any business logic, as opposed to mixing in code not related to routing.

So far we've been talking about basic routes. Most routers offer a way to greatly expand the capabilities of a single route, by turning the route path into something dynamic. The next section explores the topic of *route parameters* and how to use them in your application.

4.2.3   *Route parameters*

Most routers have the notion of route parameters. A *route parameter* is a variable defined in the route's path. This allows you to add variables to the URL, which will later execute when the route is carried out.

Why would you need this ability? Well, you might want to use the same functionality and the same view but want a different outcome for different situations. Route parameters provide this flexibility. This is a powerful tool to have at your disposal.

Let's illustrate this concept with a route that displays the office hours for the faculty members in our university-themed example. In this situation, everything is the same in your route, down to the view. But you need the view to display different information depending on which faculty member's name is clicked. To do this, you'll pass the faculty member's ID in the route's path. This situation is a perfect scenario for using a route parameter.

To make the route parameter work, you need two parts: the relative URL containing the text you're passing and the route path with the parameter on the receiving end.

CONFIGURING A ROUTE PATH WITH A PARAMETER

To tell the router that part of the path is a parameter, you define it in your route's configuration. The parameter is defined by using special characters as specified by the router. The following listing shows your office hours route with its route parameter.

Listing 4.3   Office hours route with a parameter (pseudocode)

```
ON MATCH OF "/routes/officehrs/{facultyNameParam}"      ◄─────   Route parameter to pass a faculty
    EXECUTE THIS FUNCTION :                                      member's ID denoted with {}
    function(facultyNameParam) {               ◄───────
        // get office hours for faculty member
        // with ID of facultyNameParam         The router passes the route
    }                                          parameter to the callback
                                               function so you have access to it
```

Each router has its own syntax for route parameters. Table 4.2 contains several examples of route parameter syntax for comparison. We'll stick to the same router list that you saw previously in table 4.1. Each one happens to use the same route parameter syntax.

Table 4.2   Examples of route parameter syntax

Framework/library	Path example
Sammy.js http://sammyjs.org	:facultyNameParam
Kendo UI http://www.telerik.com/kendo-ui	:facultyNameParam
AngularJS https://angularjs.org	:facultyNameParam
Backbone.js (2 steps) http://backbonejs.org	:facultyNameParam

In the frameworks/libraries represented in table 4.2, a colon is the common way to denote a route parameter. But no universal standard exists. Other routers may use a different convention. Additionally, the router you select may offer more-advanced parameter options, such as regular expressions. Consult the documentation for whichever router you choose.

THE RELATIVE URL WITH THE TEXT TO BE PASSED

If you use a route parameter, the router can discern from the path which part of the URL is the parameter and which part should be a verbatim match. For example, the following is a link that matches the route from listing 4.3. The URL matches the path exactly, except for the parameter portion.

```
<a href="#/routes/officehrs/manderson">
    Dr. Mary Anderson
</a>
```

If this were a link to your office hours route, the last part of the link's URL would represent this person's faculty ID. Each faculty member on your fictitious university web page could have a link that uses the same route pattern but includes a different ID as the URL's suffix.

MULTIPLE PARAMETERS

Most (if not all) routers allow for more than one parameter to be used at a time. For example, if you have more than one link for a faculty member, you might want to parameterize the route even further:

```
/routes/officehrs/{facultyNameParam}/{dayOfTheWeek}
```

Apart from defining specific routes, it's also possible to include a default route.

4.2.4 *Default routes*

To round out our discussion of routes and their configuration, we need to touch on default routes. These types of routes are good for catchall situations when the route isn't specified or is invalid. Without a default, your application wouldn't do anything if the user typed a URL in the address bar that had no matches in the router's configuration. With a default route in place, you're immediately redirected to a particular route from your route list. The following listing shows how you can redirect any URL back to the faculty route when no match is found.

> **Listing 4.4   Default route (pseudocode)**

```
DEFAULT ROUTE: [
    REDIRECT TO "/routes/faculty"
]
```
◄⌐ **Otherwise indicates your default. You redirect back to the faculty route when there's no match to any other path.**

Your default means that when you have a route match, route to it; otherwise, redirect to the faculty route. The default route is also a handy mechanism to specify what happens when a user types a website's base URL into the browser, with no specific paths included.

The next section explains what the router is doing when you navigate. The discussion will stay at a high level but go just deep enough for you to understand what's going on behind the scenes during routing.

4.3   *How do client-side routers work?*

Part of a client-side router's job is to allow users to use the address bar and the browser's navigation buttons as they normally would in a traditional web application. At a minimum, many client-side routers offer the following features that make this possible:

- Match patterns in the URL with paths defined by the route
- Allow for the execution of code in your application when a match is found

- Allow a view to be specified that will be displayed when the route is triggered
- Allow for parameters to be passed via the route's path
- Allow users to use standard navigation methods of the browser to navigate the SPA

These features are all that are needed to provide a minimal level of navigation in an SPA. Keep in mind, though, that there's no guaranteed standard that all client-side routers must follow. These are just the most common options you'll encounter. The documentation for the MV* framework (or independent router library) will list its full range of features.

Having summarized a basic list of features most routers offer, let's peek under the covers to see how routers provide navigation in a single-page setting.

Routers use one of two methods: either via the URL's *fragment identifier* or the *HTML5 History API*. Both methods enable the router to provide server-less navigation but in slightly different ways. Because the HTML5 History API is newer and not supported by older browsers, you'll start your foray into the world of client-side routing with the more traditional fragment identifier method.

4.3.1   *The fragment identifier method*

The traditional method for routers to provide navigation in an SPA is via a *fragment identifier.* As noted in figure 4.5, the fragment identifier is any arbitrary string of text at the end of the URL and is prefixed with a hash symbol (#). This optional part of the URL references a section of the current document, not a new document.

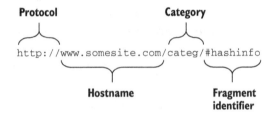

Figure 4.5   **The fragment identifier**

Browsers treat this part differently from the rest of the URL. When a new fragment identifier is added to the URL, the browser doesn't attempt to interact with the server. The addition does, however, become a new entry in the browser's history.

This is important because all entries in the browser's history, even those generated from the fragment identifier, can be navigated to via normal means, such as the address bar and the navigation buttons. To see this in action, go to any website, such as www.manning.com. Next, try executing the following in your browser's console:

```
window.location.hash = "hello";
```

As you'll see, doing this results in *hello* being added as the URL's fragment identifier. The URL should look like this after the line executes:

```
http://www.manning.com/#hello
```

This action also adds a new entry in the browser's history. Now you can navigate back and forth between the fragment identifier and the original URL.

EXPLOITING THE BROWSER'S LOCATION OBJECT

The *location object* contains an API that allows you to access the browser's URL information. In an SPA, routers take advantage of the location object to programmatically gain access to the current URL, including the fragment identifier. The router does this to listen for changes in the fragment identifier portion of the URL, via the window's onhashchange event (if available in that browser version—otherwise, it polls for hash changes).

When a change occurs, the pattern in the new hash string is compared to all the paths in each route from the router's configuration. If a match exists, the router executes any process specified and then displays the view from the matching route.

For example, imagine you have a link to your fictitious department's main contact page in your website header. The link's code points to a fragment identifier URL:

```
<a href="#routes/contact">Contact Us</a>
```

When you click this link, the browser's fragment identifier changes from its initial value to #/routes/contact.

Because the router actively listens for changes in the fragment identifier, this new hash is detected. Upon detection, the router searches all routes in its configuration for a path matching /routes/contact. When it finds a match, the route in the following listing is carried out.

Listing 4.5 Main contact route (pseudocode)

```
                     The functionality used
                     in the new route
ON MATCH OF "/routes/contact" :
    FUNCTION NAME : "displayContactNumber",
    VIEW TO DISPLAY : "App/partials/contact.html"
The path
                     The view you'll change to
```

You should now have a pretty good understanding of basic client-side routing. As I mentioned at the beginning of this section, routers can use two methods to control the application's state. You've looked at the fragment identifier method. In the next section, you'll look at the newer HTML5 History API method.

4.3.2 The HTML5 History API method

You've learned that by using the fragment identifier method to change the URL's hash information, the router can add new navigable entries in the browser's history. Each change adds a new entry in the history stack. After that, users can navigate back and forth between hashes without triggering a page refresh. But when using this method, developers are forced to create paths that revolve around the hash symbol (#).

New methods in the HTML5 History API change this. Routers can take advantage of new functionality available in HTML5 to interact with the browser's history without relying on the fragment identifier. Also, because these methods aren't available in older browsers, most routers gracefully fall back on the fragment identifier automatically.

PUSHSTATE AND REPLACESTATE

The two new methods in the History object's API that routers can take advantage of are as follows:

- `pushState()`—Allows you to add new history entries
- `replaceState()`—Allows you to replace existing history entries with new ones

These new additions allow direct access to the browser's history without relying on the fragment identifier. You'll explore them briefly to understand what happens when routers use the HTML5 History API method.

Using `history.pushState()` or `history.replaceState()`, the router can directly modify the browser's history stack. Both methods also allow the router to work with "pretty," natural-looking URL segments instead of hashes. Both methods take three parameters:

- *State object*—An optional JavaScript object associated with the history entry
- *Title*—Represents a new title for the history entry (though not implemented by most browsers as of this writing)
- *URL*—The URL that should be displayed in the browser's address bar

To see how this method works, give `pushState()` a try. Go to any website, such as www.manning.com, and type following in your browser's console:

```
history.pushState({myObject: "hi"},"A Title", "newURL.html");
```

The command results in the URL changing to this:

```
http://www.manning.com/newURL.html
```

It also adds a new entry in the browser's history. Now you can navigate back and forth between the new URL and the original URL. You'll also notice that the URL added via `pushState()` doesn't trigger a browser refresh and doesn't contain the hash symbol.

To view the state object that was added, you can type `history.state` into the console. In response, you'll see the contents of `myObject` returned.

THE POPSTATE EVENT

Finally, routers are given a way to monitor the history stack for changes: the `window.popstate` event. Browsers fire this event whenever the user navigates between history entries.

You can also experiment with this in your console. Use the `pushState()` method to add some history entries. Then execute the following code in your console:

```
window.addEventListener("popstate", function(event) {
    console.log("popstate event fired");
});
```

Next, navigate back and forth between the URLs added with `pushState()`. You should see the following log entry added to the console:

```
popstate event fired
```

Now that you understand the newer HTML5 History API method of routing, let's see how you change your code to use it.

4.3.3 Changes for the HTML5 History API method

Most routers offer the option to use the HTML5 History API method for client-side routing. Indicating to the router which method you prefer is usually as easy as setting a single configuration option. Often, however, other changes need to be made in addition to the mode switch. I talk about those in this section.

Let's start with the option to change methods. In many routers, you change a Boolean value from `false` to `true`.

HTML5 MODE

To convert our example from the fragment identifier method to this one, you need to change the appropriate setting in your router's configuration. This is where you flip the switch to use the HTML5 History API method. For example, in AngularJS, you'd use this:

```
html5Mode(true);
```

In Backbone.js, you'd use this:

```
Backbone.history.start({pushState: true});
```

Again, these are framework-specific examples. Consult your router's documentation for the exact syntax.

BASE HREF

Now that you've told the router that you want to use the HTML5 History API method, you need to set the BASE HREF in your index page's header:

```
<head>
<base href="/SPA/">
</head>
```

For the HTML5 History API to work correctly, your BASE HREF must match the deployed application's root path in its *base URL*. Otherwise, you'll get an "Error 404 not found" response when your application tries to retrieve the views in its routes.

> **TIP** You need a base URL only if you don't want to include the full path in your links/code.

In this example, /SPA/ will be the root path in your base URL. So you need to use that as the BASE HREF. A lot of different servers are out there, and applications get deployed in many ways. As long the BASE HREF is set properly, your views will be displayed.

SERVER-SIDE CHANGES

Finally, to finish off the HTML5 History API configuration, you'll need to configure your server so that it always returns content for the root. For example, if you have a catchall server-side route configured, it'll always return the correct resource to the client.

One caveat is that if a user uses a bookmark or page refresh, the browser will make a request for that same content. One possible solution is to set up a redirect on the server to internally redirect to that same URL.

REMOVING THE HASH

If the router supports it, you can now remove the hash characters from the links in your views. For example, in the link to the main office contact information, the anchor tag can be written as follows:

```
<a href="routes/contact">Contact Us</a>
```

When you click this link, you'll see what looks like a normal URL in the browser's address bar. No hash character!

Now that you know the basics of client-side routing, you can roll up your sleeves and do some coding.

4.4 *Putting it all together: implementing routing in SPAs*

In this section, you'll take the concepts discussed and illustrated with pseudocode and create a real, working project using AngularJS. In this example, you'll continue the university theme. Let's pretend you're a campus IT staff member tasked with creating a website for one of the university's departments.

You'll have three views: a landing view with faculty names to choose from, another view to display the office hours for the person the user selects, and a general contact view for the department.

The user can navigate by either clicking the name of a faculty member in the landing view's faculty list or clicking a navigation link in the header. Also, because you're incorporating an SPA navigation component, the user will be able to use the browser's address bar and navigation buttons.

I include the most relevant excerpts from the code here. The complete code is available for download when you want to give the example a try or see the complete code for this chapter's example. Figure 4.6 shows the finished product.

You'll begin with the example's first route, the faculty list route. This is your default route. As you may remember from earlier, the default route is the one used when there's no match between the current URL and any of the paths in your configuration file. Because the site's base URL

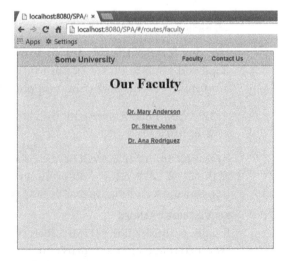

Figure 4.6   For this example, you'll create a basic website for a university department.

won't have a match, you should always execute the faculty list route by default. A direct link to the faculty route exists in the header, so this route can be accessed from there as well.

4.4.1 The faculty list (default route)

You saw the pseudocode for the faculty list in our discussion of routes, so let's create it for real now.

When you use AngularJS's router, your routes will be configured via $route-Provider. You can use the $routeProvider's when() method for normal routes and otherwise() to configure a default route. This is specific to AngularJS, though, so don't worry about that detail. If you're using a different framework or routing library, you'll add the same configuration using different syntax.

For now, let's focus on the concept presented by the route itself. In this route, you'll use the text /routes/faculty to represent the route's path (see the following listing).

Listing 4.6 Faculty list route

```
$routeProvider.when("/routes/faculty", {
    templateUrl : "App/components/simplerouter/partials/facList.html",
    controller : "facultyController"
})
```

The path

The functionality that's executed

The view that gets displayed

As mentioned earlier, you also want to display the list of faculty members by default. The next listing shows your default route.

Listing 4.7 Default route

```
.otherwise({
    redirectTo: "/routes/faculty"
})
```

Indicates your default

Redirects back to the faculty route

With this default route in place, you're immediately redirected to your faculty list when you type the application's URL into the browser.

THE FUNCTIONALITY BEHIND THE ROUTE

With AngularJS, you can give the name of a registered controller as the functionality to be executed. In other libraries or frameworks, it may be some other type of object or the name of a callback function. In this example, whenever the router finds a URL that contains /routes/faculty, the code in the facultyController controller is executed.

Your faculty list's controller will provide the list of faculty members to be displayed in the view (see listing 4.8). This controller is one of the three defined in our example's controller file, which also contains the definition for the routeControllers object:

```
var routerControllers = angular.module(
"RouterApp.controllers", []);
```

To be available in the view, your list needs to be added to AngularJS's $scope object. As you may remember from chapter 2, $scope is a built-in object, which serves as the "middleman" between the view and your data (kind of like a ViewModel).

Listing 4.8   The functionality for your route

```
routerControllers.controller(                          ◄──── Define the
        "facultyController", function($scope) {              facultyController

    $scope.deptFaculty = [ {                           ◄────
        hrefVal : "manderson",
        displayText : "Dr. Mary Anderson"              Add the data for the faculty
    }, {                                               office hour links to the $scope
        hrefVal: "sjones",                             so it's available in the view
        displayText : "Dr. Steve Jones"
    }, {
        hrefVal: "arodriguez",
        displayText : "Dr. Ana Rodriguez"
    } ];

});
```

In the array you're making available to the view, you have a list of faculty objects. Each object has two properties: hrefVal and displayText. The hrefVal property will be used in the creation of the link's URL. The displayText property contains the name the faculty member. You'll use the faculty member's name as the visible text of the link.

NOTE   The most common practice when using AngularJS is to keep any kind of business logic in an AngularJS service, but we're breaking that rule here for the sake of keeping this example as simple as possible.

THE FACULTY LIST VIEW

Finally, in listing 4.9, you see the source code for your view. As part of the state changes associated with this route, you'll display this view, which will contain the data from listing 4.8. Notice that the view's template uses the properties from the $scope object with the ng-repeat binding to iteratively create the list of links.

Listing 4.9   The route's view

```
<section id="fac_list">
   <h1>Our Faculty</h1>
   <section id="faculty">
      <ul>
         <li ng-repeat="faculty in deptFaculty">         ◄────
            <a href="#routes/officehrs/{{faculty.hrefVal}}">
            {{faculty.displayText}}
            </a>                      ng-repeat is used to stamp out anchor tags for each
         </li>                        object in the deptFaculty array. The ng-repeat binding
      </ul>                           tells the framework to create the structure of the
   </section>                         <li> element repeatedly for each item in your list. It
</section>                            works similarly to a for...in loop in JavaScript.
```

After the code fires, your view in facList.html is displayed. The view's template is rendered for each entry in the array. The following listing shows what the first object in the array would look like if you were to inspect the DOM after the template has been rendered. Each HREF in each anchor tag now has a URL and display text.

Listing 4.10 DOM view of rendered template

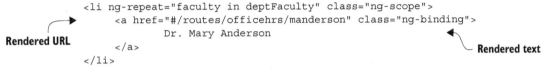

```
<li ng-repeat="faculty in deptFaculty" class="ng-scope">
    <a href="#/routes/officehrs/manderson" class="ng-binding">
        Dr. Mary Anderson
    </a>
</li>
```

Rendered URL

Rendered text

> **TIP** In AngularJS, you use the special directive ng-view to mark the area where views are to be rendered. You put this directive anywhere in your SPA's shell, and the $route service will automatically find it and place its views there. Because this is AngularJS-specific syntax, this detail will vary depending on the MV* framework you've chosen.

4.4.2 The main contact route

Also in the navigation header of your site is a link to the fictitious department's main contact view. The link's code points to a fragment identifier URL:

```
<a href="#routes/contact">Contact Us</a>
```

When you click this link, the browser's fragment identifier changes from #/routes/faculty to #/routes/contact (see figure 4.7).

Because the router is actively listening for changes in the fragment identifier, this new hash is detected. Upon detection, the router searches all routes in its configura-

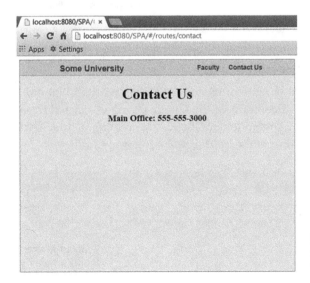

Figure 4.7 Clicking the Contact Us link produces a new fragment identifier in the browser's URL.

tion for a path matching /routes/contact. When it finds a match, the route in the
following listing is carried out.

Listing 4.11   Main contact route

```
.when("/routes/contact", {
    templateUrl : "App/components/simplerouter/partials/contact.html",
    controller : "contactController"
})
```

The path

**The functionality
that's executed**

**The view that
gets displayed**

The controller for this route is contrived, but it provides another view to demonstrate
navigation (see the next listing). Again, any real business logic would be placed in
another component, such as an AngularJS service.

Listing 4.12   The functionality for your route

```
routerControllers.controller(
        "contactController", function($scope) {

    $scope.mainOffice = "555-555-3000";
});
```

Define the contactController

**The property to be
displayed in the view**

In contactController, you have only one property: the main office's contact number.
The following listing shows the view for this route. It displays the main office's tele-
phone number via an expression binding.

Listing 4.13   The route's view

```
<section id="contact_us">
    <h1>Contact Us</h1>

    <h3>Main Office: {{ mainOffice }}</h3>
</section>
```

**An expression binding for
the main office number**

4.4.3   *Faculty office hours (parameterized route)*

Let's create one route with a parameter to show how they're used. When this route is
handled, you'll display the office hours of the faculty member selected from your faculty list view. As with our pseudocode, you'll start by creating a route with a place-
holder for the selected faculty member's ID (see the following listing).

Listing 4.14   Office hours route with a parameter

```
.when("/routes/officehrs/:facultyID, {
    templateUrl : "App/components/simplerouter/partials/hours.html",
    controller : "hoursController"
})
```

**Route parameter to pass a
faculty member's ID**

Each router will have different syntax for route parameters. Consult the documentation for whichever router you choose. This example uses `facultyID` as the variable name.

THE RELATIVE URL WITH THE TEXT TO BE PASSED

If you view the source in your browser for the links that you print out in your view, each link points to the same route except for the last segment of the URL. Here's the link for the first faculty member:

```
<a href="#/routes/officehrs/manderson" class="ng-binding">
    Dr. Mary Anderson
</a>
```

The last part of the link's URL represents this person's faculty ID. It was written dynamically with your binding. Because you have three faculty members in your list, each member's URL will contain a different ID.

THE CONTROLLER

To be able to use the information passed via the route parameter, each framework or library will provide a way to access it in your code. AngularJS has the aptly named `$routeParams` object. The next listing illustrates your controller's use of this variable.

Listing 4.15   Controller for office hours

```
routerControllers.controller("hoursController",          ◄── Define the
        function($scope, $routeParams) {                     hoursController

    var contactInfo = {};

    contactInfo["manderson"] = {                        ◄── Define the office hours
        name : "Dr. Mary Anderson",                         and contact information
        hours : "Tuesday 12-2pm",
        email : "manderson@someuniv.edu",
        phone : "555-555-1111"
    };

    contactInfo["sjones"] = {
        name : "Dr. Steve Jones",
        hours : "By Appointment",
        email : "sjones@someuniv.edu",
        phone : "555-555-1112"
    };

    contactInfo["arodriguez"] = {
        name : "Dr. Ana Rodriguez",
        hours : "Wednesday 1-3pm",
        email : "arodriguez@someuniv.edu",
        phone : "555-555-1113"                          The route parameter is
    };                                                  used to find the correct
                                                        contact information
    $scope.info = contactInfo[$routeParams.facultyID]   ◄──
})
```

The object that provides access to route parameters — *(annotation pointing to `function($scope, $routeParams)`)*

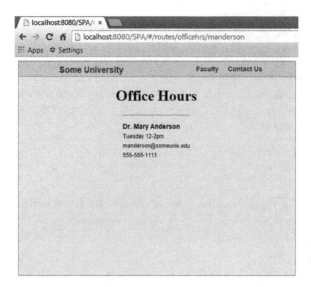

Figure 4.8 Passing `manderson` **via a route parameter results in the correct office hours being displayed.**

In this example, the route parameter passed in will match one of the three contact information entries. Passing the route parameter (the faculty ID) as the property name of the `contactInfo` object returns the correct faculty member's information. Then you can put the information returned into the `$scope` variable so the view can display it. The following listing provides the view for this route.

Listing 4.16   Office hours view

```
<section id="office_hours">
   <h1>Office Hours</h1>

   <p class="hrs_faculty_name">{{ info.name }}</p>      Display the info object's
   <p>{{ info.hours }}</p>                              properties with an
   <p>{{ info.email }}</p>                              expression bindin
   <p>{{ info.phone }}</p>

</section>
```

Now let's look at the final product. When the user clicks the first link from your faculty list view, and the faculty ID of `manderson` is passed into the controller via the route parameter, the user sees the screen shown in figure 4.8.

Now that you understand routing, you'll be using a router from this point forward. Feel free to refer to this chapter anytime you need a refresher on what you've learned.

4.5   *Chapter challenge*

Now here's a challenge for you to see what you've learned in this chapter: create a simple picture viewer. You'll take several images you have available and use client-side routing to display them. You could use a different route and resulting view for each picture. But if you want to make the challenge more interesting, try using a single route and use the name of the image as a route parameter. Then use the MV* framework to dynamically swap the pictures, using the image's name passed in via the route parameter.

4.6 *Summary*

There was quite a lot of information to digest in this chapter. Let's review to see what you've learned:

- Routers are libraries/frameworks that allow you to specify a desired state for your application for a given URL.
- Routes are configured in a router's configuration.
- Routing in an SPA occurs in the browser. No server requests are required.
- Routers use one of two methods to achieve client-side routing: the fragment identifier or the HTML5 History API.
- The HTML5 History API method for routing normally requires you to explicitly state in the router configuration that you want to use it. It also requires a few code changes, including changes on the server.
- The same route can be used to display different outcomes by incorporating route parameters in a route's path. Route parameters are variables defined in the path of the route that allow information to be passed via a URL.

View composition
and layout

This chapter covers

- An introduction to layout design
- Steps for composing views
- A guide to designing complex routes
- Insight on how to deal with nested and sibling views

So far you've learned some of the basic nuts and bolts of creating a single-page application. During this journey, you learned how to modularize your code and how to use the power of an MV* framework to create the views that your users see and interact with. You also discovered the vital role routers play in your application: they not only allow the natural navigation features of the browser to work with your single page but also provide a way to configure the functionality and views associated with your application's URLs.

To this point, however, you've grasped particular concepts rather than the bigger picture. Now that you have some tools in your SPA toolbox, let's zoom out and tackle the overall design process for creating a single-page application. Designing a successful SPA is a little like learning to speak a new language. You've learned the basics—the vocabulary and grammar—but you still haven't mastered the dynamics of holding a conversation.

In this chapter, you'll walk through the design of an SPA, from the visualization of your layout to the transformation of requirements into a real, working application. You'll learn to design the layout with views instead of pages, to design routes to connect the dots, and then to pull it all together with working code. Even though you understand the underlying mechanics of an SPA, you'll galvanize what you know by focusing more on the overall process. Along the way, you'll also learn how to deal with lifelike scenarios, such as more-complicated layouts and routes that result in multiple views.

5.1   Introducing our project

The project for this chapter is the creation of an online tool for a fictitious medical supply company. We'll pretend that this SPA will be used by sales reps to track the status of their clients' orders. Because this chapter's focus is on the overall design process, I'll make the project's layout a little more complex than in previous projects. In the application, you'll need to display several categories of information for a given route, such as customer data, order history, and the client's addresses for billing and shipping.

We'll talk more specifically about the details of the project later, when we get into the design process, but first take a glimpse at the final product (see figure 5.1). This gives you a picture of what you're building as you progress through each phase of the project.

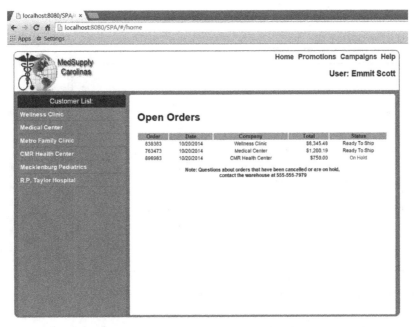

Figure 5.1   Our sample project tracks the status of orders for a fictitious medical supply company and includes a layout that's more complex and diverse than you've previously dealt with.

Before we begin, though, let's talk about some basic layout design concepts. I want to make sure we're on the same page with familiar concepts and present any new concepts before continuing.

5.2 Reviewing layout design concepts

Our discussion of SPA concepts thus far has been narrowly focused. Let's pull back now and review the SPA landscape from a holistic viewpoint. This review will also bring to light some new details that you'll need to grasp when you start this project.

5.2.1 Views

When you design an SPA's views, you're creating the individual pieces of the overall SPA puzzle. Each piece provides a particular experience for the user, whether it's merely displaying data or providing controls for user input. Generally speaking, you design views on two levels. At a basic level, you design the view itself. At a broader level, you're more concerned with how the view fits into the overall architecture.

From within the view, your design efforts are concentrated on tasks such as displaying data and possibly adding interactivity via JavaScript. As you've learned, it's the MV* framework that helps keep the various parts of your application's code separate but working together as a team. HTML elements and bindings combine to form the basis of the view's design. You can further contribute to the design of the view by applying styles to it via CSS (see figure 5.2).

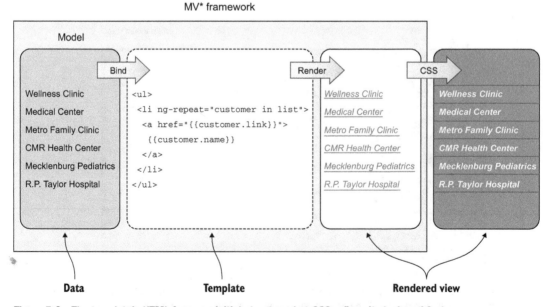

Figure 5.2   The template's HTML forms an initial structure, but CSS refines its look and feel.

When it comes to the bigger picture (the layout), you have to think about how each view will be positioned with respect to the other views in a feature. To position a rendered view in a particular area of the screen, you turn to a construct called a *region*.

5.2.2 Regions

I briefly discussed the concept of a region in chapter 1. Although certain view engines have their own notions of this term, in this chapter I use *region* to mean an area of the screen that's been designated to contain one or more views. A region can be defined using semantic elements if you're using HTML5 (see figure 5.3) or an element such as a DIV if you're not. These types of elements are ideal, because they can remain invisible to the user but can be used to define physical space within the UI.

To define a region's dimensions, as well as its aesthetic relationship with other regions, you can use Cascading Style Sheets (CSS). In figure 5.4, you can see an example of applying styles to regions to achieve a certain layout.

This example positions two regions side by side by assigning a simple float property to the regions. For a simple 2×2 layout, you can float one region to the left and the other to the right. After placing the regions, you can make decisions about the views they'll contain.

You can also assign other CSS properties to your region to further enhance the effect on your layout's design, such as width, height, padding, borders, margins, and

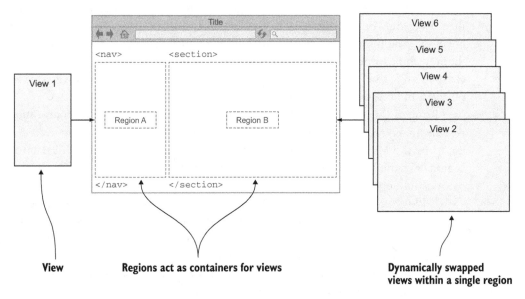

Figure 5.3 Regions give you a physical area in the UI where your views can be displayed. Within a region, views can be fixed or dynamically swapped.

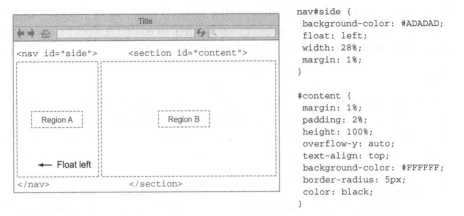

```
nav#side {
  background-color: #ADADAD;
  float: left;
  width: 28%;
  margin: 1%;
}

#content {
  margin: 1%;
  padding: 2%;
  height: 100%;
  overflow-y: auto;
  text-align: top;
  background-color: #FFFFFF;
  border-radius: 5px;
  color: black;
}
```

Figure 5.4   CSS is used to define the physical attributes of the regions in your layout, as well as to define their relationship with other regions in the UI.

background-color, to name a few. Any property applicable to the type of element you choose is fair game.

The process of deciding on the size and shape of regions and the arrangement of views within those regions to arrive at a particular layout is called *view composition.*

5.2.3   *View composition*

As part of the design process, you arrange, or compose, views in a certain way to form the UI's layout. In this regard, you can think of view composition as both art and science. On one hand, you have the technology that helps create the views and display them in the UI when a particular route is carried out. On the other hand, there's the creative aspect in which you make a subjective decision about where regions will be placed and how a view, or a set of views, will be arranged within them.

Although this process is called *view* composition, *regions* play an equally important role in the creation of a layout, as you've seen. Regions house the views that are rendered by the MV* framework. Given this, you can say that for all practical purposes, regions are the bounding boxes that frame views within your layout. That's why view composition encompasses both views and regions, hand in hand.

To illustrate how regions can affect view composition, take a look at figure 5.5. Here you see the same views that you saw earlier in figure 5.3. By reconfiguring your regions, you can display exactly the same information with an entirely different layout. In turn, this has a direct impact on your SPA's look and feel.

How your regions and views are arranged is completely subjective, tailored to the goals of your project and your design preferences.

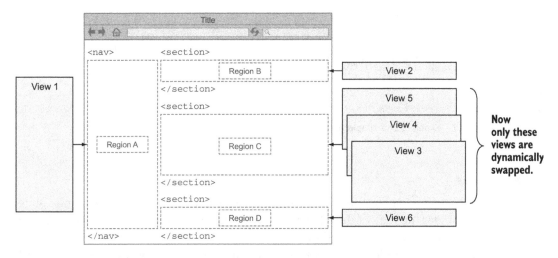

Figure 5.5 How regions and views are configured impacts view composition and ultimately the layout.

5.2.4 Nested views

An important point to bear in mind is that the use of regions doesn't have to be confined to the SPA's shell. Regions can also be employed within a view to nest other views (see figure 5.6).

Nesting views can dramatically increase the complexity of your design, but that's sometimes necessary given the nature of the feature you're building. You can also configure the application's routes so that your design is properly reflected in the UI when the application's state changes.

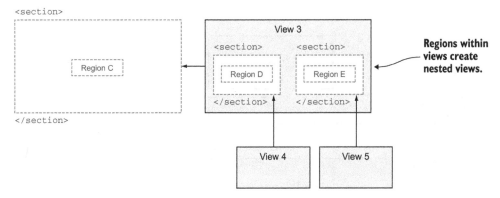

Figure 5.6 Regions can also be used in views, if you need to nest a view (or views) inside another view.

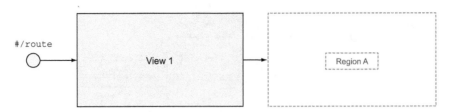

Figure 5.7   Example of a simple route

5.2.5   *Routes*

As you saw in chapter 4, the way you configure routes affects the application's state. This includes the state of the UI. This is why route configuration can also be an important aspect of your layout's design.

While you were learning about routing and how routers work, you worked with only simple examples, as in figure 5.7. In this type of route, each resulting view occupies the entire destination region. Designing a route like this is pretty cut and dry.

But as you just learned, the regions you're targeting can be placed in any number of places on the screen. This can lead to some interesting designs. You could, for example, have multiple regions positioned next to each other and display multiple views for a given route (see figure 5.8).

When you design routes that result in complex region/view configurations, things can become difficult to manage. For complicated layouts, if you're not using a one-stop-shopping framework with robust routing and view management built in, you might want to consider adding a library to your arsenal that manages the application's state specifically for the MV* framework you're using. The next section covers some of the pros and cons of bringing a view management library onboard and points out some of the options available.

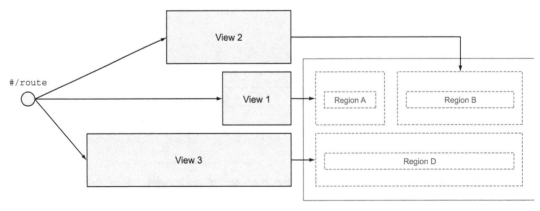

Figure 5.8   Example of a route with multiple views

5.3 Considering alternatives for advanced composition and layout

There are a few reasons why you might need a framework with a more elaborate set of features built in. The most obvious one I've already mentioned is the ability to deal with complex layouts, specifically those with multiple or nested views.

If a given MV* framework doesn't have a particular feature built in, you end up writing code to bridge the gap. Frameworks exist that expand upon the original MV* framework, though. They have the common goal of making certain complex tasks, such as advanced view composition and complex routing, as easy as possible while trying to reduce the amount of boilerplate code you have to write. This alone is a fairly compelling reason for considering outside help.

Another reason to consider this type of framework is the extra set of features it may bring to the table, such as events, messaging, and built-in objects for easy layout creation.

Finally, with complex designs, you have to deal with the view's state. Remember that when you display a view (or views), you're also interacting with the MV* framework. You rely on the MV* framework not only for the sake of handling the data and interactivity for the view but also to manage the view's lifecycle.

If you think back to our evaluation of several styles of MV* framework, each one approached the binding and rendering process differently. With Backbone.js, for example, the normal process destroys the previous view and re-creates it from the template with fresh data. In an MVVM-style framework, such as Knockout, binding is done once and the view stays active. You merely interact with the ViewModel as needed.

Each framework has specific parts of the lifecycle that need to be addressed, such as when a view is rendered, shown, hidden, and (if applicable) destroyed. Certain libraries/frameworks either take care of this for you or provide hooks for you to use.

As I mentioned, most of the large, end-to-end frameworks have most or all of these concerns addressed. If you're using one that doesn't have these capabilities built in, you might try one of these libraries/frameworks instead. But first you should consider various factors. No dependency should be added without due consideration. So before you jump in with both feet, here are a few of the pros and cons.

5.3.1 Pros

Here are some of the good points:

- If a library/framework extends or enhances a particular MV* framework, it'll be designed around the nuances of that framework right out of the box.
- These libraries/frameworks are written by people who have expertise in a certain MV* framework and understand the difficulties and pitfalls of managing complex tasks in that environment.
- You don't have to worry as much about trying to cobble together various other libraries and frameworks yourself.

5.3.2 *Cons*

Here are a few downsides to consider:

- You're at the mercy of the developer(s) of the software for bug fixes and upgrades.
- Because an outside library/framework isn't your code and isn't part of the core MV* framework, you may find debugging application errors more difficult.
- The author(s) might, for whatever reason, abandon the library/framework. This leaves you dependent on obsolete software.

If you need a more robust set of features from your SPA solution, table 5.1 presents a few options you might consider. Several of these are powerful SPA frameworks in their own right and include many more features than merely view/layout management. This isn't an exhaustive list, but it does represent some of the choices available at the time of this writing.

Table 5.1 Frameworks with built-in features for advanced composition and layout

Framework	Options for more-complex composition and layout tasks
Knockout	Durandal (http://durandaljs.com)
Backbone.js	Marionette.js (http://marionettejs.com) Geppetto (https://github.com/ModelN/backbone.geppetto) Chaplin (http://chaplinjs.org) Vertebrae (https://github.com/hautelook/vertebrae) LayoutManager (https://github.com/tbranyen/backbone.layoutmanager) Thorax (https://github.com/walmartlabs/thorax)
AngularJS	AngularUI (http://angular-ui.github.io), part of AngularJS but offered as a separate download
Kendo UI	Built in
Ember.js	Built in

You can apply the same acceptance criteria to these frameworks as you did when selecting the MV* framework itself, in terms of factors such as learning curve, bugs and fix rate, documentation, maturity, and community support.

Now that you've reviewed basic design concepts and considered possible software solutions to creating a complex layout, let's move on to our project. Because I'll be using AngularJS to illustrate, I'll be leveraging the AngularUI component. As mentioned in table 5.1, it's part of the overall Angular software, but it must be separately downloaded. I've also included it in this chapter's code available for download online.

5.4 *Designing the application*

Let's begin with a description of what you're going to design: an online reporting tool for a medical supply company. This tool will help the company's sales reps track the status of orders, view order history, and view information about clients. The following is a list of features you'll pretend you've been asked to include:

- Provide a selectable list of the sales rep's customers.
- Display all open orders by default.
- When a customer is selected, display company info, contact info, and order history.
- Initially hide the customer's billing and shipping information but make it viewable on demand. In addition, assign customers their own URLs so the user can traverse quickly to where they were previously.
- Include links in the header to the company's current campaigns, promotions, and the application's help file.

5.4.1 Designing the base layout

One of the first things you have to do is to decide on a basic structure for the application, just as you would with a regular web application. This is often called the *base layout*. Will it be a master-detail kind of application? Or would having a side column for navigation be better? Do you need a footer? Many choices would work.

You'll use a traditional three-part base layout for this project. You can put your links at the top, the list of clients in the navigation bar at the bottom left, and display the results of your routes in the main content area at the bottom right. You'll create this structure in two steps.

First, you'll divide the screen into a header and a main body. Figure 5.9 illustrates this step.

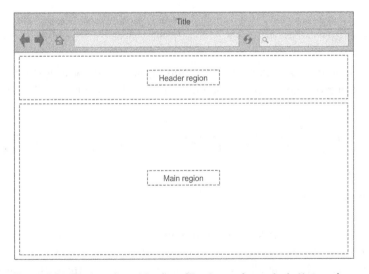

Figure 5.9 The base layout begins with a top region and a bottom region.

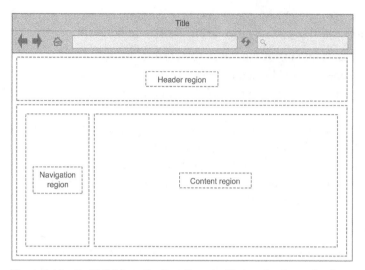

Figure 5.10   You'll finish up the base layout with a region for navigation and a region for content.

Next, you'll divide the main region into two parts: a region on the left for navigation and a region on the right to display your content (see figure 5.10).

At this point, your base layout source code looks like the following listing.

Listing 5.1   Base layout

```
<main>                                      ⌐ Header region across the top
    <header></header>              ◄

    <nav id="side"></nav>                    Main region across the bottom, split
    <section id="content"></section>         between navigation and content
</main>
```

You'll use CSS to mold these regions into the general shape you want for the base layout. To start, you'll give your header some height and a white background (see the following listing).

Listing 5.2   Header region CSS

```
header {
    height: 15%;
    background-color: #FFFFFF;
}
```

You'll also apply styles to your side navigation region and content region, floating your navigation region to the left so the two regions sit side by side. And you'll define the proportions of the regions by allocating a portion of the width to the navigation region (see the next listing).

Listing 5.3   Navigation region and content region CSS

```
nav#side {
    background-color: #ADADAD;
    float: left;
    width: 28%;
    height: 100%;
    margin: 1%;
}
#content {
    margin: 1%;
    padding: 2%;
    height: 100%;
    overflow-y: auto;
    text-align: top;
    background-color: #FFFFFF;
    border-radius: 5px;
}
```

The navigation region is floated to the left and given width to define the relationship of these two regions

After all your styles have been applied to the base layout, it looks like figure 5.11.

Having finished the basic layout for the application, you can move on to adding its content.

5.4.2   *Designing the default content*

Now that you have some regions that you can add content to, you can design views and a default route. Because your header and navigation views will be fixed (only their content will change), you'll design those two first.

Figure 5.11   The base layout with styles applied

THE HEADER

The header view is fairly simple. It has a logo, some links, and the name of the user who's logged in. Because it's a fixed view, you don't need a route for it. This view will never be swapped for another view. So all you need to do to get it onscreen is include it. In AngularJS, you do this via an attribute added to the header region's DIV. Note, however, that the MV* framework you choose may require a different method to include a view.

```
<div
id="header"
ng-include src="'App/components/customerorders/partials/header.html'">
</div>
```

The following listing provides a glimpse of the source code for your header view.

Listing 5.4   The header view

```
<section ng-controller="navController">
   <section id="logo">
      <img src="App/images/logo.png">
   </section>
   <nav id="top">
      <ul>
         <li><a ui-sref="home">Home</a></li>          ◄    The ui-sref attribute provided by
         <li><a ui-sref="promos">Promotions</a></li>        the view management library is
         <li><a ui-sref="campaigns">Campaigns</a></li>      used to execute routes
         <li><a ui-sref="help">Help</a></li>
      </ul>
      <p id="userName">User: {{user}}</p>          ◄    The name of the user is
   </nav>                                                added via data binding
</section>
```

The Home link provides a way back to your default content, and the other links satisfy the rest of the requirements for your header. With the view rendered and some styles applied, your header now looks like figure 5.12.

Figure 5.12   The layout's header after styles have been applied

With a header in place, you can design the main navigation view. For this application, the links in the navigation view will consist of a the company's current customer list.

NAVIGATION

The list of customers in the customer list view will be just as easy. It's also fixed, so no route is needed. With an include statement, it'll load with the application.

```
<div
id="navigation"
ng-include src="'App/components/customerorders/partials/customerList.html'" >
</div>
```

To create a link for each customer in your client list, you'll use a binding made for iterating over lists. This is the same kind of operation covered in chapter 2, when you learned about templates and binding. You'll also use the special link attribute from your view management component I just mentioned (ui-sref) to execute the customerInfo route when a link is clicked (see the following listing).

Listing 5.5 Navigation view

```
<div id="listheader">Customer List:</div>
<div id="navButton" ng-controller="customerListController">
    <ul>
        <li ng-repeat="customer in customerList">
            <a ui-sref=
            "customerInfo({ customerID:customer.custNum })">
            {{customer.name}}
            </a>
        </li>
    </ul>
</div>
```

For each customer in the list, create a link to the customerInfo route. When the route executes, pass the customer number as a route parameter.

Note that your companion view manager allows you to pass route parameters as you did with the core AngularJS router. In this example, customerID is the name of the variable, and customer.custNum represents the data assigned to the parameter when the ng-repeat attribute stamps out the information from the template.

With the view rendered to the screen, you can use CSS to turn your unordered list into what looks like a group of clickable panels. The following listing is a portion of the style attributes applied (the rest can be viewed in the code available for download).

Listing 5.6 Navigation styles applied

```
#navButton {
    width: 100%;
    padding: 0 0 1em 0;
    margin-bottom: 1em;
    background-color: #ADADAD;
    color: white;
}

#navButton li {
    border-bottom: 1px solid #979797;
    margin: 0;
}

#navButton li a:hover {
    background-color: #D9D8D8;
    color: #fff;
}
```

A background color is added

A subtle bottom border accepts the panel

A hover is added to the anchor for a rollover effect

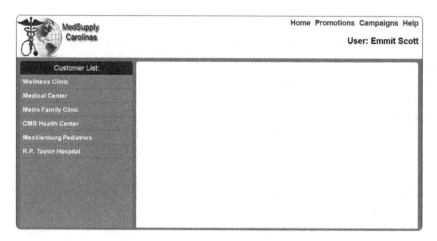

Figure 5.13   Your layout after both the header and navigation view are rendered

After your navigation view is rendered, your default content will look like figure 5.13.

With the fixed portion of your default content completed, you can work on the dynamic area.

THE DEFAULT ROUTE

According to our requirements, the user should be greeted with a list of open orders by default. For this, you'll create a default route. The view resulting from this route will be what a user sees after first entering the application or after clicking the Home link.

Listing 5.7 shows the configuration for this route. As I mentioned earlier, you're using the AngularUI router. The syntax is slightly different from the router that comes with core AngularJS, but it shouldn't feel totally alien. This router is much more powerful and was deliberately modeled around states rather than URLs. It also supports multiple views, both nested and parallel.

Keep in mind that this syntax is specific to the AngularUI router. Don't worry, though; the basic concepts carry over to most frameworks that support advanced state management.

Listing 5.7   Configuration for the default route

```
.state("home", {
    url: "/home",
    templateUrl: "App/components/customerorders/partials/openOrders.html",
    controller: "openOrdersController"
})

.otherwise("/home");
```

State name *(pointing to* `.state("home"`)*)*

Declaring home as the default *(pointing to* `.otherwise("/home");`)*)*

As you can see from the template that's being used, the requirement to show all open orders by default will be met when this route completes. The keyword `otherwise` denotes the default route.

To specify that the content region should be the recipient of the view rendered by this route, the attribute ui-view is applied to the region's DIV:

```
<div id="content" ui-view></div>
```

No matter what view management solution you're using, you'll need to identify the region the view should be inserted into. Consult the documentation to see how to do this for the view manager you've chosen.

In your open orders view, you'll once again use a repeat binding directive to tell AngularJS to repeatedly stamp out rows in a table for each order that's still open (see the following listing).

Listing 5.8   The row template from our view for open orders

```
<tr ng-repeat="rorder in recentOrders">              Repeat for each
    <td class="orderData">{{rorder.orderNumber}}</td>    open order
    <td class="orderData">{{rorder.date}}</td>
    <td class="orderData">{{rorder.name}}</td>
    <td class="orderTotal">{{rorder.total}}</td>
    <td class="orderData"                             Class binding used to
    ng-class="rorder.status == 'On Hold'              apply a different class
    ? 'orderOnHold' : ''" rorder.status}}</td>        if the status is On Hold
</tr>
```

With the meat of your default content filled in, let's take a peek at what the screen looks like at this point. You saw the opening content of your application at the beginning of the chapter, but let's look at it again now that you have all the pieces in place (see figure 5.14). It'll give you a picture of what you've accomplished so far.

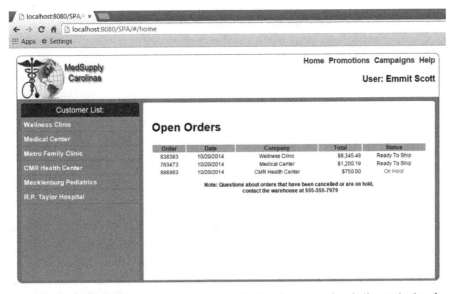

Figure 5.14   Your layout after the default route displays the open orders in the content region

With your default content complete, let's move to the last leg of your application: displaying the appropriate customer information for a selected customer. This time, the view composition will be more complicated, so you'll see the usefulness of your view manager component.

5.4.3 *Using a view manager for complex designs*

Until this point, the application hasn't been anything your regular router and MV* framework couldn't handle. Now, however, multiple views will need to be simultaneously displayed in your content region when a customer from your navigation view is selected.

The design for this feature includes a main customer view that you'll configure in your customer information route. The complexity, though, is that this new view will contain regions of its own for the placement of the customer's contact information and order history. These regions, in turn, have views of their own. You'll configure them within the *same* route as the main view. You can pretend that each of the three views in this route is complicated enough that it needs to be developed and maintained separately.

As you may recall from earlier in this chapter, the placement of regions isn't confined to the shell itself. The use of regions within a view is another view composition device you have at your disposal to design the most appropriate layout for a given set of requirements. Figure 5.15 illustrates this arrangement of the regions and views.

With a mental picture of what you're going to do, let's see how to use the extended routing and view composition abilities of the view management component you've chosen.

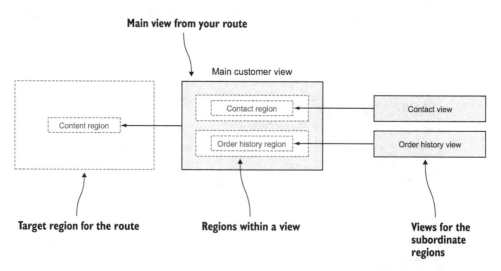

Figure 5.15   To compose the customer information feature, you're placing additional regions within the main view itself to include the related but separate contact and order history views.

Let's begin with the route. After you wrap your head around how to configure a route like this, understanding the rest of the code will be easier. The following listing shows the configuration of your route with multiple states.

Listing 5.9 Customer information route with multiple states

```
.state("customerInfo", {
    url: "/customerInfo/:customerID",
    views: {

        "": {
            templateUrl: "App/components/customerorders/partials/
                        ➥ customerMain.html",
            controller:  "customerController"
        },

        "contact@customerInfo": {
            templateUrl: "App/components/customerorders/partials/
                        ➥ customerContact.html",
            controller:  "customerContactController"
        },

        "history@customerInfo": {
            templateUrl: "App/components/customerorders/
                        ➥ partials/customerHistory.html",
            controller:  "customerHistoryController"
        }

    }
})
```

State name → `.state("customerInfo", {`

Route's path with a parameter defined ← `url: "/customerInfo/:customerID",`

Main customer view → `"": {`

Associated inner views for contact and customer history

Again, if you're using a different kind of view manager, the syntax will be different, but the concepts will be the same or relatively similar. Because this route needs a little more explanation due to its complexity, we'll analyze the syntax of the AngularUI route you just saw (at a high level) to make sure you understand it.

THE ROUTE EXPLAINED

This kind of route has the same things a normal route has (path, view, functionality)—but times three. Here's what's happening with this type of route configuration:

- The default view for this state doesn't need to be named.
- The absolute name of each view contains the ID of each region and the name of the state, concatenated using @. (You'll see the source for the main view in a moment.)

You'll also notice that each view in the view list can have its own functionality. This is optional but handy because the main reason for this kind of route is to have a feature with views that are related but developed separately. Moreover, thanks to the expanded capabilities of your view manager, you're able to share the route's parameter with each inner view and its functionality.

THE ROUTE'S MAIN/OUTER VIEW

Now that you've seen the route, let's look at the source for its main view (see the following listing). This view is important because it contains bindings for its own information, as well as the regions where the other two views will be rendered.

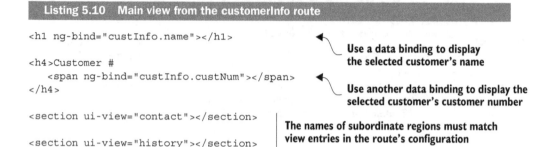

Listing 5.10   Main view from the customerInfo route

```
<h1 ng-bind="custInfo.name"></h1>                    ◄─── Use a data binding to display
                                                          the selected customer's name
<h4>Customer #
  <span ng-bind="custInfo.custNum"></span>           ◄─── Use another data binding to display the
</h4>                                                      selected customer's customer number

<section ui-view="contact"></section>                ─┐ The names of subordinate regions must match
                                                       │ view entries in the route's configuration
<section ui-view="history"></section>                ─┘
```

The source of the two inner views is typical of what you've already seen. They display data about the customer through the use of bindings. The route parameter, as I mentioned, is shared, and the inner views can also use it to locate the correct data entries. Their source can be found in the complete online source code.

Let's look at a screenshot of the application to check your progress (see figure 5.16).

The screenshot shows the three rendered views with their styles applied. It's impossible to tell where each rendered view is from the screenshot, but that's part of the

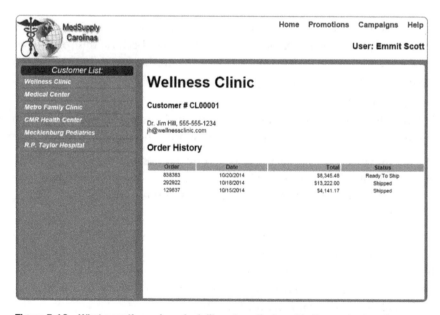

Figure 5.16   What your three views look like when displayed in the content region

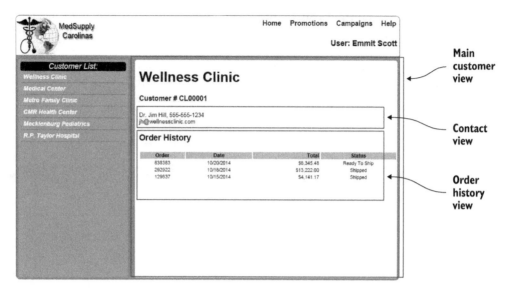

Figure 5.17   The result of the customer information route with each view highlighted

design. Although these views are developed and maintained separately, the content appears like one seamless page to the user. Look at the screenshot again, but this time I call out the location of each view in the customer information route (see figure 5.17).

One more part of the project, which I haven't discussed yet, requires you to use nested views.

5.4.4   Creating nested views with their own states

To satisfy your requirement for on-demand billing and shipping information, each having its own state, you'll once again call upon your view management software. The following listing shows the routes for these views.

Listing 5.11   Routes for billing and shipping info

```
.state("customerInfo.shipping", {
  url: "/shipping",
  templateUrl: "App/components/customerorders/partials/billShipInfo.html",
  controller: "customerShippingController"
})

.state("customerInfo.billing", {
  url: "/billing",
  templateUrl: "App/components/customerorders/partials/billShipInfo.html",
  controller: "customerBillingController"
});
```

Child routes are defined with dot notation (parentRoute.childRoute)

Notice that child routes are defined with dot notation with respect to another route in the configuration file. In this case, you're also defining the customer information route as the parent route.

Now you need to know how to construct links to get to these child routes. Here's where a bit of magic happens. To target these child routes, you also use dot notation in the link. So let's now add on to the main customer view that you saw earlier and put in these additional elements. The following listing shows the updated source for the main customer view.

Listing 5.12   The main customer view with billing and shipping added

```html
<h1 ng-bind="custInfo.name"></h1>

<h4>Customer #
    <span ng-bind="custInfo.custNum"></span>
</h4>

<section ui-view="contact"></section>

<section ui-view="history"></section>

<nav class="customerInfoNav">
    <a ui-sref=".shipping">View Shipping Info</a>        Links to nested views are
    <a ui-sref=".billing">View Billing Info</a>          defined with dot notation
</nav>

<section ui-view></section>          An empty region for displaying
                                     the billing and shipping views
```

Once again, the syntax you'll use may be different, but let's talk about this addition at a high level so you can get the main idea. You've added a NAV (navigation) element to the customer information view to display either billing or shipping information. The other element is an empty SECTION where the resulting views from the route will be displayed.

One other thing to note, just for the sake of understanding the code, is that with AngularUI's router, unnamed regions become a catchall for the route. Contact and History are named, so those views will be assigned directly to the regions of the same name. When no name matches a region, a route's views are targeted to the first unnamed region. This is specific to AngularUI, but it should be noted to avoid any confusion about this example.

Now, for a final touch, you'll add a few CSS attributes to the links so they appear more like buttons and you'll have a way to see the on-demand content. Figure 5.18 shows both button-styled links and what one of the child views looks like when the route finishes.

Now, users can click the appropriate button to show the billing or shipping information on an as-needed basis and then click the browser's Back button to return to the state the SPA was in previously.

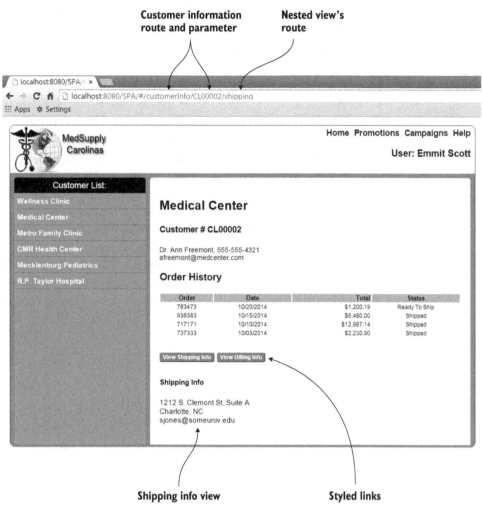

Figure 5.18   The nested shipping view with its own URL

5.5   *Chapter challenge*

Here's a challenge to see what you've learned in this chapter. Pretend you've been hired to create a website for a local landscaping company. The company wants a view for each of its services: lawn maintenance, landscaping, shrub pruning, and exterior home staging. The company also needs a products view to display the custom decks, fountains, and swimming pools they build. You can keep the details for each view as simple as a description, such as "landscaping view," or make it more lifelike with simulated content.

Divide the screen into three regions: one for the header, one for navigation, and one to display content. Each service will have its own view and corresponding navigation link. The product view also has a navigation link, but its view is subdivided into its own product header and product detail regions. The product header should have links to a view for each product, which will display in the product detail region.

5.6   Summary

Whew, that was intense! You made it, though. Let's do a quick recap:

- In an SPA, you use the view composition process to create a layout.
- The semantic elements that you've used as regions occupy physical space on the screen. CSS is used to style and position them. Their arrangement affects how views are displayed, which directly impacts the design of the layout.
- The first, underlying set of regions that give the application its basic shape is called the base layout.
- Regions can also be added to views when the layout's design calls for multiple and/or nested views.
- Routes that result in complex view and region combinations can be difficult to manage. Frameworks/libraries with robust routing and view management capabilities abstract the complexity by getting you to think in terms of the application's state.

Inter-module interaction

In chapter 3, you learned a great deal about modular programming. One of the biggest takeaways from that chapter is the idea that you can internalize the complexity of your code and provide a public API to its features by applying an architectural design pattern commonly referred to as the *module pattern*. This is a way to achieve encapsulation in JavaScript.

As you discovered, coding with modules helps organize your application's logic into small, single-purpose units, which are easier to maintain and update. This inevitably leads to greater reusability for your code. Using modules also helps with data integrity, code organization, and the avoidance of name collisions. After all, you're creating code in a single, nonrefreshing page. Without this kind of design for your application's code base, relying purely on global variables and functions would quickly become unmanageable (see figure 6.1).

129

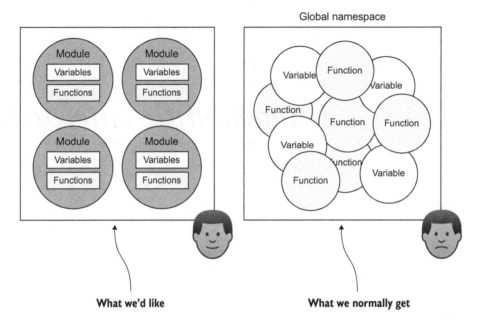

Figure 6.1   As your project grows, your code base become less and less manageable if you put all your variables and functions in the global namespace.

Even though the modules themselves are at the heart of modular programming, being able to use them to create a successful SPA requires more than knowing how they work mechanically. You also need to understand how they can interact: how one module can invoke the functionality of another module and, possibly, receive a response.

This chapter continues talking about modules but this time within the context of shaping your SPA's architecture by the way you design module interaction. The chapter begins with a review of a module's structure at a high level but mainly concentrates on the design of the inter-module interaction process.

> **NOTE**   Because modules are based on a variety of pattern styles (such as the traditional, revealing, AMD, and AngularJS-styled modules, to name a few), I'll keep our discussion as neutral as possible when covering the chapter's concepts. Also, as in the other chapters, I'll include highlights from a concrete example, with its entire source available for download.

For your project this time, you'll create an SPA for an acquaintance who wants to start an online store to sell used video games. You won't need to get into the complexities of having a shopping cart in this exercise. You'll instead focus on the store's product search feature. This application, though simple, will still give you a chance to create several modules and design how they'll interact, without drowning in source code.

As in the preceding chapter, you'll save the details of the project for later. Even though the interface is fairly trivial, we'll make sure that the modules that power the application are interesting. Before talking about methods for inter-module interaction, though, let's set the stage by reviewing some basic concepts for modular programming.

6.1 Review of module concepts

Let's begin by reviewing some basic module concepts at a high level. We'll use this as a baseline for the rest of our discussion.

6.1.1 Modules encapsulate code

Because the JavaScript specification at the time of this writing has no built-in syntax for creating modules or classes to encapsulate parts of your code, it's simulated using the module pattern.

> **NOTE** The next version of JavaScript, ECMAScript 6 (also called *Harmony* or *ES.next*), adds official support of the module to the language.

A module, as far as JavaScript goes, is a specially constructed function. This type of function is often called an *immediately invoked function expression* (IIFE).

Immediately invoked function expression

As a reminder, the module pattern's outer function is often referred to as an immediately invoked function expression, or IIFE, because it's written as a function expression (it doesn't start with the `function` keyword) instead of a function declaration and has a trailing set of parentheses to make the function get invoked immediately. The IIFE's syntax looks like this:

```
var x = (function() {
    // do something
})();
```

If you want to learn more about function expressions and how they differ from function declarations, here's a good resource: http://javascriptweblog.wordpress.com/2010/07/06/function-declarations-vs-function-expressions

---

The following listing is an example of the traditional module pattern. It creates a module to apply a discount to the price of a product. The price of the product is passed in via the `calculate` function, and the new, discounted price is returned.

Listing 6.1 Traditional module pattern

```
var pricingSvcMod = (function() {

    var discountRate = 40;

    function calculate(amt) {
        if(isNaN(amt)){
            return 1;
```

A global variable serves as the module's name (or namespace with submodules)

Code used internally by the module

```
        }else{
            return ((discountRate / 100) * amt).toFixed(2);
        }

    };

    return {
        applyDiscount : function(param) {          An object literal with public
            return calculate(param);              functions is returned, which serves
        }                                          as the module's public API
    };

})();
```

NOTE   For AMD/CommonJS modules, an assignment to a global variable isn't needed.

Chapter 3 also introduced a popular variation of the module pattern called the *revealing module pattern*. The following listing shows the same module written using this style.

Listing 6.2   Revealing module pattern

```
var pricingSvcMod = (function() {

    var discountRate = 40;

    function calculate(amt) {
        if(isNaN(amt)){
            return 1;
        }else{
            return ((discountRate / 100) * amt).toFixed(2);
        }

    };

    return {
        applyDiscount : calculate          A simplified return object
    };                                      simplifies the API

})();
```

In this version, everything is the same except for the returned object literal. Here, the public function is merely a pointer to the internal code. This makes the API cleaner and easier to read.

   With either version, the pattern's design enables the module to be used as a wrapper for a piece of functionality (see figure 6.2).

   The outer function of the module pattern forms a kind of protective barrier around your code. This is possible thanks to the limiting scope of the outer function.

NOTE   *Scope* (in a broad sense) refers to the accessibility of one part of an application to another part of that application.

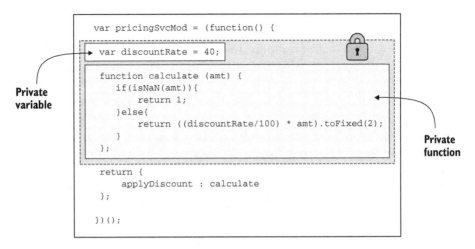

Figure 6.2   The module forms a protective barrier around your code. Variables and functions declared within the module are private.

The clever design of this function also enables you to avoid polluting the global namespace with your application's variables and functions, because they're local to the module's outer function.

6.1.2   APIs provide controlled access to internal functionality

Another nice feature of the module pattern is that it allows for the creation of an application programming interface, or API. An API is like the module's contract when another module wants to talk to it. The API defines what's publicly available. Code from other modules can use the API to gain limited and controlled access to its internal code.

The API is formed via the module's return statement (see figure 6.3). This forms a bridge between the internal functionality of the module and the outside world.

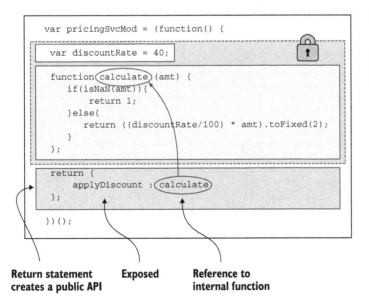

Return statement creates a public API   Exposed   Reference to internal function

Figure 6.3   Each public function in the API (left of the colon) has a corresponding reference to a private object inside the module (right of the colon).

In figure 6.3, we're returning an object defined with object literal syntax. In the returned object, any object member names to the left of the colon are exposed. Those to the right are the references to the internal code of the module.

After the object is returned, it's assigned to an external variable. This variable acts like a remote control to the module's functionality. Other modules will send messages to the object referenced by the variable. This variable will continue to hold a valid reference to that object as long as the variable persists (see figure 6.4).

Providing an API for your encapsulated code enables you to not only access the code within the module but also custom-tailor any interaction with it. You can purposely name the exposed functions of the API something meaningful to the others while naming private functions something meaningful only to the internal code. You can also choose to expose certain things about the module's inner workings while hiding others.

Remember that you're *not* hiding functionality out of secrecy. You're limiting what's exposed in the API to only what's needed for other modules to successfully use it.

6.1.3   *SRP means designing with a single purpose*

When you design a module, you try to limit the scope of its functionality to a single purpose. Having only one purpose per object is the crux of the single-responsibility principle (SRP) for software design. You can extend this idea to the modules you

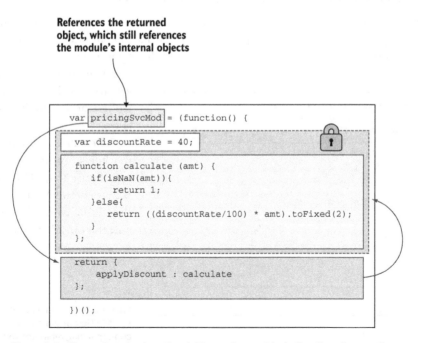

Figure 6.4   The assigned external variable can be used to indirectly reference the internal objects.

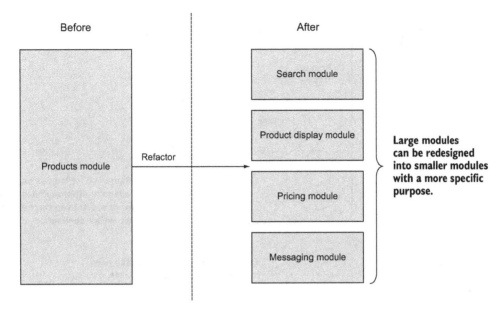

Figure 6.5   Modules can have multiple functions but should ideally have a single, overall purpose.

design: the module itself might have many variables and many functions inside it, but all of them are to support the module's overall reason for existence. When modules are designed with SRP in mind, they become like cogs in a machine. Each cog has a particular purpose but works harmoniously with the other modules of the application.

As the application grows in complexity, it's also normal for the complexity in your modules to increase. The nice thing about modules, though, is that if their code starts getting out of control in some way (becoming too large or enabling other purposes to emerge, perhaps), you can always refactor and split that module into one or more other modules.

For example, imagine that your video game application begins as a single module, but its functionality eventually grows beyond its initial purpose. The best strategy is to refactor the code, dividing it into smaller, single-purpose modules (see figure 6.5). Refactoring large, multipurpose modules helps you preserve the SRP aspect of your application's code base.

6.1.4   *Code reuse helps your project scale*

Another thing that sometimes emerges when you refactor is the potential to find functionality that can be reused either in the immediate project or in future phases of the project. Reusable components mean less work as your project evolves and grows larger, because having shared modules eliminates the need to repeat code in multiple places.

Currently, your SPA in this chapter's example displays the price of a game only after a product is selected from the search results. Imagine, however, that your

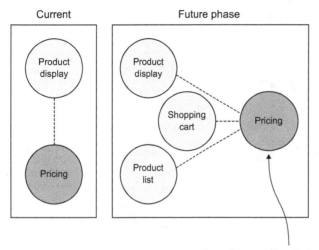

Figure 6.6 **Modules can be reused in other modules, other features, or even throughout the entire application.**

Reusable modules eliminate the need to repeat code in multiple places.

acquaintance calls you back to ask for additional features, such as a shopping cart or a product list, which also require displaying the game's calculated discount price (see figure 6.6).

With your application designed with reusable modules, you could support these types of enhancement requests with less retooling than typically required.

Being able to design your application's infrastructure in a modular fashion is well and good, but how are these self-contained units able to interact with each other? In the next section, you'll look at a couple of basic interaction methods.

6.2   Inter-module interaction methods

Modules interact in two ways: directly via module APIs, which creates a direct dependency, or through events. We've talked about module APIs in detail, so this section focuses more on how using dependencies for module interaction affects the application's architecture. This section also covers the decoupling effect of events and, more specifically, an event aggregation pattern called pub/sub.

6.2.1   Inter-module interaction through dependencies

Even though the syntax of any of the module pattern styles looks alien, a module is still just a function. As such, you can pass things into it via its parameters. Passing in another module as a parameter is one way modules can interact. This interaction method is considered *direct*, because one module is directly accessing the API of another. When one module interacts with another by directly calling the other's API, the other module is known as its *dependency*.

Each module style provides a way to declare other modules as dependencies. Although the syntax varies, the dependency list of each type serves a universal purpose: to allow a module access to the APIs of other modules so they can interact with one another. If you're using the traditional module pattern, for example, you declare dependencies in the module's trailing parentheses and gain access to them via its parameter (dependency) list.

To illustrate, let's use the pricing module shown previously. To get the price of each selected game at a discount, you need to add it as a dependency to the product display module (see the following listing). You're also adding the product data module as a dependency to gain access to your stub product data.

Listing 6.3   Traditional module pattern dependency list

```
var productDisplaySvcMod = (function(productData, pricingSvc) {          ← Access via its parameter list

    function getDetailsById(id) {
        var gameFound = null;
        var gameList = productData.usedGames;          ← Your module can now access
        for ( var i = 0; i < gameList.length; i++) {       the APIs of the dependencies
            if (gameList[i].productId === id) {
                gameFound = {
                name : gameList[i].name,
                productId : gameList[i].productId,
                summary : gameList[i].summary,
                url : gameList[i].url,
                price : pricingSvc.applyDiscount(gameList[i].price)
                };
            }
        }

        return gameFound;
    };

    return {
        getDetails : getDetailsById          ← Dependency declarations
    };                                          inside the trailing
                                                parentheses
})(productDataMod, pricingSvcMod);
```

The combined functionality can be exposed in this module's API

After a module is declared as a dependency of another, you can gain access to its API. The module's API ensures that you access its functionality as it was intended, passing in any necessary information for the call to be successful. Bear in mind that you still don't have direct access to the dependent module's module-scoped functions and other objects.

> **NOTE**   Even though adding a module as a dependency is a direct method of module interaction, you're still interacting only via the dependent module's API.

Interacting through dependencies is a good choice for many situations but not always. This method has both pros and cons.

6.2.2   *Dependency method pros and cons*

Here are a few advantages and disadvantages of direct inter-module interaction. Don't see this list as reasons to adopt this method or not, however. It's not practical to avoid using dependencies in modular programming. Think of the list as a helpful guide for when to use them.

Pros:

- No intermediary objects are involved; one module can directly call the API of another.
- Direct interaction is sometimes easier to debug.
- Using the dependency list of a module, it's easy to look at the source code and figure out which modules have been grouped together for a particular functionality or feature.

Cons:

- With dependent modules, a certain amount of coupling is involved. *Coupling* refers to how directly tied one part of your code is to another. When you couple modules, you reduce the flexibility you normally have when updating your code.
- Dependency lists can get rather long, which can sometimes make it a little hairy to keep track of what's dependent on what.
- When a module interacts with its dependency, it's a one-to-one relationship. This type of interaction is narrow and has only one recipient, as opposed to the method described in the next section, which can have multiple recipients.

The other option for module interaction is through events. The next section highlights a popular event aggregation pattern called the *publish/subscribe* (or *pub/sub*) pattern. You'll learn about what publish/subscribe is, how it works at a high level, and some of the pros and cons of using it in your SPA.

6.2.3   *Inter-module interaction through publish/subscribe*

Whether you're talking about interaction with the DOM or interaction between objects as you've seen in our discussion of MV* frameworks, events are used extensively in modern applications. You can think of the entire browser environment as being event driven. Events provide a natural way to achieve loose coupling, because recipients can choose to listen or not and also decide on how to respond.

Several design patterns around events have emerged over the years. The one this section focuses on is called the *publish/subscribe*, or *pub/sub*, pattern. Pub/sub is a common and useful pattern for interaction between disparate modules. Pub/sub is based on a classic design pattern called the *observer pattern*.

With the observer pattern, one object is directly observed (the *observable*), and any number of other objects (called *observers*) can choose to pay attention to it, as shown in figure 6.7. The observable sends out a notification (typically through events) whenever its state changes so the observers can react accordingly.

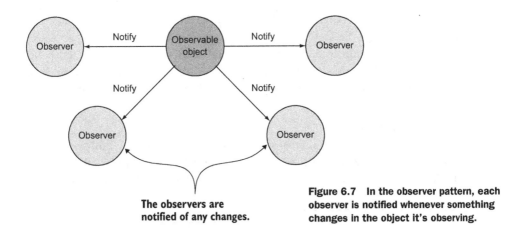

Figure 6.7 In the observer pattern, each observer is notified whenever something changes in the object it's observing.

The observers are notified of any changes.

What distinguishes pub/sub from the traditional observer pattern is that usually an intermediary service *publishes* (sends/broadcasts) the notifications on behalf of another object. Other objects in the application can choose to listen or not.

This type of brokered, indirect inter-module interaction is ideal when two unrelated modules need to interact or an application-wide message needs to be broadcast without any expectations by the publisher about what happens when the message is received.

TOPICS

Though not a requirement, notifications with most pub/sub implementations are topic based. A *topic* (or event name in AngularJS) is a simple name that's used to represent a particular notification. If another object wants to listen, it *subscribes* to that topic. When a topical message is published, the message broker delivers that notification to any of the topic's subscribers.

In the case of your application, you've created a module whose sole purpose is to broadcast system-wide messages using AngularJS's built-in pub/sub mechanism. This module will use pub/sub to publish a message with the topic userMessage.

As you can see in figure 6.8, the topic has only one subscriber: the controller for a view that displays

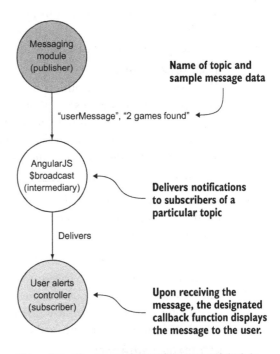

Name of topic and sample message data

Delivers notifications to subscribers of a particular topic

Upon receiving the message, the designated callback function displays the message to the user.

Figure 6.8 The messaging module uses pub/sub to publish messages, via an intermediary service, to any subscribers in the application.

user alerts. Because the controller is a subscriber of the `userMessage` topic, it will update the text in the view anytime it receives a new message.

Usually, pub/sub topic notifications and subscriptions are created programmatically by using the syntax style provided by the pub/sub implementation. If you decide to use the pub/sub method in your application, you'll need some type of pub/sub software.

PUB/SUB LIBRARIES

In your SPA, either the message broker implementation will be built into the MV* framework or you'll have to download one of the many JavaScript pub/sub libraries available. Table 6.1 lists a few of the pub/sub libraries available at the time of this writing.

Table 6.1   A sampling of pub/sub libraries

Pub/sub library	URL
AmplifyJS	http://amplifyjs.com
PubSubJS	https://github.com/mroderick/PubSubJS
Radio.js	http://radio.uxder.com
Arbiter.js	http://arbiterjs.com

As with any dependency in your application's code base, check out all available alternatives, using the usual set of criteria I've previously mentioned: learning curve, bugs and fix rate, documentation, maturity, and community support.

BASIC NOTIFICATIONS

The most basic type of notification doesn't include any data being passed. It's merely the topic name of the message that's being published. To illustrate a basic notification in pub/sub, we'll keep things vendor agnostic by using pseudocode.

We'll start with how to publish a topical message. To publish a message in module A, you include a line similar to the following:

```
pSub.publish("hello_world_topic");
```

It's that simple. Then, in module B, subscribing to that topic is equally easy. You include the topic name of the message you're interested in hearing and what you want to happen when you hear it:

```
pSub.subscribe("hello_world_topic", functionToCallWhenHeard);
```

You typically use a basic notification to inform all subscribers that something happened. Then each subscriber, upon hearing it, can react in a completely different way.

At times, however, you'll want to include data along with the topic being published. This, too, is accomplished easily using pub/sub.

NOTIFICATIONS WITH DATA

In addition to basic notifications, most pub/sub brokers let you pass data along when the message is published. In turn, each subscriber of that topic gets this data passed into its callback function by the broker. To publish with data, you use a line similar to the following in module A:

```
pSub.publish("hello_world_topic", dataObjectToSend);
```

In module B, your subscription line would be the same. The message broker passes the data sent into the function you list in the subscription:

```
pSub.subscribe("hello_world_topic", functionToCallWhenHeard);
```

The only difference when receiving data is in your callback function itself. Here, you'll need a parameter in the function's signature to represent the data being passed to it from the subscription:

```
function functionToCallWhenHeard( paramForDataPassed ) { ... }
```

With most brokers, any valid JavaScript object or value can be passed with the notification.

UNSUBSCRIBING

Another feature common to most pub/sub implementations is the ability to unsubscribe. Because subscriptions are topic based, the subscriber can invoke the broker's unsubscribe function when it doesn't want to react to that topic anymore. Once again, most pub/sub implementations make doing this super easy:

```
pSub.unsubscribe("hello_world_topic");
```

Various other options might be available, such as setting a priority for a topic, but are specialized and vendor specific. Additionally, the options mentioned thus far are the bare minimum but aren't guaranteed to be available in the pub/sub implementation you're using. The documentation for the broker you're using will specify the list of available features.

6.2.4 Pub/sub pros and cons

As noted earlier, pub/sub is a pattern that helps keep the modules of your code base decoupled. It can be a powerful and flexible tool, but it's not without its disadvantages. The following are some of the main pros and cons of using pub/sub in your SPA.

Pros:

- It promotes a loose coupling of your modules through notifications posted to a message broker, instead of having to maintain direct dependencies.
- As with using APIs, pub/sub is easy to implement.
- Notification topical messages can be broadcast to many subscribers at once.
- Different parts of the application can elect whether to pay attention to published messages.

Cons:

- If not built into the MV* framework, the message broker implementation itself is an extra dependency that must be separately maintained.

- Notifications flow in only one direction. No acknowledgement or response is sent back to the publisher (although you could create a response topic to create a kind of ping-pong effect).
- Topics are simple text strings. You must rely on a naming convention to ensure that they're routed to the correct recipient.
- It's harder to track the flow of messages through the system while debugging.
- In your code, you must ensure that the subscriber is available and listening before the notification is published, or the topic won't be heard.

Now that we've reviewed module concepts and the ways modules can interact, let's review some of the highlights of this chapter's project. For consistency with the other chapters in this book, we'll use AngularJS.

6.3   *Project details*

As mentioned at the start of the chapter, in this project you'll create a simple online store for a friend who has a small business selling used video games. You'll create only the product search portion of the SPA, because that's enough to demonstrate both methods of inter-module interaction discussed in this chapter.

In previous chapters, you've stuck to a feature or two for your sample application to stay focused on the concepts at hand. But now your application's code base is a little more elaborate. In this chapter, your application is divided into the following features:

- Search
- Product display
- Pricing
- Messaging
- User alerts

As you go through some of the code highlights, you'll see the inter-module interaction method used by each module so you can see how the application is connected. Before going over the code, though, let's discuss the objectives for this project.

For starters, figure 6.9 provides a glimpse of what the application will look like when you're finished. With that image in mind, here's a list of features that you want the application to have:

- Customers can search by both partial and complete game titles.
- Successful searches display a list of results, including a thumbnail image of the game and its title.
- In addition to the search results, a message with the number of results appears briefly at the bottom of the application after each search.
- When a game is selected, the user is taken to the product view to display the details of that particular game.
- The discounted price of the used game is based on the current retail price with a standard 40% discount (to keep things simple).

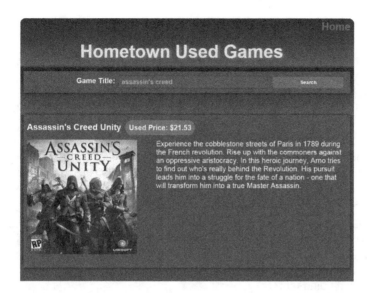

Figure 6.9 Our sample project is an online store to sell used video games.

Because previous chapters have thoroughly covered routing and views, I'll refer to them only when setting the stage for each section of our module discussion. As always, the complete project is available for download.

Because this chapter's example uses AngularJS, you'll also need a brief overview of modules and dependencies in AngularJS. Although this discussion of the sample project will be as neutral as possible, you'll need a little AngularJS knowledge to follow the source code.

High-level overview of AngularJS modules and dependencies

In AngularJS, you can create a module by calling the framework's `module()` function, supplying it with a name for your module and, optionally, including a dependency list:

```
angular.module("moduleName", ["dependency1", "dependency2"])
```

Let's compare that with the traditional module pattern:

```
var moduleName = (function(depParam1,depParam2) {
})(dependency1, dependency2)
```

If you don't have any dependencies, you provide empty brackets:

```
angular.module("moduleName", [])
```

After creating your module, you can create Angular-specific components *within* that module based on what you need your code to do. AngularJS provides the following out-of-the-box components: filters, directives, controllers, values, constants, services, factories, and providers. The details of the various AngularJS components are beyond the scope of this book but can be found in the online documentation at https://angularjs.org.

(continued)

In addition to the built-in AngularJS directives, you're using controllers, values, and factories. You're using the value component to hold your stub data, because this component is ideal for storing values used in an application. The factory components are the closest equivalent to your traditional module pattern (in terms of purpose), so you'll mostly use those for basic functionality. The controller components will, as you've already learned, act as a bridge between your application's code and the UI.

To create components for a module, you add a component function, such as `factory()` or `controller()`, to the module declaration. You can also include the name of other components in your declaration, and AngularJS will inject them into the one you're creating. This is called *dependency injection* (or DI).

To tell AngularJS you want another component injected into the component you're creating, you add the other component to the function parameter list. The names of injected components are duplicated as text strings, to decouple the name of the concrete implementation of the injected dependency from the named reference that the consuming code binds to:

```
angular.module("moduleName", [])
    .factory("componentName",
        ["otherComponent", function(otherComponent){…}]
    )
```

The components you ask AngularJS to inject for you can be any you've created in another module (if that module is in the current module's dependency list) or any one of the out-of-the-box components from AngularJS or other third-party components.

Now that you understand the bare minimum of AngularJS modules, components, and dependencies, you can move on to the source code for this chapter's SPA example.

6.3.1   Searching

When the application loads, users are greeted with a welcome message and a way to search for the games they're interested in. The header view and the search view are fixed, so they stay present as the main content changes with each search. When a title is searched, clicking the Search button invokes the route to display your search results (see figure 6.10).

Figure 6.10   Upon arrival, users are greeted with a welcome message and can immediately begin to search for games.

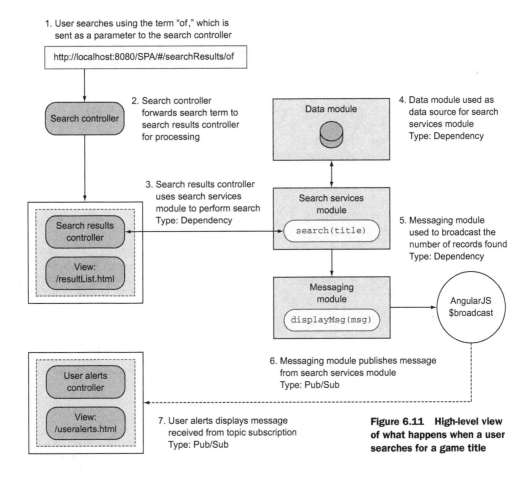

1. User searches using the term "of," which is sent as a parameter to the search controller

http://localhost:8080/SPA/#/searchResults/of

Search controller

2. Search controller forwards search term to search results controller for processing

Data module

4. Data module used as data source for search services module
Type: Dependency

3. Search results controller uses search services module to perform search
Type: Dependency

Search results controller

View: /resultList.html

Search services module

search(title)

5. Messaging module used to broadcast the number of records found
Type: Dependency

Messaging module

displayMsg(msg)

AngularJS $broadcast

User alerts controller

View: /useralerts.html

6. Messaging module publishes message from search services module
Type: Pub/Sub

7. User alerts displays message received from topic subscription
Type: Pub/Sub

Figure 6.11 High-level view of what happens when a user searches for a game title

Figure 6.11 gives you a big-picture look at this transaction, end to end, and notes the type of inter-module interaction, where relevant.

All searches are keyword searches, so any game with the search term in its title is added to the result list and displayed.

That's the high-level view of what happens when a user searches. Let's break down the steps now and look at the code behind each type of module interaction.

THE SEARCH CONTROLLERS MODULE

The search.controllers module has two controller components: one to handle the search itself and the other to display the search results. It also includes the search.services module as its sole dependency (see figure 6.12).

Inter-module interaction type: Dependency

Search controllers module → Search services module

Module dependency

Figure 6.12 The search controllers module uses the search services module to perform the searches. The search services module is its only dependency.

After searching, your search results controller uses a component in the search.services module to do the work of looking up the term a user has entered. If anything is found, the search component in the search.services module will return a list of game objects for the results controller to pass to its view for display.

The following listing shows the code for your search.controllers module. Remember that in AngularJS you add module-level dependencies in the brackets of the module declaration.

Listing 6.4   Module for search controllers

```
angular.module("search.controllers", ["search.services"])    ◄── Create the module with
                                                                 the search.services
                                                                 module as a dependency
    .controller("searchController",
        ["$scope", "$state",

            function($scope, $state){          ◄── In the UI, the Search button is bound to
                $scope.search = function() {        $scope.search. This function transitions to
                    $state.go("searchResults",      the searchResults state, passing along the
                    { gameTitle:$scope.game.name } );   search term in a parameter (gameTitle)
                };
            }

        ])
    .controller("searchResultsController",      searchResultsController
        ["$scope", "$stateParams", "searchSvc",   ◄── is the controller for the
                                                       searchResults state

            function($scope, $stateParams, searchSvc){
                $scope.results =
                searchSvc.search($stateParams.gameTitle);    ◄── The searchSvc component of
            }                                                    the search.services module is
                                                                 injected to do the data lookup
        ]);
```

Create a controller component for the search

Now that you've seen the controllers used for the search, let's review some of the code in the search.services module that you've added as a dependency. This is the module that does the heavy lifting.

THE SEARCH SERVICES MODULE

The search.services module has two dependencies: one to access your data and another to broadcast the number of search results found (see figure 6.13).

Inter-module interaction type: Dependency

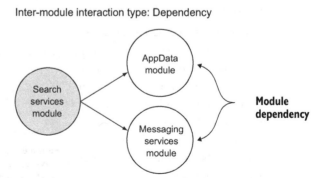

Figure 6.13   The search services module uses the app data module as a data source and the messaging services module to broadcast the number of search results.

Let's break up your analysis of the search so it's easier to read. Let's start with the dependency list:

```
angular.module("search.services",["data.appData"
,"messaging.services])
```

Here you'll notice that the search.services module also has its own dependencies. Its dependencies include the following:

- data.appData—A module that contains your game inventory
- messaging.services—A module that creates a message about the number of results found and uses pub/sub to broadcast that message

The following listing provides the entire source code for this module. It's a lot of code, but most of it is routine JavaScript used to match the search term with any of the game titles.

Listing 6.5 The search services module

```
angular.module("search.services",
["data.appData", "messaging.services"])          ◄── Create your module with
                                                       its two dependencies

.factory("searchSvc", [ "productData", "messageSvc",  ◄──
  function(productData, messageSvc) {
                                                 Create your factory component with
                                                 two components injected into it

  function searchByTitle(title) {

      if(!(title && (typeof title.trim == "function"))) {
          return [];
      }
                                                 Access the data from the
                                                 app.appData module
      if(!(productData && productData.usedGames
      && (typeof productData.usedGames.filter == "function"))) {
         return [];
      }

      var loweredTitle = title.trim().toLowerCase();

      var gamesFound =
      productData.usedGames.filter(function(game) {
         return game.name.toLowerCase().indexOf(loweredTitle) > -1;
      });

      // new user msg for lookup outcome
      messageSvc.displayMsg(                          ◄── Access the API of the
         createResultsMsg(gamesFound.length)              messageSvc component of the
      );                                                   messaging.services module

      return gamesFound;
  }


  function createResultsMsg(resultSize) {
```

The function referenced by the module API

```
    var quantifier = resultSize > 0 ? resultSize : "No";
    var noun = resultSize === 1 ? "game" : "games";
    var terminator = resultSize > 0 ? "!" : ".";

    return quantifier + " " + noun
    + " found" + terminator;
  }

  return {
    search : searchByTitle        ◄──────── Create a public API
  };
} ]);
```

This asks AngularJS to inject `productData` from the `data.appData` module and `messageSvc` from the `messaging.services` module. These are the worker bees of these two modules.

For each match of the search term, the information is returned to the caller (the search results controller). The results are then displayed for the user. Figure 6.14 shows the search results view after a successful search. In this case, the user used the term *of* in the search. This matched the game titles Call *of* Duty Advanced Warfare and Middle Earth: Shadow *of* Mordor.

Figure 6.14   Search results are displayed to the user, along with a brief user alert about the number of records found. Each search result is a link to display the item's details.

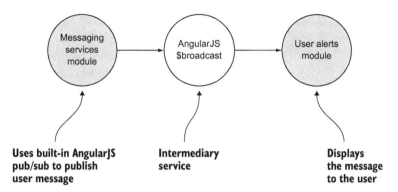

Figure 6.15 The messaging service is a generic utility, blindly broadcasting any message it's given. The only module listening in this case is the user alerts module.

Additionally, the number of records found is briefly presented at the bottom of the screen. Before the searchByTitle function returns, you'll use the messageSvc component of the messaging.services module to create a message about the number of matches in your search and broadcast it to the rest of the application. This is the message in yellow in figure 6.11. This messaging module will then use pub/sub to do the broadcast.

THE MESSAGING MODULE

The messaging module has no module-level dependencies, so no direct interaction occurs with another module. It does, however, interact indirectly with the user alerts module using pub/sub (see figure 6.15).

The code in this module is straightforward. It has a single component called messageSvc that uses the built-in pub/sub system of AngularJS to broadcast any messages passed to it, as you can see in the following listing.

Listing 6.6 The messaging services module

```
angular.module("messaging.services", [])                          ⟵ Create the module
                                                                     and give it a name,
.factory("messageSvc", [ "$rootScope", function($rootScope) {        no dependencies

        function displayMsg(msg) {
                $rootScope.$broadcast("userMessage", msg)         ⟵ Use $broadcast to publish
        };                                                           the userMessage topic, along
                                                                     with any message text
        return {
                displayMsg : displayMsg                           ⟵ Expose the functionality via the
        };                                                           displayMsg function in its API

} ] );
```

Create a factory component, ask AngularJS to inject $rootScope (topmost scope object)

With a generic, system-wide feature such as broadcasting a message, it's acceptable, if not preferable, to use pub/sub. Also, writing the module in this generic way lets you use it as a general messaging utility that can be reused anywhere you need to broadcast a message.

With the search results being displayed and the number of results being broadcasted, you're left with the module that will consume the broadcast and display it as a user alert.

THE USER ALERTS MODULE

The user.alerts module also has no module-level dependencies. As you saw in the previous section, it's communicated with indirectly by the messaging services module (refer back to figure 6.15).

Inside the module, you have one component that's a controller, so you can display any information received in the pub/sub subscription in the user alerts view (see the following listing).

Listing 6.7 The user alerts module

```
angular.module("userAlerts.controllers", [])

.controller("userAlertsController",
["$scope", "$rootScope", "$timeout",

  function($scope, $rootScope, $timeout){
    $rootScope.$on("userMessage", function(e, msg){
      $scope.msg = msg;

      $timeout(function() {
        $scope.msg = null;
      }, 2000);

    });
  }

]);
```

Create the module and give it a name, no dependencies

Ask AngularJS to inject a few out-of-the-box components you need

Subscribe to the userMessage event using $on

Display the message (via the $scope/viewmodel), and after 2 seconds remove it

At this point, you've seen how the application uses both direct and indirect methods of inter-module interaction when searching. Let's take a look at what happens when the user makes a selection from the search results list.

6.3.2 *Displaying product information*

When the user clicks one of the search results, a change in state allows the application to display the details about the selected game. Figure 6.16 shows an overview of this transaction.

After a game is selected from the search results list, its ID is sent to the product display controller as a parameter.

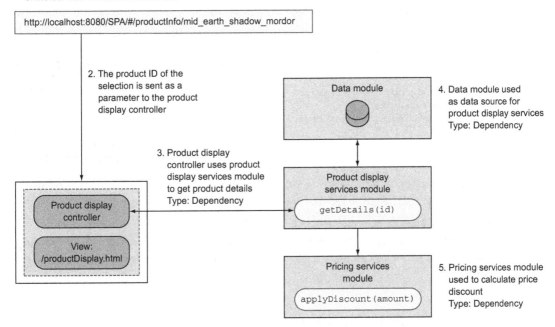

Figure 6.16   High-level view of the product display process

THE PRODUCT DISPLAY CONTROLLERS MODULE

The `productdisplay.services` module has only one module-level dependency: the product display services module (see figure 6.17).

Inter-module interaction type: Dependency

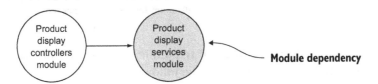

Figure 6.17   The product display services module finds the correct product information by using the selected game's ID.

As shown in the following listing, you use the `productDisplaySvc` component of the `productdisplay.services` module to look up the selected game's details, using the product ID sent in via the parameter. These details are then assigned to the `$scope` (ViewModel) for display.

Listing 6.8   The product display controller

```
angular.module("productdisplay.controllers",
  ["productdisplay.services"])
```
Create your module
with its dependency

```
.controller("productDisplayController",
  ["$scope", "$stateParams", "productDisplaySvc",
```
Ask AngularJS to inject the
productDisplaySvc component
from the other module

```
  function($scope, $stateParams, productDisplaySvc){
    $scope.results =
    productDisplaySvc.getDetails($stateParams.productId);
  }
]);
```
Use the productDisplaySvc component
to get the selected game's details

Let's take a peek at what's going on inside the product display services module in order to look up the game information and apply the price discount.

THE PRODUCT DISPLAY SERVICES MODULE

The productdisplay.services module has two dependencies: one to access your data and the other to calculate a 40% price discount for the selected used game (see figure 6.18).

Inter-module interaction type: Dependency

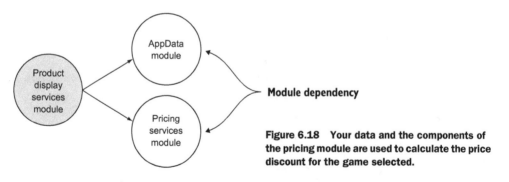

Figure 6.18   Your data and the components of the pricing module are used to calculate the price discount for the game selected.

You have some typical JavaScript coding in this module to iterate over the list of games and find the one with the matching ID (see the following listing).

Listing 6.9   Product display services module

```
angular.module("productdisplay.services",
  ["data.appData", "pricing.services"])
```
Create a new module
with two dependencies

```
.factory("productDisplaySvc", [ "productData", "pricingSvc",
  function(productData, pricingSvc) {

    function getDetailsById(id) {
```
Ask AngularJS to inject the data and pricing service
components from the dependent modules

Access the game inventory

```
        if (!(productData && productData.usedGames)){
            return null;
        }

        if (!(typeof productData.usedGames.filter == "function")) {
            return null;
        }

        var gamesFound = productData.usedGames.filter(function(game) {
            return game.productId == id;
        });

        if (!gamesFound.length) {
            return null;
        }

        var gameFound = gamesFound[0];

        return {
            name : gameFound.name,
            productId : gameFound.productId,
            summary : gameFound.summary,
            url : gameFound.url,
            price : pricingSvc.applyDiscount(gameFound.price)
        };

    }

    return {
      getDetails : getDetailsById
    };

  }

]);
```

Call the applyDiscount function of the API of the pricing component

Create an API

Having seen the product display services module, let's examine the last leg of your transaction to see how the discount is calculated and returned to the calling module.

THE PRICING SERVICES MODULE

The pricing.services module has no dependencies of its own and is straightforward. It takes in an amount from an outside module and multiplies that by the discount rate, as shown in the following listing.

Listing 6.10 The pricing services module

```
angular.module("pricing.services", [])

.factory("pricingSvc", function() {

    var discountRate = 40;
    var discount = discountRate / 100;
```

Create your module, no dependencies

```
function isNumber(n) {
   return !isNaN(parseFloat(n)) && isFinite(n);
}

function calculate(amt) {
   if(!isNumber(amt)){
      return 1;
   } else{
      return (discount * amt).toFixed(2);
   }
}

return {
   applyDiscount : calculate
};
```

Return the calculated discount

Expose the discount calculation via this API

```
} );
```

After the appropriate game has been found via its ID, and the discount has been applied to its price, a new game object is returned to the controller, where the information is passed over to the view for display. Figure 6.19 shows the outcome of the product selection.

The resulting view is the culmination of your inter-module interaction design for this project, including both the dependency method and the pub/sub method.

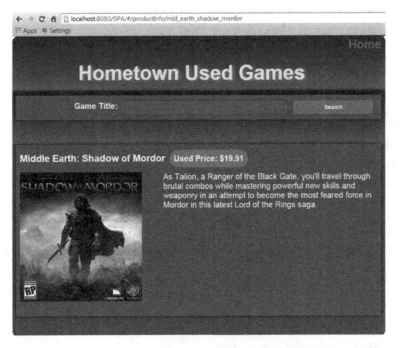

Figure 6.19 The resulting view after a matching game is found and a discount has been applied to the game's price

6.4 Chapter challenge

Now here's a challenge for you to see what you've learned in this chapter. Create a movie title search for which the matching names of movies appear in a list as the user types into an input text field. Use a single view, with the input text field at the top and an unordered list for the results below it. Use a mix of dependencies and pub/sub to create the functionality. Using your preferred MV* framework, bind a key-up event to a function that will publish the contents of the input field with every keystroke. One module should be listening for the topical message and perform the search. It should also use pub/sub to publish the results. Upon hearing the results, populate the unordered list by using your MV* framework.

6.5 Summary

You've accomplished a lot in this chapter. You've learned the following about inter-module interaction:

- Modules are a vital part of your application's infrastructure, providing encapsulation and a means for code reuse.
- A well-designed module can have many functions but should have a single overall purpose.
- Although the internal code of a module remains hidden, its API provides a central, controlled access point for its functionality.
- Two main methods exist for inter-module interaction: directly via APIs or indirectly via events. An event aggregation pattern called pub/sub was used to illustrate.
- No hard-and-fast rules exist for the type of inter-module interaction that you should choose. In general, modules related to a feature are good candidates for the dependency method. General-use modules, such as utility modules, are also OK to have as a direct dependency. Pub/sub is most suitable for unrelated modules and application-wide notifications.
- Interaction via dependencies is narrow but allows for direct access to another module's API.
- Interaction via pub/sub is broad and allows all subscribers of a topic to be notified at the same time.

Communicating
with the server

This chapter covers

- The server's role in an SPA environment
- How MV* frameworks communicate with the server
- Handling results with callback functions and promises
- Consuming RESTful services

In chapter 1, you learned how the adoption of the XMLHttpRequest (XHR) API and the AJAX movement eventually led to the emergence of SPAs. After XHR was supported in the browser—as a COM component at first and then natively—developers could use it to asynchronously load both the application's scaffolding and its data without refreshing the page. This opened many new avenues for the ways that web pages could be constructed.

Until now, you've been focusing on creating the SPA itself. In doing so, you've used XHR to dynamically retrieve the templates used to construct your views but restricted the data in your sample applications to local stub data. In this chapter, you'll take another important step forward. You're going to move the source data to the server and learn how to remotely access it from your SPA.

We'll kick things off with a brief look at the communication process between the SPA client and the server. After you're clear on the overall process, we'll look at the details of what happens on the client.

On the client side, I'll focus on how MV* frameworks try to make your life easier when you need to talk to the server. MV* frameworks that have built-in support for persistence enhance the XMLHttpRequest API with their own expanded set of features. But because each one has to go through XHR, there are certain commonalities I can point out.

What's the optimal way for an SPA to communicate with the server?

Generally, the most optimal way to communicate with the server from your SPA is to use the objects provided by your MV* framework—provided that the framework supports server communication. Because its objects are built specifically to work within the framework, they provide request and response methods that are ready-made to work with the rest of the framework. You'll need to customize these objects for your specific needs, either through configuration or by extending them in some fashion. Typically, you don't need to supplement the framework with any additional libraries.

If your framework doesn't have built-in support for communicating with the server, you can opt to work directly with the low-level methods of the `XMLHttpRequest` object itself, use a general utility library (such as jQuery), or go for a library that has fewer, more specialized components (such as AmplifyJS, http://amplifyjs.com).

After learning the basics of communicating with the server, you'll turn your attention to dealing with the results. You'll start with traditional callback functions, which describe what you want to happen when calls succeed or fail. Next, you'll learn about the use of promises. Promises are fast becoming the preferred means of dealing with XHR results by many of today's MV* frameworks. More important, though, they're part of the ECMAScript 6 version of JavaScript. They're generally considered a cleaner, more elegant way of dealing with asynchronous processes than simple callback functions.

This chapter wraps up with a look at consuming RESTful services with your SPA. REST is an architectural style for both websites and web services that has gained widespread popularity in recent years—so much so that many MV* frameworks support it out of the box. Some even use the REST style as a default.

I won't go into great detail about designing RESTful services, because that server-side topic is beyond the scope of this book. I'll talk about what REST is in the philosophical sense and discuss some of the ways in which MV* frameworks approach REST.

In the example for this chapter, you'll continue the preceding chapter's used video game store project by adding a shopping cart to it. A shopping cart is a standard feature for most sites selling goods and/or services online. It's also the perfect venue for demonstrating the server communication concepts in this chapter. You'll explore the details of your shopping cart later in the book. That being said, the sample project has some new requirements that we need to discuss.

7.1   Understanding the project requirements

Unlike in previous chapters, to run the code in this chapter you'll need a server. Because most MV* frameworks, including the one we're using (AngularJS), are server agnostic, you can pick any server you want. You can also use any server-side language you want. So whether you like JavaScript, PHP, Python, Ruby, .NET, Java, or any other of the multitude of languages out there for server-side development, that's perfectly OK.

Here are the only two hard requirements for whichever server/language combination you prefer:

- Support of RESTful services, because the example uses REST
- JSON support, either built in or via an add-on

The example's server code was developed using Spring MVC (version 4), which is a Java-based MVC framework. Don't worry, though, if you don't know Java or Spring. In our discussions within the chapter, I'll refer to the server-side code only conceptually. A guide to the server-side code's configuration is available in appendix C. If you prefer a different server-side tech stack, the appendix begins with a summary of the server-side objects and tasks so you can structure your own server-side code accordingly. The entire source for the project is available online for download.

Now that you've been introduced to the project, let's look at how your SPA can communicate with the server.

7.2   Exploring the communication process

Though many concepts around communicating with the server are the same for any type of web application, the next few sections present some of the basics within the context of a single-page application. I'll also highlight some specific ways in which the MV* framework supports the communication process.

7.2.1   Choosing a data type

In order for the SPA running in the browser to communicate with a server, both need to speak the same language. The first order of business is deciding on the type of data that will be sent and received. To illustrate, I'll use the example of a shopping cart, as I do at the end of the chapter.

When the user interacts with your shopping cart—whether it's adding an item, updating the quantity of an item, or viewing the current state of the cart's contents—you're sending and receiving JSON-formatted text. JSON is commonly used by SPAs when communicating with servers, though the data type can be anything from plain text, to XML, to a file.

Even though you're using JSON-formatted text as a common data exchange format, it's merely a representation of a system's native object or objects. For the text to be useful, conversions are happening at both ends. You'll learn about these a little later. To ensure that the conversions to native objects work, each side must do its part to make sure the agreed-upon JSON format is used in the call.

When a call is made to the server, requests can include information about the *internet media types* that are acceptable, because a resource can be available in a variety of languages and media types. The server can then respond with a version of the requested resource that it deems a best fit. This is called *content negotiation*. For this project, you're interested only in JSON. To express this, you can explicitly declare an internet media type of `application/json` for the exchange.

Internet media types

An *internet media type* (formerly a MIME type) is a standard way to identify the data that's being exchanged between two systems. It's used by many internet protocols, including HTTP. Internet media types have the format of `type/subtype`. In this case, you're using a media type of `application/json`: the type is `application`, and the subtype is `json`.

Optional parameters can also be added by using a semicolon, if required. For example, to specify a media type of `text`, with a subtype of `html` and a character encoding of `UTF-8`, you use `text/html; charset=UTF-8`.

Internet media types are specified using *HTTP headers*, which are the fields sent in the transmission that provide information about the request, the response, or what's contained in the message's body. The `Content-type` header tells the other system what to expect in the request and response. The `Accept` header can also be specified in the request to let the server know the media type or types that are acceptable to return.

After a data type has been selected, an appropriate request method must be used for the call to be successful. The next section presents common request methods for an SPA.

7.2.2 *Using a supported HTTP request method*

When a client makes a request, it can indicate the type of action it would like the server to perform by specifying the *request method*. In order for the request to be successful, though, the HTTP request method specified in the request must be supported by the server-side code for that call. If it isn't, the server may respond with a 405 Method Not Allowed status code.

Because the HTTP request method describes what should happen to the resource represented in the request, it's often called the *verb* of the call. A request method that doesn't modify a resource, such as `GET`, is considered *safe*. Any request method that ends in the same result, no matter how many times its call is executed, is considered *idempotent*. For example, you'll use `PUT` when the user wants to update the count of a particular item that's in the cart. Because `PUT` is idempotent, you can tell the server that you want two copies of *Madden NFL* 10 times in a row, but after the tenth time, you still have only two copies in the cart.

Table 7.1 defines a few common HTTP request methods used in our shopping cart example. Although it's not a comprehensive list, it does represent the ones most commonly used in single-page applications.

Table 7.1 Common HTTP methods used in an SPA

Method	Description	Example	Safe?	Idempotent?
GET	Typically, GET is used to fetch data.	View the shopping cart	Yes	Yes
POST	This method is most commonly used for creating a resource or adding an item to a resource.	Add an item to the cart	No	No
PUT	Typically, PUT is used like an update-or-create action, updating the existing resource or optionally adding it if it doesn't exist.	Update the quantity of an item in the cart	No	Yes
DELETE	This is used to remove a resource.	Remove an item from the cart	No	Yes

Other HTTP methods are specified in the HTTP protocol. For a full list, see http://en.wikipedia.org/wiki/Hypertext_Transfer_Protocol#Request_methods.

The final part of the communication process is the conversion of the data to and from the internet media type sent and received.

7.2.3 Converting the data

After the data type is agreed upon, both the client and the server must be configured to send and receive that particular type. For your shopping cart, you're using JSON exclusively, so both the code in the browser and the code on the server must be able to convert to and from this text format.

On the client, the ability to convert a JavaScript object to JSON may be built into the MV* framework. If that's the case, it's likely the default, and the conversion will happen automatically when you use the framework to make the server request. If automatic conversion is not built in, the framework may offer a utility for the conversion of its custom types. For the conversion of JavaScript POJOs, you can use the native JavaScript command JSON.stringify():

```
var cartJSONText = JSON.stringify(cartJSObj);
```

On the server, the JSON-formatted text is converted into a native object of the server-side language by a JSON parser that's either built in or available via a third-party library. Like the HTTP method, the exact method for executing the conversion process on the server will vary.

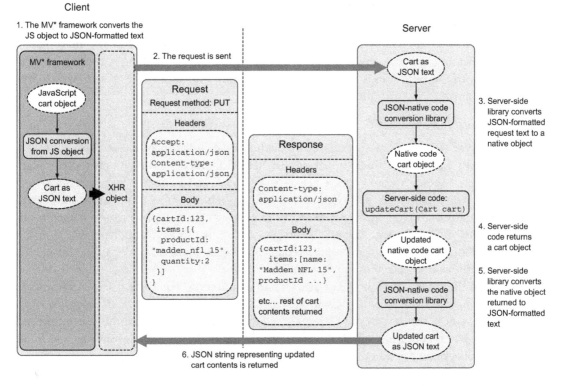

Figure 7.1 **JavaScript objects are converted to JSON and added to the request body for the request. In response, the server sends back the updated cart as JSON via the response body.**

To illustrate the process end to end, let's use the shopping cart update example again. Let's say that the user has increased the quantity of an item in the cart. For the modification to be verified and processed, you'll send the updated cart to the server. Figure 7.1 paints a picture of the conversions that happen at both ends.

After the update function is called, your JavaScript cart object is converted into JSON-formatted text by the MV* framework. Next, the MV* framework passes the data to the XMLHttpRequest API. Then the JSON payload is sent in the body of the request to the server.

On the client, after the response is received, the returned text is converted once again. This time it's converted back into a native JavaScript object. Often this is also handled automatically for you by the MV* framework. If not, you can use the native JavaScript command JSON.parse():

```
var cartJSObj = JSON.parse(returnedCartJSONText);
```

Now that we've discussed the communication process as a whole, let's go back to the client to talk about how MV* frameworks help simplify this process.

7.3   *Using MV* frameworks*

One thing MV* frameworks are great at is simplifying complex tasks by abstracting away a lot of the boilerplate code involved. This is certainly true when it comes to communicating with the server. This section specifically covers making requests and dealing with the responses. In our discussion, I'll point out some of the ways in which MV* frameworks help with the heavy lifting.

7.3.1   *Generating requests*

If server communication is supported by the framework, it may expose the XHR object directly or abstract some or all of the XHR functionality with its own proprietary objects. These custom objects act as wrappers around the XMLHttpRequest object either directly or indirectly via another library such as jQuery. They add value by hiding many of the tedious, repetitive tasks in making calls and processing the results.

Before you look at any MV* examples, let's put things into perspective by using vanilla JavaScript and the XMLHttpRequest object to make a server call. If you need a refresher on XHR, refer to appendix B.

We'll use the shopping cart again as an example. As you did earlier, you'll update the quantity of an existing item in the cart. Because you're updating the quantity of an item, you'll use the PUT HTTP request method. As you learned in the preceding section, PUT is commonly used in an update situation. To keep things simple, you'll use an abbreviated version of the cart data used in the project:

```
var cartObj = {
    cartId : 123,
    items : [ {
        productId : "madden_nfl_15",
        quantity : 2
    } ]
};
```

The following listing illustrates the plain JavaScript version of an update to the shopping cart using the XMLHttpRequest object directly.

Listing 7.1   Shopping cart update using PUT and XHR directly

```
var cartJSON = JSON.stringify(cartObj);                          Create new instance of
                                                                 XMLHttpRequest object
var xhrObj = new XMLHttpRequest();

xhrObj
.open("PUT","/SPA/controllers/shopping/carts",true);            Define the call
                                                                 properties

xhrObj
.setRequestHeader("Content-Type","application/json");           Set the content type

xhrObj
.setRequestHeader("Accept","application/json");

xhrObj.send(cartJSON);                                           Declare the data
                                                                 type you'll accept
```

Convert JS object to JSON text

Send the request

In this example, you're not even handling the results. You'll tackle that in the next section. Even so, you have to deal with several of the low-level details. You have to manually set the content type and any other headers you need (such as `Accept`). Additionally, you have to manually convert the JavaScript cart object to JSON-formatted text.

Generally, if an MV* framework has out-of-the-box support for server communication, you'll most likely be generating requests from one of two types of objects: a model or some type of utility/service object. If the framework requires you to create an explicitly defined data model, you'll most likely perform server operations by calling functions on the model itself. If the framework doesn't have an explicit data model (the framework considers any source of data an implied model), you'll probably work through the framework's utility/service. AngularJS, for example, provides a couple of services for server communication: `$http` and `$resource`. You're be using `$resource` in the project, and you'll see it in action a little later.

MAKING REQUESTS VIA A DATA MODEL

With some frameworks (Backbone.js, for example), you explicitly define a data model by extending a built-in model object from the framework. By extending the framework's model, you inherit many capabilities automatically. This includes the built-in capability to perform the full range of CRUD (create, read, update, and delete) operations on a remote resource (see figure 7.2).

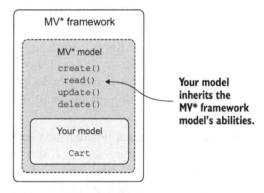

Figure 7.2   With MV* frameworks, where your model extends those of the framework, you automatically inherit abilities from the parent, such as the ability to make server requests.

Don't worry, though, if you need to make custom calls. Most frameworks let you override and customize their out-of-the box behavior.

Listing 7.2 extends `Backbone.Model` to define your shopping cart, passing in the name of the attribute you want to use as its ID. You're also defining a base URL for all server requests. You have to do this only once, because this is just the model's definition.

After the model has a definition, you can create new instances of it anytime you need to use it. All new instances of your shopping cart will then inherit everything you need for server communication.

Listing 7.2   Backbone.js version of your shopping cart update

```
var Cart = Backbone.Model.extend({
    idAttribute : 'cartId',
    urlRoot : 'controllers/shopping/carts/',
});

var cartInstance = new Cart(cartObj);
cartInstance.save();
```

Create a new model instance

Define a model with a URL and an ID

Call its inherited save() function to initiate the request

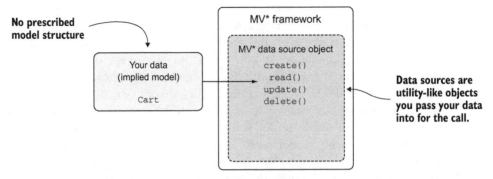

Figure 7.3   Frameworks that provide server communication, but don't provide a model to extend, will most likely provide a data source object instead.

The Backbone.js code is certainly less verbose. It's also doing several things under the covers. For starters, it assumes you're dealing with JSON (unless you tell it otherwise) and automatically converts the object passed into its constructor to JSON-formatted text. In addition, it automatically sets the Content-type and Accept headers for JSON. Finally, it can automatically decide whether to use PUT or POST based on whether the object of the request has an ID yet. Again, any of these features can be customized or overridden.

MAKING REQUESTS THROUGH DATA SOURCE OBJECTS

The other manner in which MV* frameworks make requests to the server is through a separate data source object. This is typical when a framework, such as AngularJS, allows you to use anything you want as a data model. With no parent to extend, there are no canned abilities to inherit. When this is the case, the framework provides a data source object that you'll pass your model into when making a call (see figure 7.3).

Let's see an example of this alternative MV* approach. Listing 7.3 uses an AngularJS $resource object to perform your shopping cart update. I mentioned earlier that $resource is one of AngularJS's services that can be used when communicating with the server. It has many features for easily modeling requests and dealing with the server's response. When you get to this chapter's project, you'll delve into the use of $resource in detail to understand the example. For now, let's see this style of MV* code as a comparison with your original, vanilla JavaScript server call.

Listing 7.3   AngularJS version of your shopping cart update

```
var CartDataSrc =
    $resource(
        "controllers/shopping/carts", null,
        {updateCart : {method : "PUT"}
    }
);

CartDataSrc.updateCart(cartObj);
```

Define a URL for the call and no URL parameters (null)

Use the built-in $resource object to create a data source instance

AngularJS's $resource object has all CRUD operations except update(); you can configure it

Use the updateCart() method you added

Even though you're not extending anything, the overall concept is the same as our first MV* example. You can lean on the MV* framework to help you generate the request. Like Backbone.js, under the covers AngularJS sets the appropriate headers, converts the JavaScript object into JSON, and uses the HTTP method you defined. As you saw, though, the authors of this particular framework chose to not include a method to update the cart (PUT) out of the box. It's easy enough, though, to customize the data source object to add this behavior.

Another feature that MV* frameworks provide is an easy way to deal with the results of a call to the server. Some frameworks support using callback functions, whereas others rely on promises. Promises are becoming more and more prevalent with MV* frameworks, but I'll make sure you understand using callbacks with asynchronous requests first.

7.3.2 Processing results with callbacks

When you're processing an asynchronous task, such as your server call to update the shopping cart, you don't always want the application to hang while you wait for the server to respond. You sometimes need it to continue in the background while your application handles other tasks. So instead of the update function returning a value when it's done, callbacks are passed in to handle the results when it completes. You can do this because functions can be passed around. This allows any function to take other functions as arguments.

When callbacks are passed into a function as arguments, they become like an extension of it. They can be passed control and continue processing from there. Using callbacks in this way is called *continuation-passing style.*

Let's take a look, then, at using the continuation-passing style of programming to process the results of a server call. Because Backbone.js supports callbacks, I'll use that framework to illustrate. Let's add some handlers to your previous shopping cart update. Figure 7.4 gives an overview.

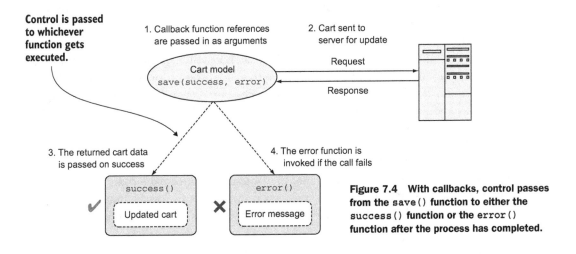

Figure 7.4 With callbacks, control passes from the save() function to either the success() function or the error() function after the process has completed.

If the call is successful, the save() function invokes the success() function via the XHR object, passing to it the returned cart data. If the call fails, save() invokes error(), passing in the details for the failure. In either case, processing is continuing from the model's save() function to one of these callback functions.

Now let's take a look at some code. You'll make exactly the same request that you did earlier with Backbone.js, but this time you'll do something with the results (see the following listing).

Listing 7.4   Processing a shopping cart update via callbacks

New Cart instance created

```
var cartInstance = new Cart(cartObj);

cartInstance.save(null, {
    success : function(updatedCart, reponse) {
        console.log("Cart ID: " + updatedCart.id);
    },
    error : function(cartUnchanged, response) {
        console.log("Error: " + response.statusText);
    }
});
```

No model attributes to change before saving (null)

Define callbacks for save()

Not only is this code a little easier to read, but you're also able to pass in a configuration object to the save() function itself. In this object, you can define success and error callback functions and any other configuration options supported by save() that are needed. Backbone.js also helps out by automatically passing the results of the server call to the callback functions you've defined.

In a successful call, you have access to the updated cart object as well as the response from the server. When the call fails, you can use the response to find out the reason for the failure. Moreover, if you need any low-level details about the call, the save() method also returns a jQuery jqXHR object, which is a wrapper for XHR. For more details about jqXHR, see http://api.jquery.com/jQuery.ajax/#jqXHR.

Callbacks are easy to work with and great for simple results, but continuation-passing style can sometimes become cumbersome if you have multiple tasks to perform when the call completes.

Fortunately, a trend with many MV* frameworks is to return a promise instead of relying on continuation-passing style callbacks. Like callback functions, promises are nonblocking: the application doesn't have to stop and wait for the call to finish. This makes them also ideal for asynchronous processing. As you'll see in the next section, they have additional properties and behaviors that make your life much easier when you have complex requirements for handling results.

7.3.3   Processing results with promises

A *promise* is an object that represents the outcome of a process that hasn't yet completed. When an MV* framework supports promises, its functions that perform asynchronous server calls will return a promise that serves as a proxy for the call's eventual results. It's through this promise that you can orchestrate complex result-handling routines. To understand how to use a promise, you must first understand its internal state before and after the call is made.

WORKING WITH PROMISE STATES

The good news about working with promises is that they exist in only *one* of the following three states:

- *Fulfilled*—This is the state of the promise when the process resolves successfully. The value contained within the promise is the result of the process that ran. In your shopping cart update, this would be the updated cart contents returned by the server.
- *Rejected*—This is the promise's state when the process fails. The promise contains a reason for the failure (usually an `Error` object).
- *Pending*—This is the initial state of the promise before the process completes. In this state, the promise is neither fulfilled nor rejected.

These three states are mutually exclusive and final. After the promise has been fulfilled or rejected, it's considered settled and can't be converted into any other state. Figure 7.5 uses the shopping cart project to illustrate the three states of a promise.

A variable assigned to a promise doesn't remain a null reference while it waits for the function to return. Instead, a full-fledged object gets returned immediately in a pending state with an undetermined value. When the process finishes, the promise's

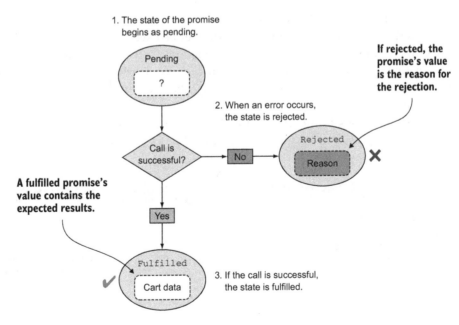

Figure 7.5 A promise has three mutually exclusive states: pending, fulfilled, and rejected.

state changes to either fulfilled, with its value containing the results of the call, or rejected, with the reason for the failure.

ACCESSING THE RESULTS OF YOUR PROCESS

I haven't talked about what you do with a promise after it's returned, in order to access a process's results. The Promise API has several useful methods, but the one you'll use the most is its then() method.

The then() method lets you register callback functions that allow the promise to hand you back a process's results. The functions you define here are called *reactions*. The first reaction function represents the case in which the promise is fulfilled. The second is optional and represents the case in which the promise is rejected:

```
promise.then(
    function (value) {
        // reaction to process the success value
    },
    function (reason) {
        // reaction to optionally deal with the rejection reason
    }
);
```

Because the rejected reaction is optional, the then() method can be written in short-hand:

```
promise.then(function (value) {
    // process the success value, ignore rejection
});
```

Here's the point to remember about reaction functions: no matter how the code is formatted, only *one* of the two functions will ever be executed—never both. It's one or the other. In this regard, it's somewhat analogous to a try/catch block. It's also worth noting that the parameter of the reaction function is what the promise hands you back (with either the fulfilled value or the rejection reason). When that happens, you have your results.

Let's take a look at the then() function in action. The following listing updates your shopping cart and uses a promise instead of a callback function to process the results.

Listing 7.5   Processing a shopping cart update via a promise

```
CartDataSrc.updateCart(cartObj).$promise
    .then(
        function(updatedCart) {
            console.log("Cart ID: " + updatedCart.id);
        },
        function(errorMsg) {
            console.log("Error: " + errorMsg);
        }
    );
```

The update returns a promise

Use the promise's then() function to access the results

Having a promise returned is built into AngularJS's $resource methods. As you can see in the example, you're writing out the results of the call to the console as you did before—only this time you're able to use the returned promise object instead of diverting control over to a callback function. The then() method passes the success results or the rejected reason to the functions you give it.

Another perk of using promises is that you can chain multiple then() methods together if more than one thing needs to happen after your call has been made.

CHAINING PROMISES

Often after a process has run, you want several things to happen after the fact. In addition, you may need these things to happen in order, ensuring that the next event happens only if the one before it succeeds. This is not only possible but also easy to do with promises.

> **NOTE** jQuery's implementation of promises doesn't support every scenario described in this section. See https://blog.domenic.me/youre-missing-the-point-of-promises for more details.

So far in your shopping cart update, you've been printing the results to the console. In a real application, you want to perform the following tasks after the server call finishes:

1 Recalculate the cart's total, applying necessary discounts.
2 Update the view with the results.
3 Reuse the message service to update the user that the call was a success.

Moreover, you want these tasks performed in order, and only if each task is successful should the next one begin. This ensures that the user won't be erroneously notified that everything went swimmingly if an error happens to occur along the way (see the following listing).

Listing 7.6 Using promises to force control flow

```
var promise = CartDataSrc.updateCart(cartObj).$promise

promise.then(function( updatedCart ) {
    return shoppingCartSvc
    .calculateTotalCartCosts(updatedCart);
})
.then(function(recalculatedCart) {
    replaceCartInView(recalculatedCart);
})
.then(function() {
    messageSvc.displayMsg("Cart updated!");
})
["catch"](function(errorResult) {
    messageSvc.displayError(errorResult);
});
```

$resource returns a promise

Return recalculated cart for use in next then()

Display recalculated cart

Display a user message

Handle any errors that occurred along the way

This works because each then() returns a promise. If the reaction of the previous then() returns a promise, its value is used in the subsequent promise handed to the next then(). If the reaction returns a simple value, this value becomes the value in the promise passed forward. This allows you to chain them all together and makes for a straightforward and clean approach.

Being able to chain together multiple tasks in sequence in a few lines of code is amazing, but chaining can help you in other ways. Another amazing thing about chaining promises is that you can have more than one asynchronous process in the chain.

CHAINING MULTIPLE ASYNCHRONOUS PROCESSES IN SEQUENCE

Sometimes when you need several tasks to run in order, more than one may be asynchronous. Because you don't know when asynchronous processes will finish, trying to place one into a sequence with other tasks might be pretty challenging. It's easy, though, using promises. Because each then() is resolved before the next one is executed, the entire chain executes sequentially. This is still true even if multiple asynchronous processes are in the chain.

To demonstrate, let's pretend that the server APIs require you to use the cart ID that's returned by the shopping cart update in a subsequent GET call in order to properly display the cart onscreen. The following listing illustrates how to use promises to do this.

> **Listing 7.7   Executing more than one server call in order**

```
var promise = CartDataSrc.updateCart(cartObj).$promise

promise.then(function( cartReturned ) {
    return shoppingCartSvc                      ◀── Use the cart returned in the
    .getCartById(cartReturned.cartId);              update for the next server call
})
.then(function(fetchedCart) {
    return shoppingCartSvc                      ◀── Use the fetched cart
    .calculateTotalCartCosts(fetchedCart);          for the recalculation
})
.then(function(recalculatedCart) {
    replaceCartInView(recalculatedCart);
})
.then(function() {
    messageSvc.displayMsg(userMsg);
})
["catch"](function(errorResult) {
    messageSvc.displayError(errorResult);
});
```

In this chain, your update happens first. Then, after it returns, your next server call fires. Because the GET call from $resource already creates a promise, its value will be used in the promise passed to the next then().

Before finishing this discussion of promises, let's get a quick overview of error handling. You saw error handling in some of the examples, but I didn't go over any details.

7.3.4   *Promise error handling*

You can handle rejected promises in two ways. You saw the first way early on. Option 1 is to use the second reaction function of the promise's then() method. The second reaction is the one triggered when there's a rejection:

```
promise.then(
    function (value) {
    },
    function (reason) {
        // deal with the rejection
    }
);
```

Option 2 is to add an error-handling method called catch() to the end of your chain:

```
.catch(function (errorResult) {
    // deal with the rejection
});
```

Some browsers take issue with a method called catch(), because it's a preexisting term in the JavaScript language. Alternatively, you can use this syntax:

```
["catch"](function(errorResult) {
    // deal with the rejection
});
```

> **TIP**   Writing .catch() as ["catch"] looks strange but will help you avoid potential issues for any older browsers that don't support ECMAScript 5. If you use this syntax, as shown in these examples, notice that it *doesn't* have a dot in front of it.

You saw the second option being used with your shopping cart call. It used the message service to log the error and broadcast a user-friendly message to the user:

```
["catch"](function(errorResult) {
    messageSvc.displayError(errorResult);
});
```

With either method of error handling, rejections are passed down the chain to the first available error handler. This behavior seems obvious with the catch() method. What's less obvious is that this is true even when using the optional reaction function for error handling. If a rejection occurs somewhere up the chain, and *either* type of error-handling method is encountered somewhere down the chain (even if it's several then()s later), that error handler will be triggered and passed the error thrown.

As illustrated in our shopping cart examples, promises are powerful yet easy to use if you understand them. Frameworks and libraries sometimes add even more functionality, on top of what this chapter covers on promises. See their documentation for specific details.

Even if you have a project that requires you to support older browser versions, you can still use promises via your MV* framework if promises are supported or via a third-party library. The following are a few of the many popular promise third-party libraries at the time of this writing:

- *bluebird*—https://github.com/petkaantonov/bluebird
- *Q*—https://github.com/kriskowal/q
- *RSVP.js*—https://github.com/tildeio/rsvp.js
- *when*—https://github.com/cujojs/when
- *WinJS*—http://msdn.microsoft.com/en-us/library/windows/apps/br211867.aspx

Aside from all of these being promise libraries, they also conform to the current preferred promise standard called *Promise/A+*. This is the same standard that native JavaScript promises are based on. If you'd like to read more about the Promise/A+ specification, a good resource is https://github.com/promises-aplus/promises-spec.

As an aside, jQuery also has its own version of promises, but as of this writing they aren't Promise/A+ compliant. With jQuery, promise functionality is done via its Deferred object. If you're interested, a great resource is the jQuery site itself: http://api.jquery.com/category/deferred-object.

Promises are also being implemented into the ECMAScript 6 (Harmony) version of JavaScript. Even before the specifications have been finalized, they already have limited support in many of today's browsers.

At this point, you're almost ready for our project. But you need to review the consumption of RESTful services first.

7.4   Consuming RESTful web services

This section covers consuming RESTful web services from your SPA. In many single-page applications today, these types of services are extremely common.

7.4.1   What is REST?

REST stands for *Representational State Transfer.* REST isn't a protocol or even a specification but an architectural style for distributed hypermedia systems. It has gained such widespread popularity that many MV* frameworks not only provide out-of-the-box support for it but also favor this style by default.

In a RESTful service, APIs define the media types that represent resources and drive application state. The URL and the HTTP method used in the API define the processing rules for a given media type. The HTTP method describes what's being done, and the URL uniquely identifies the resource affected by the action. REST can best be defined by describing its set of guiding principles.

7.4.2   REST principles

This section presents a few of the REST principles that most affect how you consume RESTful web services. This will also give you a good idea of what REST is about.

EVERYTHING IS A RESOURCE

One of the fundamental concepts in REST is that everything is a resource. A *resource* is represented with a type and conceptually maps to an entity or set of entities. A resource could be a document, an image, or information that represents an object such as a person. The notion of a resource could also extend to a service such as *today's weather* or, in our case, *a shopping cart.*

EVERY RESOURCE NEEDS A UNIQUE IDENTIFIER

Each resource in a RESTfull service should have a unique URL to identify it. This often entails creating and assigning unique IDs to the resource. You want to make sure that any ID you use in a URL in no way jeopardizes the security or integrity of your application. A common security measure is to assign a randomly generated ID for any resource that's personal or confidential. To ensure that the ID is used by only the intended user, the server-side code makes sure the requester is the authenticated user assigned to the resource and has the proper authorization to perform the action on the resource.

REST EMPHASIZES A UNIFORM INTERFACE BETWEEN COMPONENTS

You've already seen how HTTP methods are considered the verb of a web service call. Resource identifiers and HTTP methods are used to provide a uniform way of accessing resources. Table 7.2 gives some examples from the project.

Table 7.2　URLs in REST uniquely identify a resource, and the HTTP method describes that action being performed on the resource.

REST
URL: /shopping/carts/CART_ID_452 Method: GET Purpose: Fetch cart
URL: /shopping/carts/CART_ID_452/products/cod_adv_war Method: POST Purpose: Add an item to the cart
URL: /shopping/carts/CART_ID_452 Method: PUT Purpose: Update the entire cart's contents
URL: / shopping/carts/CART_ID_452/products/cod_adv_war Method: DELETE Purpose: Remove all instances of a particular product from the cart

It's important to note that the style of URL used isn't part of REST, even though you sometimes see the phrase *RESTful URL* used in articles about REST.

INTERACTIONS ARE STATELESS

Session state for your application should be held in your SPA and shouldn't rely on client context being stored on the server between requests. Each request made by the

SPA to the server should convey all the information needed to fulfill the request and allow the SPA to transition to a new state.

Again, we've barely scratched the surface of REST here. For more information about REST and REST architecture, see http://en.wikipedia.org/wiki/Representational_state_transfer.

7.4.3   *How MV* frameworks help us be RESTful*

Thinking in terms of REST can take a little getting used to. Fortunately, MV* frameworks such as Backbone.js and AngularJS support REST right out of the box. For example, when you used Backbone.js for your shopping cart update, it automatically added the ID from your model to your URL so that the URL uniquely identifies the resource in the request. Frameworks that don't have explicit models, such as AngularJS, might allow you to use path variables in a URL template to create a RESTful URL. You'll see examples of path variables in a moment, when you look how AngularJS's $resource object is used in your project.

MV* frameworks also help you consume RESTful services by making it easy to send the correct HTTP request method. They usually either come with canned functions for GET, POST, PUT, and DELETE or allow you to effortlessly generate them via configuration.

Now that you have a general idea of RESTful services and their guiding principles, you're finally ready to tackle the project. In this project, you'll get to see firsthand how promises and REST work together to maintain a shopping cart.

7.5   *Project details*

You'll continue building on the preceding chapter's used video game project by adding a shopping cart. As usual, you'll use AngularJS for your MV* framework. It has built-in support for both promises and the consumption of RESTful services. As indicated at the beginning of this chapter, we discuss the server side of the application only conceptually here.

Because many server-side languages and frameworks might be used instead of what you're using, I include a small summary of the tasks the server will need to perform for each call in appendix C. This way, you can create the server-side code by using a different tech stack if you wish. As always, the complete code is available for download. Let's begin by walking through the setup of your data source.

7.5.1   *Configuring REST calls*

Earlier in this chapter, you learned about the $resource object from AngularJS. It makes consuming RESTful services easier, and its methods all return promises. You'll use it for every server call in your project. Although I try to keep our discussions framework neutral, you'll have to take a moment to further review how $resource works. It can be a little intimidating at first. After you walk through how it works, though, you'll see how easy it is to use. After a gentle introduction to $resource, you'll proceed with how it'll be configured in your example SPA's shopping cart service.

Creating URLs with AngularJS's $resource

Like some of the other MV* frameworks, AngularJS offers support for RESTful service web service consumption out of the box by using its $resource object. This object adds a lot of sugar coating for the underlying XMLHttpRequest object to hide much of the boilerplate code you'd have to otherwise write yourself.

The main goal of $resource is to make it easy to work with RESTful services. Having a consistent and uniform way to represent resources is one of the principles of REST. After a URL style has been established, the $resource factory will help you create URLs that conform to this style easily.

The $resource factory enables you to define a template that will create resource URLs for each type of REST call you need to make. To use $resource, you can pass a URL, optional default parameters, and an optional set of actions to its constructor:

```
$resource(DEFAULT URL, DEFAULT URL PARAMS, OPTIONAL ACTIONS)
```

The following will serve as your default URL:

```
"controllers/shopping/carts"
```

The default will be used if you don't override it. But in this project, you're defining custom functions that will override it with their own URLs. Each custom action can have its own. To construct the URLs in the structure needed by your RESTful web services, you can use URL path parameters. As with routes, using a colon in front of a string in the URL indicates a parameter. Here's an example URL from your configuration that includes URL path parameters:

```
"controllers/shopping/carts/:cartId/products/:productId"
```

The next argument, the optional parameter list, acts like a data map. It tells the $resource object that in one or more of these calls, this optional parameter list *may* be used. This list is in the form of key-value pairs. The left side is the name of a parameter in the URL. The right side is the value for the parameter. The @ symbol tells $resource that the value is a *data property name*, not just a string. With it present, the data object passed in will be scanned for a property with that name, and its value will be used in the URL's path.

```
{
    cartId : "@cartId",
    productId : "@productId "
}
```

For example, if you passed in an object called myCart for the call, then the value for the URL parameter cartId would come from myCart.cartId. The value for the URL parameter productId would come from myCart.productId.

The nice thing about using $resource as a REST URL template is that you get a set of REST calls out of the box that are preconfigured with the following HTTP methods:

```
get()—GET
query()—GET (intended for a list; by default it expects an array)
save()—POST
```

(continued)

`delete()`—DELETE

`remove()`—DELETE (identical to `delete()`, in case the browser has a problem with the `delete()` action)

If you want to customize your calls as we're doing, you can pass in the optional set of named functions (or *actions* in Angular-speak). You can use the action to create a completely customized call or override one of the out-of-the-box functions. For example, to create a custom action called `updateCart()`, you can include the following in your set of actions:

```
updateCart : {
    method : "PUT",
    url : "controllers/shopping/carts/:cartId"
}
```

After you have the `$resource` object configured, any calls you make with it automatically return a promise. You've already seen how to use them to work with the results of your calls.

In this chapter's examples, you're using `$resource` inside your shopping cart service because you have additional processes taking place before the data is returned to the controller. For simple data returns, you might want to wrap the `$resource` in another AngularJS object (such as a factory) and include it directly in your controller.

To see the complete documentation for `$resource`, visit the AngularJS site at https://docs.angularjs.org/api/ngResource/service/$resource.

Now that you've looked at `$resource` basics, let's look at the entire code for the `$resource` instance used for your shopping cart (see the following listing). This will give you a picture of the type of calls that will be made inside the shopping cart service.

Listing 7.8 Configuration for your REST calls

```
var Cart = $resource("controllers/shopping/carts", {       Assign the $resource
    cartId : "@cartId",                                    created to a variable
    productId : "@productId"          Define default
}, {                                  parameters
    // cart methods
    getCart : {
        method : "GET",                                    Define actions for
        url : "controllers/shopping/carts/:cartId"         the rest of your calls
    },
    updateCart : {
        method : "PUT",
        url : "controllers/shopping/carts/:cartId"
    },
    // item-level methods
    addProductItem : {
        method : "POST",
```

```
         url : "controllers/shopping/carts/:cartId/products/:productId"
    },
    removeAllProductItems : {
        method : "DELETE",
        url : "controllers/shopping/carts/:cartId/products/:productId"
    },
});
```

With `getCart()`, you can get the cart's content anytime you need it. You'll use `add-ProductItem()` to add a new product to the cart or use `removeAllProductItems()` to remove all quantities of a given product type. You can use `updateCart()` to update the entire cart.

> **TIP** Though you're not implementing security in this application, usually each call you make is validated for security and data integrity in the server-side code.

Because the previous chapter covered the application, in this section you'll focus only on the code around your server calls and how to process the results. Let's begin with adding new product items to the cart.

7.5.2 *Adding product items to the cart*

Following the URL format chosen earlier, you include the cart ID and the product ID in your RESTful service call to add a product item to the shopping cart (see table 7.3). If the product already exists in the cart, the quantity increases.

Table 7.3 RESTful call to add a product to the shopping cart

Method	URL	HTTP method	Request	Response
`Cart.addProductItem()`	/shopping /carts/ CART_ID_89/products/ cod_adv_war	POST	Products	Cart

You've modified the product display page to include a new button that will make the call to add a product item to the cart. When this button is clicked, it calls the `addItem()` action in your shopping cart's `$resource`'s configuration. The following listing shows the modified view containing the new button.

Listing 7.9 Updated product display view

```
angular.module("data.appData", [])

<section class="product_info">
    <h2>
        {{results.name}}

        <span class="price">
          Used Price:
```

```
      {{results.discountPrice | currency:"$":0}}
    </span>

    <button id="product_info_add_btn"
      ng-click="addToCart('{{results.productId}}')">
      Add to Cart
    </button>
  </h2>

  <section id="product_info_img_container">
    <img id="product_info_img"  ng-src="{{results.url}}">
  </section>

  <section id="product_info_summary">
    {{results.summary}}
  </section>
</section>
```

◄──── **Pass the product ID of the game found**

Figure 7.6 shows what the finished view looks like.

Using an `ng-click` binding, you've bound the button click to a function called `addToCart()` on the `$scope` (ViewModel) in the controller to handle the new user action. In turn, this function calls the `addToCart()` function of your shopping cart service (see listing 7.10). As a reminder, the AngularJS `$stateParams` object allows you to access parameters from the route that was executed.

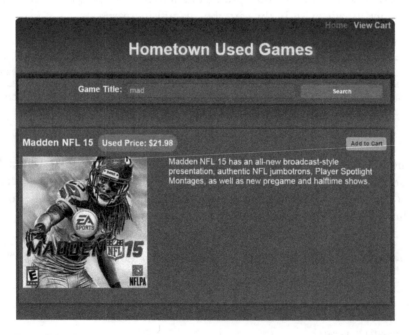

Figure 7.6   The product display page now features a button to add the item to the shopping cart.

Listing 7.10   Application's data holds cart ID

```
$scope.addToCart = function() {
    shoppingCartSvc.addToCart($stateParams.productId);
};
```
◄───── **Use the shopping cart
service to add the item**

After the function call is made, the `addToCart()` function in the shopping cart service makes the RESTful call to the server for processing (see the following listing).

Listing 7.11   Function to make the `addItem()` call

```
function addToCart(productId) {
    return Cart.addProductItem({
        cartId : createorGetExistingCart(),
        productId : productId
    }).$promise.then(function(cartReturned) {

        messageSvc.displayMsg("Item added to cart!");

        console.log("Item added successfully to cart ID "
        + cartReturned.cartId);
    })

    ["catch"](function(error) {
        messageSvc.displayError(error);
    });
}
```
**Pass the cart ID and the
product ID as call parameters**

**Promise chain: display
user message**

Handle any errors

The product ID and the cart ID get mapped to the default parameters of your `add-ProductItem()` custom action in the `$resource` configuration that you saw earlier. After the user has added items to the cart, a new view needs to display the cart's contents. For this, you've added a brand-new view to the application.

7.5.3   Viewing the cart

In this call, you use the cart ID that was generated locally when the user landed on the welcome page. You can use it to get the current state of the cart. Table 7.4 lists this call's properties.

Table 7.4   RESTful call to get the shopping cart to display its contents in the view

Method	URL	HTTP method	Request	Response
`Cart.getCart()`	/shopping /carts/CART_ID_89	GET	Empty	Cart

To be able to view the cart from anywhere, a new link is added to the header. Clicking the link executes the `viewCart` route, which takes you to the shopping cart view:

```
<a id="viewCartLink" ui-sref="viewCart">View Cart</a>
```

When the controller behind the shopping cart view is called, the first thing it does is make a GET call to retrieve the cart from the server. You'll look at this call from the controller first and then the shopping cart service.

In the controller where the call originates, the getCart() function returns the promise generated by the $resource call. As you may remember from our discussion of promises, the promise referenced here will be pending until the call completes:

```
var promise = shoppingCartSvc.getCart();
handleResponse(promise, null);
```

You're also handing off the promise to a generic JavaScript function in the shopping cart controller that will handle the promise returned. The nice thing about promises is that they can be passed around like any other JavaScript object. In each call, whether it's fetching the cart, updating it, or removing an item, you'll process the promise in the same way every time (see the next listing).

Listing 7.12   Generic function to handle all cart promises

```
function handleResponse(promise, userMsg) {

    promise.then(function( cartReturned ) {    B       ← Promise and optional
        return shoppingCartSvc                            user message passed in
        .calculateTotalCartCosts(cartReturned);       ← Recalculate cart
    })

    .then(function(recalculatedCart) {
        replaceCartInView(recalculatedCart);          ← Update the view
    })

    .then(function(recalculatedCart) {
        messageSvc.displayMsg(userMsg);               ← Display user message
    })

    ["catch"](function(errorResult) {
        messageSvc.displayError(errorResult);         ← Handle any errors
    });
};
```

In the shopping cart service, your call to get the cart becomes a one-liner thanks to the magic of the out-of-the-box support for REST in your MV* framework. Here you're passing an object with the ID of your cart as the payload of your call. The object will be scanned by $resource for a property name that matches the cartId URL parameter. Because you've stored the cart ID in the cartData object in the client, you can use it when you need the ID in the URL:

```
function getCart() {
    return Cart.getCart({cartId : cartData.cartId})
    .$promise;
}
```

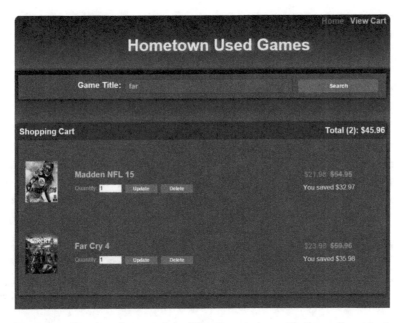

Figure 7.7 The shopping cart view allows the user to modify the cart's contents.

Also remember that Cart is the variable name assigned to the $resource object you created. When the Cart.getCart() call completes, the promise is returned to the controller for the processing you saw previously. If all the promises are fulfilled in the promise chain when the call completes, the view displays all the items currently in the cart. It also shows the original price of each item, its used price, as well as the cost savings. At the top of the cart is a running total of all items and their used prices (see figure 7.7).

With your cart returned, the user can use the UI controls to update it or delete items from it.

7.5.4 Updating the cart

When you update the cart, you're not sending only the new items; you're sending and receiving the entire cart. The RESTful URL identifies the cart you're updating, and the request body has the updated cart data. Table 7.5 has this call's properties.

Table 7.5 RESTful call to update the shopping cart with new input from the user

Method	URL	HTTP method	Request	Response
Cart.updateCart()	/shopping /carts/CART_ID_89	PUT	Cart	Cart

For each entry, you provide an input control to let the user enter a new item count. You also have a button that will update the entire cart by each item. Each update button updates the entire cart in the same manner. It's repeated beside each item only for convenience.

```
<span class="cartQuantityLabel">Quantity: </span>

<input type="text" ng-model="game.quantity" size="4">

<button class="cartItemButton" ng-click="updateQuantity()">
   Update
</button>
```

The `updateQuantity()` function needs no parameters because it always passes the entire cart. In the controller, you rely on the shopping cart service to make the update and pass the promise returned to your generic promise handler (see the following listing).

Listing 7.13   Controller code for cart updates

```
$scope.updateQuantity = function() {                          ⟵ Create a request object
   var uCart =                                                   for the request body
   shoppingCartSvc.createCartForUpdate($scope.cart);

   var promise = shoppingCartSvc.updateCart(uCart);           ⟵ Pass the promise and user
                                                                 message to the generic handler
   handleResponse(promise, "Cart updated!");
};
```

Make the update call, return the promise →

In the shopping cart service, you have a JavaScript function to create a cart object to send to the server. To make the request leaner, in the next listing you include only IDs and updatable properties.

Listing 7.14   Building the update request object

```
function createCartForUpdate(cartFromView) {                  ⟵ Create the object with a
                                                                 placeholder for the items array
   var cart = {
      cartId : cartFromView.cartId,
      totalCount : cartFromView.totalCount,
      items : new Array()
   };

   angular.forEach(cartFromView.items, function(item) {       ⟵ Iterate over the cart
      var pItem = {                                             items and add them
         productId : item.productId,                            to the request
         quantity : item.quantity
      };
      cart.items.push(pItem);
   });

   return cart;
};
```

When the request object is ready, you can make the update request. Again, thanks to our MV* framework's support for REST, you have a one-liner:

```
function updateCart(cart) {
    return Cart.updateCart(cart).$promise;
};
```

Like the other call, the update returns the promise to the controller so the promise chaining can process the results.

The last thing you need to do in the cart is provide the ability to remove items from it. In the next section, you'll examine how to remove all quantities of a particular product type from the cart.

7.5.5 Removing products from the cart

To remove all items of a product from the cart, the most obvious choice in HTTP methods is DELETE. You need to make sure that you're identifying both the cart and the product, just as you did when you added it. Table 7.6 has this call's properties.

Table 7.6 RESTful call to remove all items of a product from the shopping cart

Method	URL	HTTP method	Request	Response
Cart.removeAllProductItems()	/shopping /carts/ CART_ID_89/ products/ cod_adv_war	DELETE	Empty	Cart

In addition to users having the ability to update the quantity, the Delete button next to each product enables users to remove it completely. In the view, you've bound the button's click to the removeItem() function on the controller. The function call passes forward the product ID of the product that's being deleted.

```
<button class="cartItemButton"
ng-click="removeItem(game.productId)">Delete</button>
```

In the controller, as with getting the cart or updating it, you make the call and pass the returned promise to the generic promise handler (see the following listing).

Listing 7.15 Controller code for cart deletes

```
$scope.removeItem = function(productId) {
    var promise =
    shoppingCartSvc.removeAllProductItems(productId);        Pass the product ID,
                                                             get a promise back

    handleResponse(promise, "Cart removed!");        Pass the promise and user
};                                                   message to the generic handler
```

Finally, you get to the matching code in the shopping cart service where the call is made (see the following listing). The cart's ID from your cart data object is mapped to the cartId URL parameter, and the product ID passed in is mapped to the productId parameter.

Listing 7.16   Controller code for cart deletes

```
function deleteItem(productId) {
    return Cart.removeItem(                     Pass the cart ID and
                                                product ID to the call
    {
        cartId : cartData.cartId,
        productId : productId
    }
                                                Return a promise
                                                to the controller
    ).$promise;
};
```

Don't forget that if you want to create the project in your own environment, the server-side supplement in appendix C begins with a summary of the objects and tasks. This is included in case you're using a different tech stack than the example's code. Also, as usual, the complete source code is available for download.

7.6   Chapter challenge

Now here's a challenge for you to see what you've learned in this chapter. In the preceding chapter's challenge, you created a movie search. You displayed movie titles that matched wholly or partially the text the user typed into an input field. A key-up event was bound to a function that published the field's contents with each keystroke. A search module subscribed to that topic and performed a search accordingly. The search also used pub/sub to publish the results, which were displayed in an unordered list below the input field.

Extend this exercise by putting the stub data and the search logic on the server. You'll still have a client-side module listening for the input field contents to be published. In turn, it will fire the server call every time it hears the topic. On the server, you can use any technologies you're comfortable with. Make the server call a RESTful service call. Use a RESTful URL and an appropriate HTTP request method for this type of request. Use a promise to process the server call. Upon success, publish the results of the search. Write any errors to the console.

7.7   Summary

We covered a lot of ground in this chapter. Let's review:

- The server is still important to the single-page application, providing features such as security, validation, and standard APIs for accessing back-end data.
- Having an agreement between the client and the server on the data type and the HTTP methods is essential for a call to be successful.
- Native objects on both ends are converted to the agreed-upon data format in both the request and the response.

- MV* frameworks that support server communication often take care of routing tasks, such as providing standard request types out of the box and handling data conversions.
- MV* frameworks typically support server communication either through extending a parent model or via a data source object.
- Call results are handled either through callbacks using continuation-passing style or through promises, depending on the framework or library used.
- A promise represents the outcome of a pending asynchronous process. It starts as pending but eventually transitions to either fulfilled or rejected when the call completes.
- A promise has several methods, but the most commonly used one is then(). This method allows you to register two functions (called *reactions*) to process a fulfilled or rejected promise.
- The reaction for a fulfilled promise gives you access to the result data of a process. The reaction for a rejected promise contains the rejected reason (usually an Error object).
- Reactions can be chained together to control the flow of a group of processes, even if other asynchronous calls are in the chain.
- Promise errors can be handled either through the rejection reaction or via a catch() method.
- *REST* stands for *Representational State Transfer* and is an architectural style for developing web services.
- In REST, everything is a resource and should have a unique URL representing it.
- HTTP methods describe the action for the resource. The four most common are GET, POST, PUT, and DELETE.

Unit testing

When you create software, regardless of the platform or language used, you want to do your best to ensure that you're delivering a quality product. In this book, you've looked at various ways to create a maintainable, robust SPA, such as dividing your code into modules and using the power of MV* frameworks. Another vital facet of SPA programming is testing. Testing what you write is just as important to the delivery of the end product as the code itself. Putting your code through the paces does a lot more than uncover bugs. When you see that your code does what you expect it to and can handle failures gracefully, this helps you write better code and improves your confidence in the application.

Although an application can be subjected to a variety of tests, this chapter focuses specifically on unit testing. The upcoming sections cover what a unit test is, how to create code that's more conducive to unit testing, and what some of the benefits are. Even though certain aspects of unit testing are subjective, we can zero in on some of its most common features.

We'll frame our discussions around unit testing applications built using MV* frameworks and modular code. After we've covered some basic unit-testing concepts, we'll talk about writing unit tests for an SPA using a framework called QUnit. QUnit is powerful but still easy to use and doesn't have a steep learning curve.

The project in this chapter keeps things extremely simple. This will help you stay focused on the unit-testing aspect of your project's development. You'll create the project by using Backbone.js, Knockout, and AngularJS to illustrate testing across a variety of MV* framework styles.

8.1 Understanding the project

For this project, you'll create a basic tip calculator. I'll introduce various parts of this project when you begin writing unit tests later in this chapter. Before you begin, let's take a moment to see what the final product looks like (see figure 8.1).

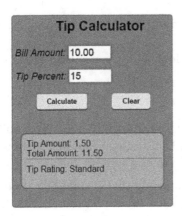

Figure 8.1 Our sample project calculates the amount of the tip and the total amount to be paid. It also rates the tip given.

Keep this image in your mind as you go through each section. As usual, the entire code (this time with tests) is available for download.

8.2 What is a unit test?

In a broad sense, a *unit test* is a test performed on the smallest testable part of an application. This type of test is a low-level test performed during development by the developer. Additionally, whether the test subject is an MV* object or a general module you've created, unit tests typically make assertions about how code behaves.

A unit test can also be characterized by its relationship to other types of tests. A pyramid structure is often used to describe different test types in terms of measurements such as scope, time, and level of effort. Because unit tests are narrow in focus and

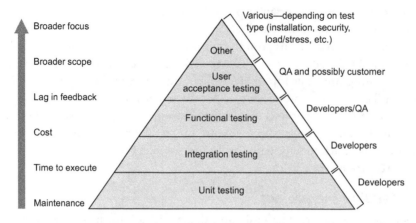

Broader focus

Broader scope

Lag in feedback

Cost

Time to execute

Maintenance

Various—depending on test
type (installation, security,
load/stress, etc.)

Other

User
acceptance testing — QA and possibly customer

Functional testing — Developers/QA

Integration testing — Developers

Unit testing — Developers

Developers

**Figure 8.2   A unit test is a low-level, focused test created during development that's
quick to execute and offers the least lag in getting test results.**

scope, are quick to run and easy to maintain, and provide fast feedback for results, they're at the pyramid's base (see figure 8.2).

Now that you know what unit tests are, let's look at why you should care about creating them.

8.2.1   Benefits of unit testing

Unit testing is about a lot more than finding bugs in your code. In reality, you'll likely find more bugs in other, more high-level tests. Unit testing is about designing better software. This list highlights some of the benefits of unit testing:

- *Can lead to better software designs*—Creating code that's easily unit tested helps reinforce the idea that software components should be loosely coupled with highly specialized parts. This can lead to a better-designed application as a whole.

- *Helps detect issues early on*—A passing unit test, which is well written and useful, is proof that the code you write is working as expected. The sooner you can detect code bugs, the easier and less costly it is to correct the problem.

- *Gives you more confidence to make changes*—Sometimes you might be hesitant to make changes because you don't want to break something that's already working. Unit tests can help bolster your confidence in this area. A good unit test is one that's repeatable with consistent results. As you refactor, the same unit tests that were successful before the changes should still be successful after the changes.

- *Provide great examples of how your code works*—Although you'll still want to document your application, unit tests provide a convenient way for others to see how your code should work. Well-written unit tests illustrate proper usage for other developers who might want a quick dive into the code. They can also serve as an introduction to the code base for new team members.

Having highlighted some of the benefits, let's talk about how to get the most out of the tests you write.

8.2.2 Creating better unit tests

Although there's no official rulebook on unit testing, you can follow general best practices to make your unit tests be *good* unit tests.

FOCUS EACH TEST ON A SPECIFIC BUSINESS-RELATED CONCEPT

Ideally, each unit test should focus on specific concepts in your code. If the scope of the unit test is too broad or focuses on things beyond specific business requirements, you'll have a hard time pinpointing specific areas in your code that aren't working as designed.

For example, don't try to initiate a unit test through automated user actions, such as the filling out of a form or the clicking of a button. Even though processes in an SPA are often initiated by user-driven events, UI-level testing is much broader in scope than unit testing, because it often generates multiple activities at once at various levels in the application. It's far better to test the lower-level parts of your code.

You also may be tempted to test that third-party software works as advertised if you're using it in your own code. But the focus of your unit test should be only on logic you've written. If the third-party software has a bug, it's incidental to your unit test and should be considered out of scope for a unit test.

Let's consider for a moment our tip calculator project as an example. Figure 8.3 provides a high-level picture of what you might want to consider in scope when unit testing this application.

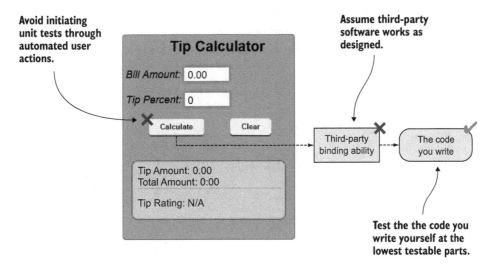

Figure 8.3 Focus unit tests on the lowest level of the application's logic.

Another way to create more easily testable code is by avoiding ambiguous or nonspecific APIs. These types of APIs generally aren't well designed. This will become evident when you try to test them.

AVOID CREATING APIS THAT ARE AMBIGUOUS OR TOO GENERAL

Poorly written APIs are not only bad for the application but also extremely difficult to unit test. If you can't easily test the individual parts of your business logic, this is a sign that you should consider refactoring your code.

For example, the tip calculator application displays several values at once when the Calculate button is clicked. You should be able to test the logic behind each calculation independently. Because the application is so simple, it would be easy enough to calculate everything in one function (see figure 8.4).

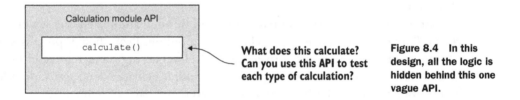

What does this calculate? Can you use this API to test each type of calculation?

Figure 8.4   In this design, all the logic is hidden behind this one vague API.

Now let's refactor things a bit and give each area of concern in the business logic its own function in the API. Figure 8.5 separates the tasks that were formerly lumped together.

When developers create APIs that are easy to unit test, one pleasant side effect is that the code is often more readable, more specialized, and more easily maintained.

In addition to being vigilant with your code, you also can structure the unit tests themselves to make them better.

NO TESTING ORDER SHOULD BE REQUIRED

You'll often find yourself writing many unit tests for a feature. Most testing tools allow you to then divide tests into groups (or *suites*). You should avoid including tests that

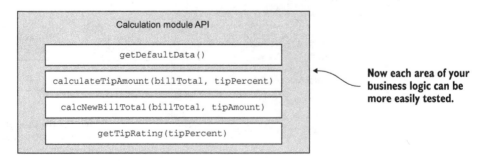

Now each area of your business logic can be more easily tested.

Figure 8.5   Smaller, specialized functions are a better fit for unit testing.

will work only if they're in a particular order within the test suite. The position of a unit test within your suite shouldn't matter. If you've created a suite of good unit tests for your SPA, you should be able to run them in any order and achieve the same results consistently. In your tip calculator tests, for example, testing the calculation for the tip amount should produce the same results whether it's run first, last, or somewhere in the middle of all the other tests.

In the case of the tip calculator, your test suite might include the tip amount calculation first, the new bill total calculation second, and the tip rating third. But if for some reason you decide to rearrange this order, the results of each test should still be the same as they were with the previous test order.

UNIT TESTS SHOULD BE SELF-RELIANT

Good unit tests should be repeatable with consistent results. The only real way to ensure this is to have tests that can be contextually isolated and don't rely on outside dependencies in order to work properly.

For starters, unit tests should be repeatable even when run in an environment other than the one they were originally written in. For example, your tip calculator unit tests should yield the same results when run in your local development environment as they would if the tests were automated on a dedicated machine.

Second, your unit tests shouldn't rely on any external systems or even other tests. You're not using server-side code in this simple project, but let's imagine you were. Suppose that your tip ratings came from a database instead of being hardcoded in your application logic. If you were to create a unit test to make sure that a particular tip would yield the correct rating, you shouldn't make a call to the server every time your test runs. Remember that a good unit test needs to be fast and reliable, with consistent results. External systems affect tests because call responses vary, which can make the execution time of your tests unpredictable. Relying on external systems also makes your tests vulnerable to outside issues, such as network problems or a server being down. Additionally, any changes made in a remote system, such as a data change or configuration change, could lead to inconsistent results. To avoid reliance on external systems, you can use mocks instead. *Mocks* are objects with preprogrammed expectations that can take the place of real ones in your unit tests. For example, you can use mocks as stand-ins for your live web service calls. They can behave as system calls but with the response you need for your tests.

Finally, if additional functions are required for the primary function you're testing to work properly, you can isolate your test function by temporarily replacing any other functions with stubs. *Stubs* are temporary replacements with predetermined behavior. They allow you to focus a unit test on your primary function without worrying about the behavior of other parts of your code.

THE FOCUS OF EACH TEST SHOULD BE EASILY UNDERSTOOD

A good unit test can also be measured by how easily its objective is understood just by looking at the test title and comments. People tend to forget things over time, so it's immensely helpful to be able to glance at a unit test and know why it exists.

Here's an example from this chapter's project. For the traditional unit test on our tip amount calculation, table 8.1 shows the title of the suite and the test, as well as its comments. From this information, the purpose of the test should be clear, whether the person looking at the test is a business analyst, a QA tester, another developer, or a business owner.

Table 8.1   Example of clear, easily understood titles and comments for a unit test

Suite title	Test title	Test comments
Tip Calculations	Calculate Tip Amount	15% tip for $10 should yield $1.50

Having discussed various aspects of unit testing, it's time to see some unit tests in action. You'll build a good foundation by starting with some traditional unit testing before moving on to testing for behavior-driven development.

8.3   *Traditional unit testing*

You can approach unit testing in various ways. The traditional method is to write your code first and then create unit tests around what you've written (see figure 8.6). This approach is also simple and easy to follow.

The traditional approach is just one style of designing unit tests. Some people prefer this approach because they like tackling the code first and then creating tests to make sure the design is solid. Because the goal of unit testing is to create better software, others argue that traditional unit tests are too removed from the design process. Just for comparison, let's contrast this with unit tests written for test-driven development (TDD).

The tests you create, TDD or otherwise, define the behavior of what you're creating. With TDD, you're associating the unit test with

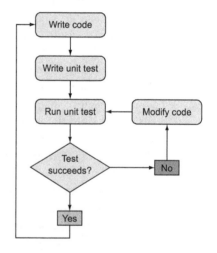

Figure 8.6   With traditional unit testing, tests are written after the code has been created.

the design process even more by putting it up front. Because you're relying on a well-written test to help in the design of the code, you're forced to have a deep understanding of the requirements up front.

The test will fail at first, because you haven't written code yet. The next step is to create the minimum amount of code needed to make the test pass. This develops a baseline for the new feature or enhancement. Next, you keep refactoring the code so it goes from minimally acceptable to well-designed, production-ready code. Every time you refactor, all tests are run again. This keeps you confident that with every improvement you haven't inadvertently broken anything or created code that no longer satisfies the point of the test. Figure 8.7 illustrates this cyclical process.

Because traditional unit testing is straightforward, let's use this approach to get your feet wet with creating some basic unit tests for this chapter's project.

To unit test your SPA, you'll need to choose a JavaScript testing framework. There are many to choose from, and we'll talk about some of the other options in a later section. You'll begin, though, with one of the oldest and easiest to use frameworks, called QUnit.

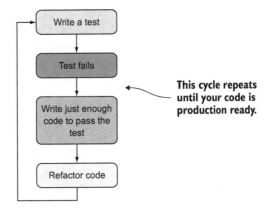

This cycle repeats until your code is production ready.

Figure 8.7   In test-driven development, tests are written before the code is created.

8.3.1 Getting started with QUnit

The first thing you need to do is download the software. QUnit can be found at http://qunitjs.com. You'll need both the JavaScript file and the CSS file. Next, you need to get your testing environment ready. Your first task is to create a directory structure within your project to house your test scripts.

CREATING A TEST DIRECTORY

As with the project itself, your directory structure for your test scripts is a matter of personal taste. One common approach is to set up a directory structure similar to that of the application. This test directory is usually separate from the application's source code.

To get exposure to testing using various MV* frameworks, I've created this chapter's project using Backbone.js, Knockout, and AngularJS. To give you an idea of what a test directory might look like, figure 8.8 demonstrates the directory structure of the

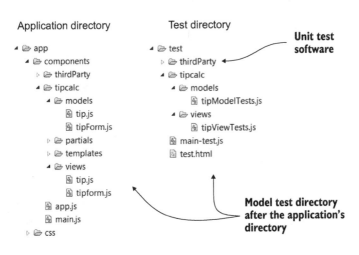

Figure 8.8   The test directory will have a similar structure but is usually kept separate from the application's source.

Backbone.js version of the application. You'll follow the same approach for the Knock-out and AngularJS versions. This same approach can also be applied to whichever type of MV* framework you ultimately decide to use in your own project.

With your directory set up, you need a place to display the output of your tests. You'll need to create a new HTML page for this.

DEFINING A TEST RESULTS PAGE

After you have a test directory, QUnit also needs an HTML page to display the results of your unit tests. For this demo, I've created a file called test.html. To view the page, you'll go directly to its URL in the browser. You *don't* want a link to any test pages in the application.

Listing 8.1 shows the structure of your test results page. In real-world solutions, you'll most likely use a build tool to gather the required includes. Because we're not covering the build process until the next chapter, you'll include any files needed directly in the HTML for the test results page with your AngularJS version. You'll include references to both the test scripts and the source files for the application in your test results page.

Listing 8.1   test.html—AngularJS version

```
<!DOCTYPE html>
<html>
<head>

<title>QUnit tests</title>
                                             ⟵ Include QUnit style sheets
<link rel="stylesheet"
href="../test/thirdParty/qunit/QUnit_Styles.css">

</head>
<body>
                                             ⟵ HTML elements used by QUnit
    <h1 id="qunit-header">QUnit Test Suite</h1>
    <h2 id="qunit-banner"></h2>
    <div id="qunit-testrunner-toolbar"></div>
    <h2 id="qunit-userAgent"></h2>
    <ol id="qunit-tests"></ol>
    <div id="qunit"></div>
    <div id="qunit-fixture"></div>
                                             ⟵ Include application files
    <script src="../app.js">
    </script>
    <script src="../tipcalc/services/calculateSvc.js">
    </script>
    <script src="../tipcalc/controllers/tipCalcCrtl.js">
    </script>

    <script src="./thirdParty/qunit/QUnit_1_17_1.js">      ⟵ Include QUnit
    </script>                                                  and AngularJS
    <script src="../thirdParty/angular.min.js">
```

```
    </script>

    <script src="./services/calculateSvc_tests.js">
    </script>
    <script src="./controllers/tipCalcCrtl_tests.js">
    </script>

</body>
</html>
```

◀── **Include test scripts**

The Knockout and Backbone.js versions use AMD-style modules and RequireJS. When using RequireJS, your HTML page will be nearly identical except that the other SCRIPT tags are replaced with a single SCRIPT tag referencing RequireJS (see listing 8.2). Its data-main attribute defines the location of the main application file. This file (main-test.js) contains references to the locations of your frameworks, application source files, and test scripts.

Listing 8.2 test.html—Knockout and Backbone.js version

```
<!DOCTYPE html>
<html>
<head>
<title>QUnit tests</title>
<link rel="stylesheet"
href="../test/thirdParty/qunit/QUnit_Styles.css">
</head>
<body>
    <h1 id="qunit-header">QUnit Test Suite</h1>
    <h2 id="qunit-banner"></h2>
    <div id="qunit-testrunner-toolbar"></div>
    <h2 id="qunit-userAgent"></h2>
    <ol id="qunit-tests"></ol>
    <div id="qunit"></div>
    <div id="qunit-fixture"></div>

    <script
        data-main="../test/main-test.js"
        src="../thirdParty/require.js">
    </script>
</body>
</html>
```

◀── **Include RequireJS, specify
configuration file location**

Also, when using AMD-style modules, unit tests are defined like any other module, using define(). The suite itself is kicked off inside require(), just like the project. Listing 8.3 shows what the require() definition looks like for our Knockout version. The Backbone.js version is similar and follows the same approach. If you need to see the complete file, you can find it in the downloadable source code for this chapter.

In this case, you've created custom addTests() APIs for each module. These do nothing more than execute the QUnit test functions, which add the tests to the list of tests that the framework will run. You'll see an example of these in a moment.

Listing 8.3   main-test.js—Knockout version using AMD modules and RequireJS

```
require(["QUnit",
    "utilTests/tipCalculatorUtilTests",
    "viewmodelTests/tipViewModelTests" ],

    function($,
        QUnit,                        ◀        Make sure dependencies
        tipCalculatorUtilTests,                get loaded
        tipViewModelTests) {

        tipCalculatorUtilTests.addTests();
        tipViewModelTests.addTests();       ◀    Explicitly add any tests
                                                 that QUnit will run
        QUnit.load();          ◀
        QUnit.start();
    }                            └─ Manually load/start QUnit
);
```

NOTE   QUnit's autoStart needs to be set to `false` in the RequireJS configuration file, and its `load()` and `start()` functions manually executed, after your tests have been added.

With your environment all set up, you can finally start writing some test scripts. In the next section, you'll learn what QUnit asserts are and how to use them to create a unit test.

8.3.2   Creating your first unit tests

All three versions of your project perform two calculations: one for the tip amount and the other for a new bill total. In addition, logic in each version gives a rating such as "Standard" or "Great!" to the tip percent entered. I've tried to make each version of the project as similar as possible, though some differences exist because of the differences in each framework. For example, in the AngularJS version, your business logic is in a service component of the AngularJS module. In the Knockout version, the business logic resides in an ancillary AMD module. Last, for your Backbone.js version, your business logic can be found in the model used by the view for the entry form.

With that said, let's get started. To create your first unit test, you'll need to understand assertions in QUnit.

MAKING AN ASSERTION

The basic idea behind the unit tests you'll create is that you're going to assert that something is true. When a QUnit test is executed, each assertion is evaluated. QUnit either passes or fails each unit test by verifying its assertion. The assertion you're making can be anything you want it to be. For example, it could be as simple as verifying that a particular object exists or it might be verifying the result of an operation.

QUnit provides many types of assertions. The full list can be found at http://api.qunitjs.com/category/assert. For these unit tests, you're using only one type of assertion:

> `strictEqual()`—This assertion compares the first and second parameters for equality. Its third parameter is for a comment. It uses the strict equality operator `===`.

Let's create your first test by using the calculations from the Knockout version of the application. In this version, your business logic is in a standard AMD module. No special setup is needed. For the Backbone.js version, your calculation logic is in the model, and in the AngularJS version, it's in a service. We'll discuss testing MV* objects a little later.

WRITING A UNIT TEST

Your first unit test will test the output of your tip amount and new bill total calculations. To give the test script some context, the following listing shows what that code looks like. Remember that the entire source for the project is available for download should you need it.

Listing 8.4   Logic to calculate the tip amount and new bill total

```
function calcTipAmount(billTotal, tipPercent) {
    var tipAmount =
    Number(billTotal) * (Number(tipPercent) / 100);

    return tipAmount.toFixed(2);          ◀
}

function calcNewBillTotal(billTotal, tipAmount) {
    var newBillTotal
    = Number(billTotal) + Number(tipAmount);

    return newBillTotal.toFixed(2);       ◀
}
```

> **Perform the calculations and round result to two decimal places**

Now let's write the unit test. The syntax of a QUnit test is simple. You call a `test()` function, giving the test a title and a function containing your assertions, as shown in the following listing.

Listing 8.5   Unit test to verify the `roundTipPercent()` function

```
test("Tip Calculations", function() {        ◀  Give the test a title
    var tipAmount
    = tipCalculator.calcTipAmount(10.00, 15);     ◀  Call the API

    var newBillTotal
    = tipCalculator.calcNewBillTotal(10.00, 1.50);  ◀

    strictEqual(tipAmount,
    "1.50",
    "When the tip is 15% and the bill is $10,      ◀  Test the result against
      the tip amount should be $1.50");              the expected value

    strictEqual(newBillTotal,
    "11.50",
    "When the bill is is $10 and the tip amount is $1.50,
    the new bill total should be $11.50");     ◀
});
```

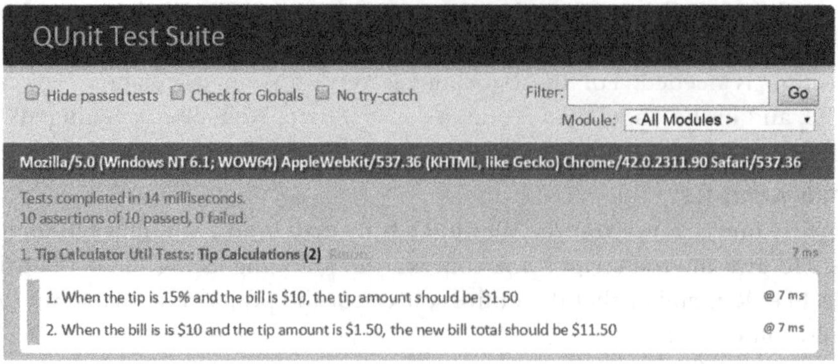

Figure 8.9   QUnit test report after your first unit test is run

When the test runs, you should see the test report displayed in your test's HTML page you set up earlier. By default, each test doesn't show the test comments. In figure 8.9, I've clicked the test title to display the passing assertions for this test as well.

If one of your tests failed, the test report would look similar to figure 8.10. QUnit displays what was expected, the result, the difference between those two, and the stack trace leading to the line that was executed.

Creating a unit test is that simple. Now let's finish writing tests for the rest of the utility. Before we do that, though, let's group these tests under a single heading.

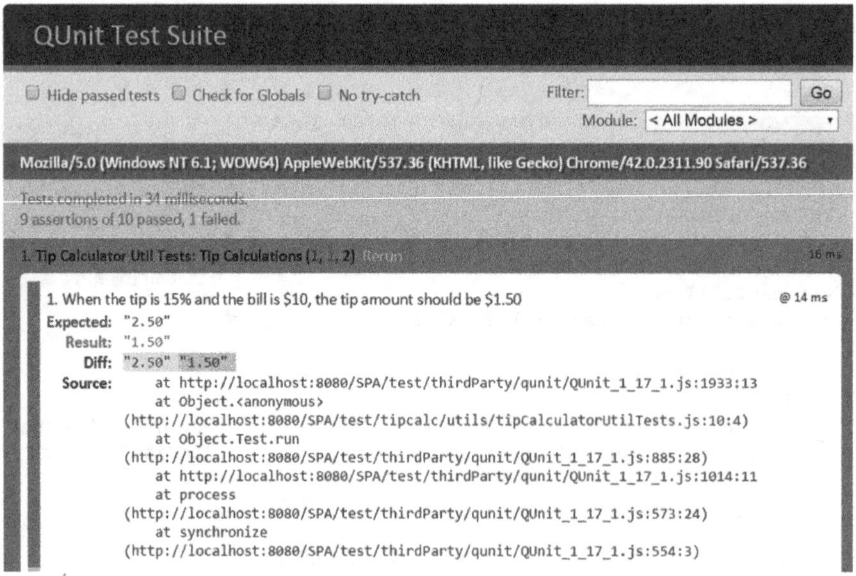

Figure 8.10   QUnit test report with a failed test

GROUPING TESTS

Another nice feature of QUnit is that it lets you group tests by using its `module()` method. In this case, you're going to group all the calculation utility tests under a single heading. This will help you later, when you add tests for other areas of the application. In QUnit, grouping your tests into a module is a simple one-liner:

```
module("Tip Calculator Util Tests");
```

The following listing shows the complete set of tests for your tip calculator's utility module.

Listing 8.6 Utility tests grouped within a module

```
module("Tip Calculator Util Tests");                              ◀── Define the module

test("Tip Calculations", function() {
    var tipAmount = tipCalculator.calcTipAmount(10.00, 15);
    var newBillTotal = tipCalculator.calcNewBillTotal(10.00, 1.50);

    strictEqual(tipAmount,
    "1.50",
    "When the tip is 15% and the bill is $10,
    the tip amount should be $1.50");

    strictEqual(newBillTotal,
    "11.50", "When the bill is is $10 and the tip amount is $1.50,
    the new bill total should be $11.50");
});

test("Tip Ratings", function() {                                 ◀── Test the rating logic
    var rating = tipCalculator.getTipRating(5);
    strictEqual(rating,
    "So so",
    "When the tip amount is below $15, the rating should be So So");

    rating = tipCalculator.getTipRating(15);
    strictEqual(rating,
    "Standard",
    "When the tip amount equals $15, the rating should be Standard");

    rating = tipCalculator.getTipRating(20);
    strictEqual(rating,
    "Great!",
    "When the tip amount is between $15 and $20 (inclusive),
    the rating should be Great!");

    rating = tipCalculator.getTipRating(50);
    strictEqual(rating,
    "Super!",
    "When the tip amount is between $20 and $50 (inclusive),
    the rating should be Super!");

    rating = tipCalculator.getTipRating(60);
    strictEqual(rating,
    "WOW!",
```

Test the calculations

```
    "When the tip amount is greater than $50,
    the rating should be Wow!");
});
```

Figure 8.11 shows what your test report looks like now, with all the tests for this one test module. Keep in mind that each test initially displays collapsed but can be expanded, as shown previously, to see the comments.

Business-related code inside an MV* object can also be tested similarly. The only trick is the amount of setup you might need to do.

8.3.3   Testing code built with MV* objects

As far as the mechanics of crafting the unit test go, unfortunately no magic formula fits everything. Because each framework/library is different, and each object type within a framework/library has a different purpose, the amount of setup needed for the test to run varies. Setup is usually minimal, though.

You also can follow a few simple rules of thumb when unit testing MV* objects:

- *Don't share objects between tests*—Avoid trying to share MV* objects among tests. Our brains as developers are hardwired to find ways to reuse objects and avoid duplicate code. But in the case of unit testing, don't share.
- *Keep tests DRY*—As you would with your production code, avoid repeating the same code in every test. Factor out repeated code into separate functions. Many testing frameworks have a type of setup process as well for any code that needs to run before each test.
- *Consult the MV* documentation for any special instructions around testing*—For frameworks such as Backbone.js or Knockout, you merely create new instances of any

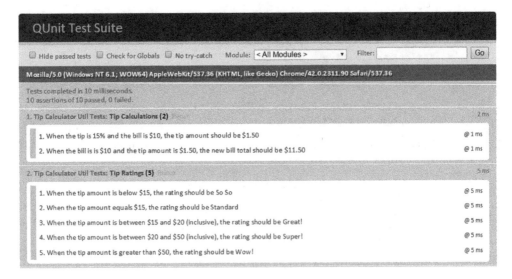

Figure 8.11   QUnit test report shows tests grouped together as a test module.

MV* objects you need to use. For some frameworks, such as AngularJS, you'll need to take care of some specific setup tasks to be able to test components correctly. You'll see this in a moment when you test the AngularJS version of your tip calculator SPA.

With these points in mind, let's try unit testing a few types of MV* objects. I won't cover the gamut of MV* objects here. The source for each version of the project, along with the entire suite of tests for each, is available for download. You will, however, take on a couple to get the idea.

Let's start with the Backbone.js business logic of your tip calculator. You'll test the same type of calculations that were in the utility module of the Knockout version of the project. The time, the code for this logic is in a Backbone.js model, as shown in the following listing.

Listing 8.7   Unit test for a Backbone.js model's business logic

```
module("Tip Form Model Tests", {
    beforeEach: function() {
        this.tipFormModel = TipForm;          ◀—— The TipForm module returns
    }                                              a new instance of the model
});

test("Tip Calculations", function() {
    this.tipFormModel.calcTipAmount(10.00, 15);   ◀—— Use the model to
                                                       perform calculations
    strictEqual(this.tipFormModel.get("tipAmount"),
    1.50,
    "When the tip is 15% and the bill is $10,
    the tip amount should be $1.50");

    this.tipFormModel.calcNewBillTotal(10.00, 1.50);

    strictEqual(this.tipFormModel.get("newBillTotal"),
    11.50, "When the bill is is $10 and the tip amount is
    $1.50, the new bill total should be $11.50");
});
```

In the listing, notice the beforeEach() function. QUnit has an optional beforeEach() function for any pretest setup and an optional afterEach() function for teardown/cleanup work. With the new instance created in the beforeEach() function, you can now test the model's logic.

Continue with your model and create the tests for the rating logic, as shown in the following listing.

Listing 8.8   Rating logic for the Backbone.js model

```
test("Tip Ratings", function() {
    this.tipFormModel.applyTipRating(5);         ◀—— Change the rating value
    strictEqual(this.tipFormModel.get("tipRating"),   for each assertion
    "So so",
    "When the tip amount is below $15, the rating should be So So");
```

```
    this.tipFormModel.applyTipRating(15);
    strictEqual(this.tipFormModel.get("tipRating"),
    "Standard",
    "When the tip amount equals $15, the rating should be Standard");

    this.tipFormModel.applyTipRating(20);
    strictEqual(this.tipFormModel.get("tipRating"),
    "Great!",
    "When the tip amount is between $15 and $20 (inclusive),
    the rating should be Great!");

    this.tipFormModel.applyTipRating(50);
    strictEqual(this.tipFormModel.get("tipRating"),
    "Super!", "When the tip amount is between $20 and $50 (inclusive),
    the rating should be Super!");

    this.tipFormModel.applyTipRating(60);
    strictEqual(this.tipFormModel.get("tipRating"),
    "WOW!", "When the tip amount is greater than $50,
    the rating should be Wow!");
});
```

Because you can group things into QUnit modules, you have one for the model's validation logic and the other for the calculations. Figure 8.12 shows what the test suite looks like at this point.

Now let's look at unit testing an AngularJS object. AngularJS is an example of when specific steps for setting up your test scripts are provided in the MV* frameworks documentation. In this example, you'll unit test the AngularJS version of your calculation utility. In the Backbone.js version of your application, your calculations were in a

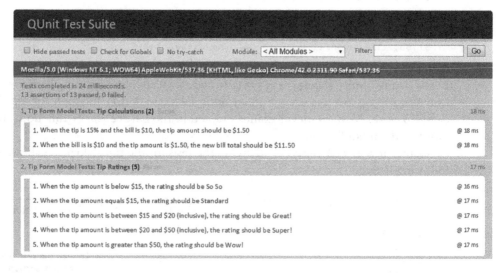

Figure 8.12   QUnit testing against a Backbone.js model

model housed in an AMD module. In the AngularJS version, your calculations are in an AngularJS service component of an AngularJS-style module.

When the application is running, AngularJS's dependency injection mechanism will automatically hand you instances of the objects you need. But because you're running your tests outside the application, you must manually invoke the dependency injection. There are several ways to manually inject AngularJS objects. This is just one of them:

```
var injector = angular.injector([ 'ng', 'tipcalculator' ]);
```

You'll need to pass in the AngularJS core module ng and the name of your application as dependencies for the injector. Then in your setup you can use the injector to get an instance of your calculation service:

```
beforeEach: function() {
    this.CalcTestSvc = injector.get("calculateSvc");
}
```

Now let's look at the complete unit test for your calculation service (see the following listing).

Listing 8.9   Unit test for an AngularJS service

```
var injector = angular.injector([ 'ng', 'tipcalculator' ]);          ◀── Get an instance
                                                                          of the injector
module("Tip Service Tests", {
    beforeEach: function() {
        this.CalcTestSvc = injector.get("calculateSvc");    ◀── Ask for an instance of
    }                                                           your calculation service
});


test("Tip Calculations", function() {                       ◀── Define your test scripts
    var tipAmount =
    this.CalcTestSvc.calcTipAmount(10.00, 15);

    var newBillTotal =
    this.CalcTestSvc.calcNewBillTotal(10.00, 1.50);

    strictEqual(tipAmount,
    "1.50",
    "When the tip is 15% and the bill is $10,
    the tip amount should be $1.50");

    strictEqual(newBillTotal,
    "11.50",
    "When the bill is is $10 and the tip amount is
    $1.50, the new bill total should be $11.50");
});

test("Tip Ratings", function() {
    var rating = this.CalcTestSvc.getTipRating(5);
```

```
        strictEqual(rating,
        "So so",
        "When the tip amount is below $15,
        the rating should be So So");

        rating = this.CalcTestSvc.getTipRating(15);
        strictEqual(rating,
        "Standard",
        "When the tip amount equals $15,
        the rating should be Standard");

        rating = this.CalcTestSvc.getTipRating(20);
        strictEqual(rating,
        "Great!",
        "When the tip amount is between $15 and $20 (inclusive),
        the rating should be Great!");

        rating = this.CalcTestSvc.getTipRating(50);
        strictEqual(rating,
        "Super!",
        "When the tip amount is between $20 and $50 (inclusive),
        the rating should be Super!");

        rating = this.CalcTestSvc.getTipRating(60);
        strictEqual(rating,
        "WOW!", "When the tip amount is greater than $50,
        the rating should be Wow!");
});
```

In figure 8.13, you can see that the tests did indeed run, which means the extra step of using the AngularJS injector worked.

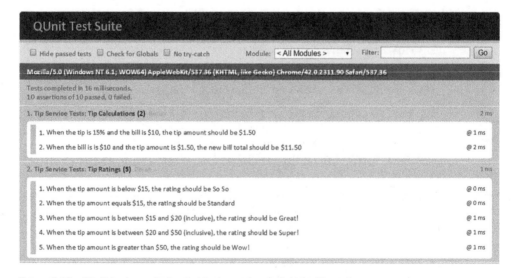

Figure 8.13 QUnit test report showing tests run for an AngularJS service

With the `injector` at your disposal, you can run tests on any AngularJS object that you need to in order to unit test your application's code.

8.3.4 Testing changes to the DOM

At times you also might need to test modifications made to the DOM in your SPA. In your tip calculator, you're using the `render()` function of the view to reflect the state of your model in the UI. To test that your calculator's output is propagated to the DOM accurately, QUnit provides a DIV element that has an ID of `qunit-fixture`. This element, referred to as a *fixture*, can be used to append DOM-related output. QUnit automatically cleans up the fixture element after each test, removing anything that's been added. The following listing shows the setup and teardown for your tests on the view.

> **Listing 8.10   Setup/teardown to perform fixture testing on a Backbone.js view**

```
module("Tip View Tests", {
    beforeEach: function() {
        $( "#qunit-fixture" ).append( "<section></section>" );
    }
});
```

Manually add the element; the view will render its output

To perform unit testing in the UI, you can check for the existence of DOM elements, CSS classes, or certain text. The next listing gives an example.

> **Listing 8.11   Unit testing your tip amount output by a Backbone.js view**

```
test("Tip Display", function() {
    TipForm.setBillTotal("10");
    TipForm.roundTipPercent("15");
    this.tipView = new TipView({
        model : TipForm
    });
    this.tipView.render();

    strictEqual(
        $("section").children("p").eq(0).text(),
        "Tip Amount: 1.50",
        "When the tip is 15% for a $10 bill,
        'Tip Amount: 1.50' should display"
    );

    strictEqual(
        $("section").children("p").eq(1).text(),
        "Total Amount: 11.50",
        "When the tip is 15% for a $10 bill,
        'Total Amount: 11.50' should display"
    );

    strictEqual(
        $("section").children("p").eq(2).text(),
```

Seed the view's model with values to output

Use jQuery to select what you expect as output from the view

Test the output against what you expect

```
        "Tip Rating: Standard",
        "When the tip is 15% for a $10 bill,
        'Tip Rating: Standard' should display"
    );
});
```

We've covered a lot of ground with QUnit. It's a great testing framework with many more capabilities than I can cover in a single chapter. But even when you have a powerful JavaScript testing framework like QUnit, you may still want (or need) to use one or more other frameworks for particular tasks.

8.3.5   *Adding other testing frameworks to the mix*

Sometimes not all of your testing needs are covered in a single JavaScript testing framework. That's OK, though. It's common to augment your main testing framework with a testing utility framework. To give you a brief example, let's pretend that at some point you added the ability to save the tip and bill amount entered by a user for trending purposes. This is stretching things a bit. But nevertheless, let's just pretend to illustrate this point. You'll use our Backbone.js version again for this one.

You learned at the beginning of the chapter that you don't want to include live server calls in unit tests. So what can you do? As it turns out, JavaScript frameworks/ add-ons can give you the ability to mock a server call easily without having to modify your code. One such testing software is called Sinon.js.

SUPPLEMENTING QUNIT WITH SINON.JS

The purpose of the section isn't to cover Sinon.js. Like QUnit, Sinon.js is powerful and has many great features in its own right. In this section, I'll show how easy and painless it is to use other testing frameworks to extend your unit-testing arsenal. In this section, you're going to supplement QUnit with Sinon.js to mock the server call of your new (pretend) feature. You'll need to download the framework and add it to your code base. The software can be found at http:// sinonjs.org. You can add it alongside QUnit in your test directory (see figure 8.14).

▲ 🗁 App
  ▲ 🗁 components
    ▲ 🗁 test
      ▲ 🗁 thirdParty
        ▷ 🗁 qunit
        ▲ 🗁 sinon
          📄 sinon_1_12_2.js

Figure 8.14   Your test directory after adding your second JavaScript testing framework

You won't go through the motions of creating server code for this example, because it's illustrating how to fake it out anyway. This will save you from having to set up a server and server-side code for one simple example. Instead, imagine you had a server call already working that's used to save user input in your tip calculator. To create a mock server call, you first ask Sinon.js to create a fake server (see the following listing).

Listing 8.12   Create a fake server to mock server requests

```
module("Tip Form Model Tests", {
    beforeEach: function() {
        this.tipFormModel = TipForm;
```

```
        this.server = sinon.fakeServer.create();
    },
    afterEach: function() {
        this.server.restore();
    }
});
```

Create the fake server

Perform cleanup and restore
the XHR constructor

You can add that command to your unit test setup. With the fake server created, you can tell Sinon.js how you'd like for it to respond. Keep in mind that you're not testing the fake server's output, because you're mandating how you want the fake server to respond for your unit-test scenario. You're testing the business logic related to the call. This could be whether the call was created or initiated properly or maybe how your application behaves, given different types of server responses. The following listing shows a mock server and a couple of simple unit tests using its response.

Listing 8.13 Using a mock server in a Backbone.js model's unit test

```
test("Save Request", function() {
    this.server.respondWith(
        [200,
            {"Content-Type":"text/html"},
            "{'save_status':'saved'}"
        ]);

    this.tipFormModel.save();

    this.server.respond();

    equal(this.tipFormModel.urlRoot,
    "/mockrequest",
    "When the model is saved,
    the URL should be /mockrequest");

    equal(this.server.requests.length, 1,
    "When the model is saved,
    the request length should be 1");

    equal(this.server.requests[0].requestBody,
    JSON.stringify(this.tipFormModel.attributes),
    "When the model is saved,
    the request body should equal the model attributes");
});
```

State how you need the
fake server to respond

Save the model data

Ask the fake server to respond

Make sure save() constructed
the URL correctly

Test for duplicate calls

Test the request

Sinon.js has many other features that make it a powerful, standalone product. As you can see, it can also be the perfect companion to other testing frameworks such as QUnit. Because we've broached the topic of other frameworks, I'll mention a few others you might want to explore. I'll also include QUnit for comparison.

MAKING JAVASCRIPT UNIT-TESTING CHOICES

Though not an exhaustive list, table 8.2 lists a few of the JavaScript testing frameworks that are popular at the time of this writing and that support unit testing.

Table 8.2 Popular JavaScript frameworks that support unit testing

Name	URL	Comments
QUnit	http://qunitjs.com	Mature framework, lots of other features I didn't get to cover in this chapter, easy to set up and use.
Mocha	http://mochajs.org	Mocha has many features but leaves it to you to pick an assertion library such as Unit.js (http://unitjs.com) or Chai.js (http://chaijs.com).
Buster.js	http://busterjs.org	Though still in beta at the time of this writing, this framework contains many promising features.
Jasmine	http://jasmine.github.io	Another easy-to-use framework, but this one is focused on behavior-driven development.

Don't be afraid to explore other frameworks even if you've found one that's your favorite. Others might have particular strengths that supplement your preferred framework.

8.4   *Chapter challenge*

Here's a challenge for you to see what you've learned in this chapter. Create a small survey SPA that could be used to poll users on what they like best about a particular topic. The topic could be which movie is the best, which food, and so on. The output should keep tallying the results with each survey submission, showing how each item in the survey is ranked. It can be as simple or as complex as you'd like. Then, using either a JavaScript unit-testing framework covered in this chapter or another that you like better, create a suite of unit tests for your application.

8.5   *Summary*

You made it through a crash course in client-side unit testing. Let's review what you learned:

- A unit test is performed on the individual parts of your code. This could be an entire module but is often individual functions.
- Unit tests provide examples of how your code works.
- Unit tests should be focused on individual concepts related to the behavior and purpose of the software.
- Unit tests shouldn't require any particular order, should be self-reliant, and should be easily understood.
- One approach to creating unit tests is to create the tests after the software is written.
- With test-driven development (TDD), the test is created first.

Client-side task automation

This chapter covers

- Understanding what task runners are and how they help you
- Working with task runner tasks for development
- Creating a client-side build process

When you develop software, you'll often find yourself repeating certain tasks over and over throughout the development lifecycle. These tasks can include performing particular development steps for a given language, running tests, and creating builds. To assist in the automation of these tasks, many task-based automation tools (or *task runners*) have been created. Some, such as Make, have been around for a long time. Others, such as the one used in this chapter's examples, are fairly recent by comparison.

Task runners come in all shapes and sizes, metaphorically speaking. Some run on a particular platform, whereas others are cross-platform. Some target a particular build language, and others are cross-language tools. Many of these tools have traditionally focused more on the build process.

In modern web applications, such as your SPA, JavaScript professionals require more than just a build tool. The landscape for today's developer is incredibly vast and complex, requiring task runners to automate a myriad of development-oriented tasks as well.

A new breed of task runner has emerged, however, that puts client-side development front and center and treats client-side tasks as first-class citizens. This chapter covers these client-oriented task runners and the types of tasks commonly automated by these tools. I'll split the discussion between how they're used during development and how they're used to create a client-side build.

For this chapter's project, you'll use a JavaScript-based task runner called Gulp.js. To have some source code to work with, you'll use the SPA created in chapter 6. For convenience, the Gulp.js files and the source code for chapter 6 are available together in the downloadable source for the chapter.

There are other task runners to choose from. I'll talk about some alternatives a little later. Before you jump into selecting a tool, though, you need a better understanding of what task runners do for you.

9.1   Common uses for task runners

When you use a task runner, you're creating a set of precise, repeatable instructions (or *tasks*) that describe the type of actions you need automated. As I mentioned previously, task runners can be used to automate the build process but can be used during development as well. Figure 9.1 provides an overview of common tasks you might perform, either during development or to create a client-side build. You could have more or fewer tasks, depending on your needs, but this gives you an idea.

You'll see some of these in action later, when you create this chapter's project. For now, let's break down each of these and discuss what they mean.

9.1.1   Live browser reloads

While creating a web application, such as your SPA, one particular development task that you'll find yourself doing all the time is reloading the browser. On their own,

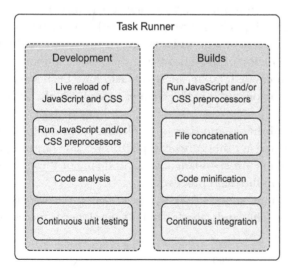

Figure 9.1   Common uses for JavaScript-based task runners

browsers have no way to know when a CSS or JavaScript file has changed. Every time you make a file change, you're out of sync with the browser. For your changes to take effect, you have to reload the browser.

To automate this process, tools such as LiveReload (http://livereload.com) and Browsersync (www.browsersync.io) can be used to automatically update the browser when a file changes. You can imagine the amount of time you could save by not having to stop and manually reload the browser in order to see the results of a change in your code. These tools can be used standalone, but invoking them from your task runner gives you the ability to run any number of tasks before triggering the reload of the browser.

9.1.2 *Automatic JavaScript and CSS preprocessing*

Preprocessors are programs used to create new or custom versions of an existing language by extending or changing the original syntax to include new features. The type of compilation preprocessors perform is sometimes referred to as *transpiling, transcompiling,* or *source-to-source compiling.*

Sass (http://sass-lang.com) and Less.js (http://lesscss.org) are examples of popular CSS preprocessors. They give you the ability to extend CSS with such features as variables, mix-ins, and nested rules. CoffeeScript (http://coffeescript.org) and LiveScript (http://livescript.net) are examples of independent programming languages that compile into JavaScript by using a preprocessor.

If you're using languages that require a preprocessor, you can use a task runner to automate the preprocessing step.

9.1.3 *Automatic code analysis from linters*

Code analysis tools (or *linters*) for JavaScript and CSS check your code for errors and other problems with the code. These tools can also be used to make sure code adheres to a standard set of coding practices. For JavaScript, JSHint (http://jshint.com) and JavaScript Lint (www.javascriptlint.com) are common choices. For CSS, CSS Lint (http://csslint.net) is a popular tool. As with preprocessors, using a tool for code analysis is a manual step in your development routine that can be automated with a task runner. This not only saves you time but also helps detect problems as you code.

9.1.4 *Continuous unit testing*

With some development styles, such as test-driven development, you're continuously unit testing the code you write. One of the hassles with unit testing is that you have to stop what you're doing whenever you want to run a test or group of tests. Test runners can be configured to watch for file changes and automatically trigger unit tests. Moreover, using headless test runners in your tasks enables you to see test results without having to swivel back and forth with the browser.

> **NOTE** The term *headless* refers to being able to access a program's output without a graphical user interface (for example, from the command line).

9.1.5   File concatenation

The term *concatenate* means *to combine*. When you combine files into as few as possible, you save on server bandwidth, reduce the amount of network traffic, and improve the user experience by having the application load faster.

A common step you can instruct your task runner to perform while creating a build for your SPA is to concatenate your JavaScript files into as few files as makes sense. This might mean that all files are combined into a single file or a small handful of files. You can do the same for your CSS files.

9.1.6   Code minification

Another step your task runner can perform during the front-end build process is to minify your application's source code. This process of removing any characters from the source file that aren't needed for the application to run is called *minification*. This includes characters such as whitespace, new lines, and comments. Minification tools can also be instructed to produce even more compact versions of your source files by changing the source code to reduce the length of variable and function names (sometimes down to a single letter).

9.1.7   Continuous integration

Continuous integration, or *CI*, is a software development practice whereby team members frequently check in code throughout the day. CI also uses an automated build process for the application that performs a code build at least once a day.

Many development teams use a centralized code repository and a centralized CI server, such as Jenkins (http://jenkins-ci.org), to establish a continuous build process. With a product like Jenkins, builds and associated tests can be run at scheduled intervals or whenever new code is checked in. Though the implementation details are beyond the scope of this book, your client-oriented build and testing tasks can also be invoked by the CI server. Your task runner needs to also be installed on the CI machine.

Having reviewed some common uses for task runners, let's talk about some of the things to consider when selecting the task runner that best suits your development needs.

9.2   Choosing a task runner

As I mentioned at the beginning of the chapter, a staggering number of task runners are available. Even narrowing the discussion to only JavaScript-based tools, you have a growing number to choose from. Unfortunately, no clear winner emerges when it comes to picking one over another. It ultimately boils down to preference. You can consider some general differences, though, when deciding. I'll use Grunt.js and Gulp.js in these descriptions, because they represent opposing task-runner architectures and are also arguably the most popular JavaScript-based task runners available.

- *Task creation*—One deciding factor is whether you prefer describing tasks by using configuration or programmatically through function calls. Whereas the other differences between task runners may be more nuanced, this difference is dramatic. Grunt.js is an example of a task runner that relies heavily on configuration for the creation of tasks. With other task runners, such as Gulp.js, tasks are created in code.

- *Temp files versus pipelines for processing*—Another difference you might consider when selecting a task runner is the method in which it processes data. With some task runners, such as Grunt.js, temporary files are created for intermediate processing. In contrast, tools such as Gulp.js also use I/O streams. These streams can be piped together to orchestrate task flow, bypassing the need for temporary files. Streams are generally considered a faster way to process tasks.

- *Number of plugins*—Not all but most task runners allow their base functionality to be extended via plugins. Plugins are add-on modules that extend the out-of-the-box functionality of a given task runner. The sheer number of plugins for a tool doesn't necessarily mean it's better, but it does speak to the variety of choices you'll have when creating your task-runner scripts. At the time of this writing, Grunt.js has nearly three times as many plugins as Gulp.js.

To get a feel for a particular task runner, you should spend some time perusing the websites for each tool. There you can get the latest information on a tool and download it to give it a trial run. Table 9.1 lists some of the JavaScript-based task runner/build frameworks that are available at the time of this writing.

Table 9.1   Some of the JavaScript-based task runner/build tools available today

Tool	URL
Grunt.js	http://gruntjs.com
Gulp.js	http://gulpjs.com
RequireJS Optimizer (r.js)	http://requirejs.org/docs/optimization.html
Mimosa	http://mimosa.io
Broccoli	https://github.com/broccolijs/broccoli
Brunch	http://brunch.io

Having reviewed task runners and some common uses for development and builds, it's time to create some tasks. So let's work on our project. We'll take things slow, though, to give you time to become familiar with your task runner's syntax and methodology.

9.3   Our project

Unlike previous chapters, in which you were creating an SPA, in this project you'll use a JavaScript-based task runner to demonstrate live browser reloads and test automation. You'll also create a client-side build script. As I mentioned earlier, you'll use

Gulp.js for this project. It's super easy to install, and its programmatic approach to creating tasks is easy to follow.

Gulp.js needs Node.js to run. So before you get started, you'll need to install both Node.js and Gulp.js. See appendix D for details on their installation. The installation commands for any plugins used are given during the discussions in each section.

9.3.1   *Introducing Gulp.js*

As I mentioned earlier, Gulp.js is a task runner. Its primary job is to automate tasks for you. Out-of-the-box Gulp.js has four basic methods, which you'll learn more about as you go:

- `gulp.src`—Specifies the files to be piped to plugins for processing
- `gulp.dest`—Writes the output of the piped processes
- `gulp.task`—Creates a task
- `gulp.watch`—Monitors files so you can react (for example, invoke a task) when changes occur

This is a high-level overview of these methods. Although you'll learn how to use them in this chapter, you can also review their functionality in detail by reading the API documentation for Gulp.js at https://github.com/gulpjs/gulp/blob/master/docs/API.md.

For any other functionality not covered by the core APIs, you'll have to get it from Gulp.js's growing library of plugins (see http://gulpjs.com/plugins). In the upcoming sections, you'll use plugins to perform some of the development and build tasks introduced earlier in the chapter.

In Gulp.js, tasks are defined through function calls rather than through configuration. When you process your application's source files with Gulp.js, the data is processed by using Node.js I/O streams. These streams can be connected (or piped) together to form a task pipeline; the output of each operation in a task can be connected to the input of another. This makes it easy to daisy-chain multiple processes in a streaming fashion to arrive at the final output (see figure 9.2).

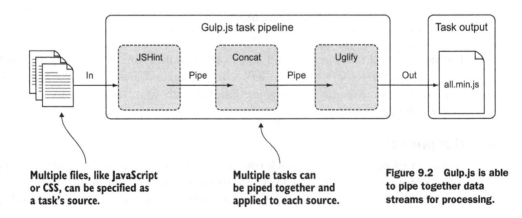

Multiple files, like JavaScript or CSS, can be specified as a task's source.

Multiple tasks can be piped together and applied to each source.

Figure 9.2   Gulp.js is able to pipe together data streams for processing.

With introductions out of the way, let's create your first task.

9.3.2 Creating your first task

To begin working on a new task, you need to create a file that will contain your task definition. Gulp.js will automatically look for a file named gulpfile.js in the directory where you run its commands. So go ahead and create a new, empty file called gulp-file.js in your local project directory. You can use any directory you want. Just make sure you're in that directory when installing plugins or executing tasks.

Next, you'll add a task to your gulpfile.js file. Before you jump into creating any build-related tasks, you'll create a simple task just to test-drive Gulp.js. Tasks in Gulp.js are written using JavaScript and have the following syntax:

```
gulp.task("task-name", [optionalArrayOfDependentTasks], function() {
  // task operations here
});
```

For your first task, you'll just write the obligatory "Hello world" to the console. You don't have any dependencies, so your gulpfile.js file looks like the following listing at this point.

Listing 9.1   Writing "Hello world" from a task

```
var gulp = require("gulp");                                    ◄── Require Gulp.js

gulp.task("say-hello", function() {                           ◄── say-hello is the task name
   console.log("Hello world");
});
```

Notice the call to `require()` at the top. Because your runtime is Node.js and it uses the CommonJS module system, this is how you include references to any external modules. This includes Gulp.js itself.

Gulp tasks are invoked from the command line. Open your favorite command-line tool and navigate to the local directory where you created the gulpfile.js file. From there, use the `gulp` command followed by the task name:

```
C:\chpt9\AngularJS-proj> gulp say-hello
```

This produces output similar to the following:

```
[00:00:39] Using gulpfile C:\chpt9\AngularJS-proj\gulpfile.js
[00:00:39] Starting 'say-hello'...
Hello world
[00:00:39] Finished 'say-hello' after 141 µs
```

NOTE   The symbol µs stands for *microseconds*.

Next, let's see how to specify task dependencies in Gulp.js. To tell Gulp.js that one or more tasks should run before a task is executed, you add the names of each dependent task to an array of task names. This array is an optional second parameter for a task:

```
gulp.task("task-name", ["task-b", "task-c", "task-d"], function() { ... });
```

To test this out, you'll create a second task. This time, you'll write "How are you?" to the console, but you'll specify in this task that your previous task must be executed first (see the following listing).

Listing 9.2   Specifying dependent tasks

```
var gulp = require("gulp");

gulp.task("say-hello", function() {
    console.log("Hello world");
});

gulp.task("how-are-you", ["say-hello"], function() {
    console.log("How are you?");
});
```

say-hello is now a
dependency for
how-are-you

The say-hello task can still be run by itself. But if you run the how-are-you task, both tasks will be executed. First, say-hello will run, because it's the dependency, and then how-are-you. The output from running your new task looks similar to the following:

```
C:\chpt9\AngularJS-proj> gulp how-are-you
[00:13:37] Using gulpfile C:\chpt9\AngularJS-proj\gulpfile.js
[00:13:37] Starting 'say-hello'...
Hello world
[00:13:37] Finished 'say-hello' after 144 µs
[00:13:37] Starting 'how-are-you'...
How are you?
[00:13:37] Finished 'how-are-you' after 58 µs
```

Now that you've gotten your feet wet with some simple tasks, let's create a more useful task. You'll start with an easy one.

9.3.3   Creating a code analysis task

Code analysis, or *linting,* is the process of using a program to analyze your code for errors and other problems. Table 9.2 contains the plugin you'll use for this task and the command to install it locally. You'll use the @latest option to grab the latest version available.

Table 9.2   Gulp.js plugin for the JSHint JavaScript code linter

Plugin	To install
gulp-jshint www.npmjs.com/package/gulp-jshint	`npm install gulp-jshint@latest --save-dev`

To use the plugin, you need to include it. Add this call to the top of your gulpfile.js file:

```
var jshint = require("gulp-jshint");
```

Now you can create the task itself in your gulpfile.js file (see the next listing). This example names the task `lint`, but you can call it anything you want.

Listing 9.3   A linter task using the gulp-jshint plugin

```
gulp.task("lint", function() {

    return gulp.src(["App/components/**/*.js",
        "!./App/components/thirdParty/**"])
        .pipe(jshint())
        .pipe(jshint.reporter('default'))

});
```

Specify which files to use → (arrow pointing to `gulp.src`)

Apply plugin → (arrow pointing to `.pipe(jshint())`)

Report the output → (arrow pointing to `.pipe(jshint.reporter('default'))`)

The listing uses `gulp.src()` to specify which set of files should be used in your linting task. The `gulp.src()` function takes either a string or an array. Inside the string or array, you can use complete file paths or *glob* patterns to represent files and folders that are included or excluded. The `pipe()` function is used to connect the I/O streams during processing.

> **NOTE**   Globbing is a way of expressing file or folder names by using patterns and wildcard characters. Gulp.js supports globbing via `node-glob`. This site has a good primer on the glob patterns it supports: https://github.com/isaacs/node-glob.

Using globbing, you define the source as all files with the extension .js under the App/ components directory (*.js) or any folders underneath that directory (/**). You're also excluding anything in the thirdParty folder by using the exclamation point (!).

You probably also noticed a call to `jshint.reporter('default')`. For this plugin, you have to use its `reporter()` function to print the results from your linter to the console. You're using the default results reporter from the plugin, but it allows external ones to be used as well.

With your task defined, you can return to the command line and type the following command:

```
C:\chpt9\AngularJS-proj> gulp lint
```

When the task runs, you see output similar to the following:

```
C:\chpt9\AngularJS-proj> gulp lint

[10:09:38] Using gulpfile C:\chpt9\AngularJS-proj\gulpfile.js
[10:09:38] Starting 'lint'...

C:\chpt9\AngularJS-proj\App\components\messaging\services\messageSvc.js:
line 7, col 6, Unnecessary semicolon.

1 error
[10:09:38] Finished 'lint' after 112 ms
```

The task runs through all the files you specified, looking for problems. In this case, the linter finds an extra semicolon at the end of a function that isn't needed. In addition to the issue itself, the plugin tells you which file to look at and the line number where you'll find the problem.

Now let's look at something that's crazy cool that will help you tremendously during development. Let's see how to get the browser to automatically reload while you're coding.

9.3.4   *Creating a browser-reload task*

During development, an annoying (yet necessary) activity is to reload the browser after you've made changes in your application. This process can be made less painful by using a program such as LiveReload or Browsersync. This example uses Browsersync (see table 9.3), because it's easy to set up. Browsersync isn't a plugin for Gulp.js; it's a completely standalone product that can be used by itself or integrated with your favorite task runner.

For this project, you're going to integrate it with Gulp.js. You'll also make the linting task you just created a dependency for the browser-reload task. This project illustrates how to use your task runner to automatically do any necessary processing on your application's source files before the reload happens.

Table 9.3   Application for automatic browser reloads

Application	To install
Browsersync www.browsersync.io	`npm install browser-sync@latest --save-dev`

What makes this program nice is that it doesn't require any special add-ons/extensions to be added to your browser. It can also keep multiple browsers and multiple devices in sync, all at the same time! I'm not going into all of its features here, but you can visit the website to see a great video illustrating the things this product can do.

Let's create your task now. Start by including the program by using `require()` just as you saw previously with the linter plugin:

```
var browserSync = require("browser-sync");
```

As I mentioned earlier, you might want to perform certain tasks before the reload occurs. To integrate Browsersync with your task runner, you wrap it in a task and specify any dependent tasks you want to run prior to this one:

```
gulp.task("reload", ["lint"], browserSync.reload);
```

Browsersync has its own built-in ability to watch files for changes, but for the integration with Gulp.js, you're going to use `gulp.watch` to execute the `reload` task when any CSS or JavaScript file changes:

```
gulp.watch(["./App/css/*.css", "App/components/**/*.js"], ["reload"]);
```

The first argument to gulp.watch() is the string or array containing the file paths or globs to use. The second argument is the name of the task that should be called when any file being watched changes. Here you're saying that if any CSS file or JavaScript files change, then execute the reload task.

Browsersync can proxy your local virtual host server or spin up its own mini server for your application. In this case, you're not using a server, so you'll let it use its own server for viewing and reloading your SPA. All you need to do is tell Browsersync where the base directory for your application is located:

```
browserSync({
    server: {
        baseDir: "./"
    }
});
```

Now let's put everything together in a task (see the following listing).

Listing 9.4 Automatically reloading the browser from a task

```
gulp.task("reload", ["lint"], browserSync.reload);          ← The reload task

gulp.task("file-watch", ["lint"], function () {             ← The task to watch
                                                              for file changes
    browserSync({                                           ← Browsersync server setup
        server: {
            baseDir: "./"
        }
    });

    gulp.watch(
        ["./App/css/*.css", "App/components/**/*.js"],     ← Files to watch
        ["reload"]                                          ← The task to call when
    );                                                         a file change occurs
});
```

Because reload is a task by itself, you can reuse it in other tasks. You can also use it to manually reload the browser. While developing code, you want the reload to automatically happen as you change files, so you'll run the file-watch task from the command line. You should see output similar to the following when it's run:

```
C:\chpt9\AngularJS-proj> gulp file-watch
[11:27:07] Using gulpfile C:\chpt9\AngularJS-proj\gulpfile.js
[11:27:07] Starting 'lint'...
C:\chpt9\AngularJS-proj\App\components\messaging\services\messageSvc.js:
line 7, col 6, Unnecessary semicolon.

1 error
[11:27:08] Finished 'lint' after 105 ms

[11:27:08] Starting 'file-watch'...
[11:27:08] Finished 'file-watch' after 133 ms
[BS] Access URLs:
```

```
------------------------------------
      Local: http://localhost:3000
   External: http://192.168.1.68:3000
------------------------------------
         UI: http://localhost:3001
UI External: http://192.168.1.68:3001
------------------------------------
[BS] Serving files from: ./
```

Because you have your linting task as a dependency, it's executed first, and then the browser is started. You didn't specify to Browsersync which browser to auto-open, so it opens your default browser. Next, if you make a change to any file in the list, you'll instantly see the change happen in the browser. You also see output similar to the following:

```
[11:33:35] Starting 'lint'...
C:\chpt9\AngularJS-proj\App\components\messaging\services\messageSvc.js:
line 7, col 6, Unnecessary semicolon.

1 error
[11:33:35] Finished 'lint' after 76 ms

[11:33:35] Starting 'reload'...
[BS] Reloading Browsers...
[11:33:35] Finished 'reload' after 1.54 ms
```

Again, your dependent task runs first. You also see at what point the browser is reloaded.

Now that you know how to have the browser reload automatically while you're coding, let's look at another task that's quite common during development.

9.3.5 *Automating unit testing*

As you saw with the automatic browser reloads, having the task runner automatically take care of repetitive tasks saves you time and hassle. Now let's look at how to design a task that automatically runs a unit test for the code you're creating. Because we used QUnit in chapter 8, we'll stick with it for this chapter. Feel free, though, to use any JavaScript testing software you wish.

In the SPA code you're using for your source files to play with, there's an AngularJS module that's used to calculate the discounted price for a used video game. You'll pretend that code hasn't been written yet, so for now you'll remove this function's code:

```
function calculate(amt) {

}
```

This function should take in an amount and multiply it by a standard discount value that's available in this module. You've created a unit test for this function as well. Its source can be found in the downloadable source for this chapter under the /test folder.

For your automated testing, you'll need a way to display the results of your QUnit tests. Normally you'd need to open the test results HTML page in a browser, but you don't want to have to do that while you're coding. You just want to see the results.

What you need is a program that will run the tests and report the results in the command line without the need for a graphical user interface. You'll use one called node-qunit-phantomjs (see table 9.4). It uses a headless browser called PhantomJS internally.

Table 9.4 Application to run QUnit tests in PhantomJS

Application	To install
node-qunit-phantomjs https://github.com/jonkemp/node-qunit-phantomjs	`npm install node-qunit-` `phantomjs@latest --save-dev`

This particular program can be run standalone from the command line, but you'll wrap it in a task and set up a watch on your application's JavaScript source files. This is similar to what you did with Browsersync in the preceding section. As usual, you'll need to include this program as a dependency for your gulpfile.js script:

```
var qunitp = require("node-qunit-phantomjs");
```

The program is simple to use. You pass to it the name of the HTML page that you'd usually use in the browser to see the results of your QUnit tests:

```
qunitp("./test/test.html");
```

Now let's put everything together in a task (see the following listing).

Listing 9.5 Automatically running unit tests when a file changes

```
gulp.task("unit-test", function() {
    qunitp("./test/test.html");
});

gulp.task("watch-js", function() {
    gulp.watch("App/components/**/*.js", ["unit-test"]);
});
```

Display the test results from the command line

Run the unit-test task when a JavaScript file change occurs

Let's first run your unit-test task manually. It fails because you haven't implemented the body of the function yet. It spits out the same verbose error that you'd normally see in the browser. A small part of the result is shown here:

```
Testing ..\..\test\test.html
Took 4 ms to run 1 tests. 0 passed, 1 failed.

Test failed: Pricing Service Tests: Pricing Calculations:
Failed assertion: When the regular price is $10.00,
the discounted price should be $4.00, expected: 4.00,
but was: undefined
```

Now let's start your watch task. When the watch-js task starts, you'll see output similar to the following from the command line:

```
C:\chpt9\AngularJS-proj> gulp watch-js
[15:08:40] Using gulpfile C:\chpt9\AngularJS-proj\gulpfile.js
[15:08:40] Starting 'watch-js'...
[15:08:40] Finished 'watch-js' after 25 ms
```

This task does nothing else until you change one of the watched files. In this unit test, you're supplying $10 as the price of the video game. The standard discount is 40%, so the correct result should be $4. Let's see what happens if you add the code back for your function so that it calculates the correct result. You get the following output in your command line:

```
[15:17:19] Starting 'unit-test'...
[15:17:19] Finished 'unit-test' after 5.67 ms
Testing ..\..\test\test.html
Took 12 ms to run 1 tests. 1 passed, 0 failed.
```

You've set the watch for any JavaScript files, so as you continue to code and add more unit tests, your tests results will keep printing out to the console as you go.

Having looked at using a task runner for development, let's switch gears and create a client-side build process with it. Each project may have different requirements, so you may have more or fewer tasks in your build. I'll use a few common build tasks to illustrate.

9.3.6   *Creating a build process*

In the preceding section, you saw how to automate your testing. Automated testing is also a task you might want for your build, so you'll make sure it's invoked by the build process. But what else might you want to include? Well, a common task for a build is to optimize source code. You'll start by optimizing your JavaScript files.

OPTIMIZING JAVASCRIPT FILES

A fairly common set of optimization steps performed on JavaScript source files includes the concatenation and minification of your source files. You'll use a plugin called gulp-concat for the concatenation of your code and one called gulp-uglify for its minification. You'll also need one more specifically for AngularJS so that your AngularJS code still works after the minification process (gulp-ng-annotate).

> **NOTE**   If minification is configured to shorten function argument names, this can prevent AngularJS's dependency-injection process from working correctly. The gulp-ng-annotate plugin makes sure that all application components are annotated properly to prevent this issue.

For the output of your build process, you'll add a new folder to your project directory called dist (as in *distribution*). You'll also use a package called del to clear out the dist folder before each new build. Table 9.5 lists your new plugins/programs.

Table 9.5 Plugins to process JavaScript and clear the build's destination folder

Plugin/application	To install
gulp-concat www.npmjs.com/package/gulp-concat	`npm install gulp-concat@latest --save-dev`
gulp-uglify www.npmjs.com/package/gulp-uglify	`npm install gulp-uglify@latest --save-dev`
gulp-ng-annotate www.npmjs.com/package/gulp-ng-annotate	`npm install gulp-ng-annotate@latest --save-dev`
del www.npmjs.com/package/del	`npm install del@latest --save-dev`

The following listing shows the build-related tasks in your gulpfile.js. It has one task for clearing your dist directory and another to optimize your JavaScript source files.

Listing 9.6 Adding tasks to optimize JavaScript

```
var gulp = require("gulp");
var del = require("del");
var concat = require("gulp-concat");
var uglify = require("gulp-uglify");
var ngAnnotate = require("gulp-ng-annotate");

gulp.task("clean", function(done) {
    console.log("cleaning dist dir");          ◀── Remove all files and folders
    del(["dist/**/*"], done);                        from the dist directory
});

gulp.task("scripts", ["clean"], function() {
    console.log("processing scripts");         ◀── Task for your
                                                    JavaScript processing
    return gulp.src(["App/components/**/*.js",
        "!./App/components/thirdParty/**"])
            .pipe(concat("all.min.js"))        ◀── Give concatenated file a name
            .pipe(ngAnnotate())
            .pipe(uglify())                    ◀── Specify a folder to place
            .pipe(gulp.dest("./dist/"));            the processed file
});
```

The output of your task is the all.min.js file defined in the concat() function. You specified the dist folder as the destination for the task's output via the gulp.dest() function.

In addition to your scripts task, you have one other task in your gulpfile.js file: the clean task. You can use your clean task to delete all the files and folders from your dist folder before each new run of the build process. This task uses the del package you installed. To tell Gulp.js that you want the clean task to run before your scripts task is run, you declare it as a task dependency.

OPTIMIZING CSS

So far, you've used Gulp.js only to optimize your JavaScript source files. To optimize your style sheets, you'll need to use npm once again to locally install a plugin called gulp-minify-css (see table 9.6).

Table 9.6   Plugin to minify CSS

Plugin	To install
gulp-minify-css www.npmjs.com/package/gulp-minify-css	`npm install gulp-minify-css@latest` `--save-dev`

The following listing shows the new task to add to your growing build script in the gulpfile.js file.

Listing 9.7   Adding a task to optimize CSS

```
var minifyCss = require("gulp-minify-css");

gulp.task("css", ["clean"], function() {
   console.log("processing css");

   return gulp.src("./App/css/*.css")
      .pipe(concat("styles.min.css"))
      .pipe(minifyCss())
      .pipe(gulp.dest("./dist/"));
});
```

Concatenate and minify all style sheets as styles.min.css

That takes care of the optimizations you're going to do for the scripts and CSS. While you're optimizing things for your build, you can also include a task to optimize your SPA's images.

OPTIMIZING IMAGES

For your images, you'll use a plugin called gulp-imagemin (see table 9.7).

Table 9.7   Plugin to reduce the size of images

Plugin	To install
gulp-imagemin www.npmjs.com/package/gulp-imagemin	`npm install gulp-imagemin@latest --save-dev`

The following listing shows your task for optimizing your SPA's image files for deployment.

Listing 9.8   Adding a task to reduce image size

```
var imagemin = require("gulp-imagemin");

gulp.task("images", ["clean", "html"], function() {
   console.log("processing images");
```

```
return gulp.src("App/images/*.png")
.pipe(imagemin())
.pipe(gulp.dest("./dist/App/images"));
```

◄─── **Optimize your .png files**

```
});
```

Your build process so far optimizes your source files and images and moves them to a dist folder. To complete a build, you'll need to have the entire application available for distribution to another environment. You'll need to create a task to move the rest of your SPA's files.

MOVING THE REST OF THE APPLICATION

Not all files went through an optimization process, but they're still part of the application. These include your HTML files and any third-party code. They'll all need to move to the same dist folder as your optimized code and images for distribution. For this, you don't need a plugin. You can use `gulp.src` and `gulp.dest` to move the files (see the next listing).

Listing 9.9 Adding a task to move the rest of the files

```
gulp.task("html", ["clean"], function(done) {
   console.log("copying over HTML");

   return gulp.src(["App/components/**/*.html",
      "./App/components/thirdParty/**"], {base: "./"})
      .pipe(gulp.dest("./dist/"));
```

◄─── **Move any application HTML or third-party code**

```
});
```

With the rest of the application taken care of, wouldn't it be nice if you could use Gulp.js to automatically create a new version of index.html that has references to the new optimized files? There's a plugin for that as well.

DYNAMICALLY UPDATING FILE REFERENCES

You can use several script replacement plugins to dynamically replace existing script and CSS references with references to the optimized versions. For this project, you're going to use one called gulp-html-replace (see table 9.8).

Table 9.8 Plugin to update the references in index.html to reflect the build files

Plugin	To install
gulp-html-replace www.npmjs.com/package/gulp-html-replace	`npm install gulp-html-replace@latest` `--save-dev`

What's nice about this plugin is that you can use HTML-style comments to annotate regions within the source file that should be replaced. There are beginning and ending comments to mark an area as a replacement block, with the syntax of `build:xxx` to denote the start of a new block. This way, you can unobtrusively mark an arbitrary number of references as candidates for replacement.

To begin, let's add the comment blocks around the places you want to replace in your index.html file from your local project directory. The following listing shows the annotated CSS include. The listing shows only the relevant portions, but you can see the entire file in the downloadable source code for the chapter.

Listing 9.10   Annotated CSS include for gulp-html-replace

```
<!-- build:css -->

<link rel="stylesheet" href="App/css/default.css">

<!-- endbuild -->
```

◄── Replace any CSS references here
with the optimized reference

You can do the same thing with your JavaScript files (see the next listing).

Listing 9.11   Annotated JavaScript includes for gulp-html-replace

```
<!-- build:js -->
<script src="App/components/app.js"></script>
<script src="App/components/data/appdata.js"></script>
<script src="App/components/useralerts/controllers/useralertsCrtl.js">
</script>
<script src="App/components/search/controllers/searchCrtl.js"></script>
<script
 src="App/components/productdisplay/controllers/productDisplayCrtl.js">
</script>
<script src="App/components/pricing/services/pricingSvc.js"></script>
<script src="App/components/messaging/services/messageSvc.js"></script>
<script src="App/components/search/services/searchSvc.js"></script>
<script src="App/components/productdisplay/services/productDisplaySvc.js">
</script>

<!-- endbuild -->
```

◄── Replace any JavaScript references
here with the optimized reference

With the blocks around your includes, you can create a Gulp.js task to dynamically update your index.html file and move it to the dist folder. You'll call this your `build` task (see the following listing).

Listing 9.12   Task update file references in index.html

```
gulp.task("build", ["clean", "scripts", "css", "images" ], function() {
    console.log("updating index");

    return gulp.src("index.html")
       .pipe(htmlreplace({
          "css": "styles.min.css",
          "js": "all.min.js"
       }))
       .pipe(gulp.dest("./dist/"));
});
```

◄── Replace any references in comment
blocks with references to these files

If you were to examine the index.html file in the dist folder after this task runs, your CSS references would have been replaced with a reference to your single, optimized CSS file:

```
<link rel="stylesheet" href="styles.min.css">
```

All of the JavaScript includes would have been replaced with just one that references the optimized JavaScript file:

```
<script src="all.min.js"></script>
```

The last thing you can do is define a default task. This isn't mandatory. If you create a default task, you're telling Gulp.js what to do if the gulp command is executed without a task name. You'll fire off your build process when the default task is invoked.

```
gulp.task("default", ["build"]);
```

It's worth mentioning that when creating your own build process, you might need to use fewer or more tasks than what you've included. Each project has its own requirements, and each development team has its own preferences. Ultimately, you'll have to decide what works best for your application.

9.4 *Chapter challenge*

Now here's a challenge for you to see what you've learned in this chapter. Pick one of the existing projects from this book or one of your own, and create several tasks. Make sure some tasks are defined as dependencies for others. Experiment with some plugins also. Be creative.

9.5 *Summary*

In this chapter, you got an introduction to task runners and client-side task automation. Let's quickly recap:

- Task runners are tools to automate repetitive tasks you'd otherwise have to perform manually.
- You can use a task runner during client-side development to perform tasks such as live browser reloads, code analysis, applying CSS and/or JavaScript preprocessing, and automated testing.
- Task runners can also be used to create a build process. A build is a set of consistent, repeatable steps to prepare an application for deployment to another environment.
- In a web-based application, such as your SPA, the build process often includes the CSS and/or JavaScript preprocessing, file concatenation, and code minification.
- Task runners such as Gulp.js or Grunt.js may use plugins, which dramatically increase the range of tasks the tool is able to perform.
- Many task runners are able to perform the same kinds of tasks, in different ways. Choosing a task runner often boils down to personal preference and the type of project/environment for which the tool is being used.

appendix A
Employee directory
example walk-through

This appendix covers

- Walk-through of the Backbone.js example
- Walk-through of the Knockout example
- Walk-through of the AngularJS example

You saw various code examples illustrating the components of our employee directory throughout chapter 2. In doing so, you gained a better understanding of the role MV* libraries/frameworks play in the creation of an SPA.

In this appendix, you'll walk through the complete source code for our directory by using each of our selected MV* frameworks. This will help you understand the complete picture if you decide to try one of these yourself. Before you start, let's go over your objectives again:

- Create a simple SPA to enter employee information.
- Build an easy-to-use UI for entering each employee's first name, last name, title, email, and phone.
- Keep track of each entry as part of a list, with the screen split between the entry form on the left and the directory's entry list on the right.

- Have two buttons on the entry side of the SPA: one to add a new entry and one to clear the form.
- Have one button next to each entry to remove the entry from the list.
- Have indicators next to each entry field to denote whether the field's entry requirement has been met (each indicator should update as the user types).

In other parts of the book, you'll learn more-advanced topics, such as routing and server transactions. For your first foray into the world of the SPA and MV*, you'll avoid the use of the router to keeps things simple. You'll also keep your employee data in memory.

Now that you've reviewed the objectives, let's take another look at the screenshot you first saw in chapter 2. This screenshot, shown in figure A.1, is the final product. The application will look and behave the same for each MV* framework used.

This design, though simple, takes you through the paces of designing views, templates, bindings, and models, as well as other framework-specific components. It's also

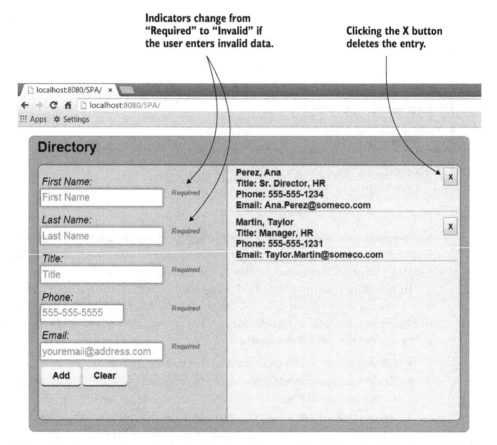

Figure A.1   Screen capture of the online directory. The user enters information in the form on the left. Valid entries appear in a list on the right.

nice in the sense that, although you're not communicating yet with the server, you're still carrying out CRUD operations on a list of items.

A.1 CSS

You'll use the same CSS files for all three versions. The following listing is your default style sheet. You're merely setting the stage with the font and the styles for your main section and header.

Listing A.1 default.css

```css
html, body {
    font-family: arial;
}

main {
    display: block; /* for IE */
    width: 800px;
    border: 1px solid #909092;
    background-color: #B7B8BA;
    border-radius: 10px;
    margin: 15px;
    padding: 5px 15px 15px 15px;
    box-sizing: border-box;
}

main > header {
    font-size: 25px;
    font-weight: bold;
    margin-bottom: 15px;
}
```

The following listing defines the styles for the entry form and the set of entries that will be displayed when the user adds directory entries.

Listing A.2 entries.css

```css
.entries {
    background-color: #D9D9D9;
    border: 1px solid #6D6D6D;
    border-radius: 10px;
    overflow: hidden;
    box-shadow: inset 0 0 3px 0 #6B6B6B;
    box-sizing: border-box;
}

.entries * {
    box-sizing: inherit;
}

.entries form {
    float: left;
    width: 45%;
```

```
    padding: 5px 0 0 5px;
    font-size: 18px;
}

.entries p {
    margin: 12px 0;
}

.entries label {
    font-style: italic;
    line-height: 1.4em;
}

.entries input {
    padding: 2px;
    box-shadow: 0 0 8px rgba(0, 0, 0, 0.3);
    border: 1px solid #999;
    line-height: inherit;
    font-size: inherit;

}

.entries .error-message {
    float: right;
    padding: 1px;
    margin-right: 15px;
    color: #DC3E5E;
    font-size: 12px;
    font-weight: bold;

}

.entries button {
    cursor: pointer;
    background-color: #EFEFEF;
}

.entries button::-moz-focus-inner {
    padding: 0;
}

.entries form button {
    box-shadow: 0px 2px 0px rgba(0, 0, 0, 0.5);
    font-size: 16px;
    border-radius: 5px;
    padding: 7px 20px;
    font-weight: bold;
    border: none;
}

.entries .entry-list {
    margin: 0 0 0 45%;
    width: 55%;
    height: 458px;
    border-left: 1px solid #9F9F9F;
```

```
    background-color: #EFEFEF;
    box-shadow: inset 0 0 3px 0 #6B6B6B;
    padding: 5px 0 0 0;
    overflow-y: auto;
}

.entries .entry-list li {
    list-style-type: none;
    margin: 5px 15px 15px 15px;
    border-bottom: 1px solid #9F9F9F;
    font-weight: bold;
}

.entries .entry-list .remove-entry {
    float: right;
    border: 1px outset #D9D9D9;
    padding: 5px;
}
```

Because it's such a small application, I've given it a fixed size on the screen. This also gives you just one general area of the screen to focus on while you get your bearings with MV*.

A.2   Backbone.js example

Let's begin with Backbone.js. Remember that it's our MVC/MVP-like framework. It's a little more feature rich than Knockout, but it doesn't have nearly as many bells and whistles baked in as AngularJS. It has an open design, though, allowing you to extend it through code or through third-party plugins to add features.

A.2.1   Downloading your dependencies

To start, you'll download what you need. You'll use several third-party libraries/frameworks to extend Backbone.js in this example. I won't cover all of the third-party libraries/frameworks in depth, but I'll discuss how they're being used here (see table A.1).

Table A.1   Dependencies for the Backbone.js version of the example

Framework/library	URL	Comments
Backbone.js	http://backbonejs.org	You can select either the minified (compact) version or the nonminified (readable/formatted) version. Both work the same. The readable version is helpful for understanding the source code. For deployment, always use the minified version.
jQuery	http://jquery.com	A great overall utility library that excels at DOM manipulation and event handling.
Underscore.js	http://underscorejs.org	Another utility library. This one is loaded with all sorts of programming helpers. You'll specifically use it as your template engine.

Table A.1   Dependencies for the Backbone.js version of the example *(continued)*

Framework/library	URL	Comments
Handlebars.js	http://handlebarsjs.com	Handlebars is another template library. At the time of this writing, Handlebars is a requirement for using Backbone.js, even if you don't use it yourself.
RequireJS	http://requirejs.org	I discuss RequireJS in chapter 3. For now, just know that it's used for asynchronous JavaScript module loading and dependency management. Using it, you'll create code using the AMD specification (also discussed in chapter 3). You'll also use two RequireJS plugins: domReady.js, which makes sure the DOM is ready before your JavaScript code acts on it, and text.js, which asynchronously downloads templates. Both plugins can be found at http://requirejs.org/docs/download.html.

A.2.2   *Directory structure*

I've tried to keep the directory structures fairly similar between the three versions. I do, however, use framework-specific folders where it makes sense. Figure A.2 is the directory structure for our Backbone.js version.

This design is still by feature, as I talked about in chapter 1, with the feature being the directory (under *components*). Your feature folders under *components* can grow with the application. But within the feature, the directory structure represents a somewhat typical Backbone.js layout.

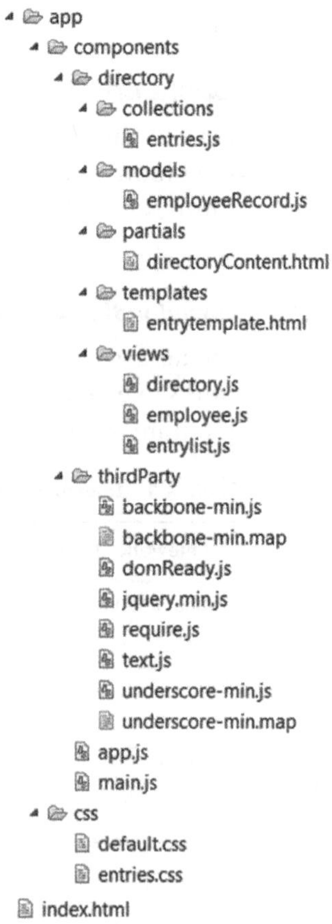

```
▲ 📂 app
    ▲ 📂 components
        ▲ 📂 directory
            ▲ 📂 collections
                📄 entries.js
            ▲ 📂 models
                📄 employeeRecord.js
            ▲ 📂 partials
                📄 directoryContent.html
            ▲ 📂 templates
                📄 entrytemplate.html
            ▲ 📂 views
                📄 directory.js
                📄 employee.js
                📄 entrylist.js
    ▲ 📂 thirdParty
        📄 backbone-min.js
        📄 backbone-min.map
        📄 domReady.js
        📄 jquery.min.js
        📄 require.js
        📄 text.js
        📄 underscore-min.js
        📄 underscore-min.map
    📄 app.js
    📄 main.js
    ▲ 📂 css
        📄 default.css
        📄 entries.css
📄 index.html
```

Figure A.2   Directory structure for the Backbone.js version of the application

A.2.3   The shell

In typical SPA fashion, your index.html welcome file, shown in the following listing, is
almost bare. Its main features are the style-sheet reference, the shell DIV for the application, and the RequireJS entry to kick-start the application.

> **Listing A.3   index.html**

```
<!DOCTYPE html>
<html>
<head>
    <link rel="stylesheet" href="app/css/default.css">
    <link rel="stylesheet" href="app/css/entries.css">      SPA's style sheets
    <!--[if IE]>
    <script>
       document.createElement("main");
    </script>                                        IE HTML5 fix
    <![endif]-->
</head>
<body>                                   Shell for the rest of the application
    <main />
    <script                                      RequireJS configuration file
       data-main="app/components/main.js"
       src="app/components/thirdParty/require.js">
    </script>                                     Reference to RequireJS itself
</body>
</html>
```

RequireJS dynamically and asynchronously loads any dependent files the application
needs, including modules and templates. It also makes sure they're ready for use before
any code tries to use them. This way, you don't have to worry about script order and the
synchronous and blocking nature of SCRIPT tags. Again, don't worry about RequireJS at
this point. It's just wrapping your JavaScript code into neat, self-contained modules.

A.2.4   main.js

This file contains the configuration preferences for RequireJS, shown in the next listing. Here you define a base URL and the paths relative to that where RequireJS can
download each file and assign an alias to that path.

> **Listing A.4   main.js—RequireJS configuration**

```
"use strict";
requirejs.config({
   baseUrl: "app/components",
   paths: {                                    Define a base URL for your SPA
      // third party
      jquery: "thirdParty/jquery.min",
      domReady: "thirdParty/domReady",         File paths and their aliases
      text: "thirdParty/text",                 relative to the base URL
      backbone: "thirdParty/backbone-min",
      underscore: "thirdParty/underscore-min",
```

```
        // application
        collections: "directory/collections",
        models: "directory/models",
        views: "directory/views",
        templates: "directory/templates",
        partials: "directory/partials"
    }
});

require([ "app" ], function(app) {
    app.init();
});
```

Kick-off point for your SPA
with app.js as a dependency

The last line is the starting point for the SPA. RequireJS makes sure that app.js is
loaded before calling your application's init() function.

A.2.5   *app.js*

Your app.js file, shown in the following listing, loads the user's first viewable area with
the SPA's first HTML content file. The file doesn't have to be called app.js, but that's a
typical naming convention for the first real code file. Any kind of pre-application work
or setup goes in this file.

Listing A.5   app.js

```
"use strict";
define([ "jquery", "collections/entries",
        "views/entrylist", "views/directory",
        "text!partials/directoryContent.html",
        "domReady"],

    function($, Entries, EntryList, Directory,
            directoryHTML, domReady) {

        function init() {
            domReady(function() {
                var entries = new Entries({});

                $("main").html(directoryHTML);

                var container = $("main .entries");

                new Directory(
                    { el: container,
                      collection: entries
                    }
                );

                new EntryList(
                    { el: container.find(".entry-list"),
                      collection: entries
                    }
                );
            });
```

The text.js
plugin used to
download a non-
JavaScript file

Dependency names match
file aliases from main.js

Parameter names for
each dependency

Make sure the
DOM is ready
before you begin

Use jQuery to insert the
HTML fragment (partial)

```
    }

    return {
        init: init
    };

  }
);
```

RequireJS downloads all dependencies in your list to begin with. After the dependencies are in place, the application's `init()` function is called. Here, you use jQuery to insert your first HTML content. When the DOM is ready, you create a new instance of your main Backbone.js view.

A.2.6 *directoryContent.html*

As you can see in the following listing, your HTML file looks clean. Backbone.js helps you interact with it without embedding JavaScript code.

Listing A.6   directoryContent.html

```
<section class="entries">

    <form name="entryForm">                          ◀── The input form for
        <p>                                              the application
            <label for="firstName">First Name:<br/>
                <input name="firstName" id="firstName"
                placeholder="First Name"/>
                <span class="error-message"></span>   ◀── SPAN contains the indicators
            </label>                                      of each input's validity checks
        </p>
        <p>
            <label for="lastName">Last Name:<br />
                <input name="lastName" id="lastName"
                placeholder="Last Name"/>
                <span class="error-message"></span>
            </label>
        </p>
        <p>
            <label for="title">Title:<br />
                <input name="title" id="title"
                placeholder="Title"/>
                <span class="error-message"></span>
            </label>
        </p>
        <p>
            <label for="phone">Phone:<br/>
                <input name="phone" id="phone"
                placeholder="555-555-5555"/>
                <span class="error-message"></span>
            </label>
        </p>
        <p>
            <label for="email">Email:<br />
```

```
            <input name="email" id="email"
            placeholder="youremail@address.com"/>
            <span class="error-message"></span>
        </label>
    </p>
    <p>
        <button type="submit">Add</button>
        <button type="reset">Clear</button>
    </p>
</form>

<ul class="entry-list"></ul>
</section>
```

A button to clear the form

A button to add an entry

The element for your collection of employee views/models

So far, so good. The HTML is nice and clean, void of JavaScript. It's also readable. In the next section, you'll see what the Backbone.js view looks like for this content.

Backbone.js objects

As you look at the JavaScript code for your Backbone.js version, one thing to keep in mind is that objects created using this framework extend an out-of-the-box object. You'll define the prototype first and then use the new keyword to create a new instance of it anytime you want to use an object of that type. Your views extend `Backbone.View`, your lists extend `Backbone.Collection`, and your models extend `Backbone.Model`. By doing this, you inherit many out-of-the-box features. To see the full set of features and examples, visit http://backbonejs.org.

A.2.7 *directory.js view*

As you may remember from our discussion of Backbone.js views, a view is created in code. A template and a model are used to create the visual content (see the following listing). Also note that function calls beginning with an underscore (_) are functions from Underscore.js. This framework makes certain tasks, especially those related to arrays, easier.

Listing A.7 directory.js view

```
"use strict";
define([ "backbone", "models/employeeRecord" ],
 function(Backbone, EmployeeRecord) {

    var Directory = Backbone.View.extend({
        events : {
            "keyup :input" : "handleInputKeyup",
            "submit" : "handleClickAdd",
            "reset" : "handleClickReset"
        },
        initialize : function() {
            this.scheduleReset();
        },
```

View's events

Reset upon initialization

```
handleInputKeyup : function() {
   this.buildAndValidateModel();
},
handleClickReset : function() {
   this.scheduleReset();
},
handleClickAdd : function(e) {
   e.preventDefault();

   var employee = this.buildAndValidateModel();

   this.collection.create(employee, {
      wait : true
   });

   if (!_.contains(this.collection.models, employee))
   {
      return;
   }

   this.$("form").trigger("reset");
},


scheduleReset : function() {

   this.$(":text:visible:first").focus();

   setTimeout(this.buildAndValidateModel.bind(this), 0);
},
buildAndValidateModel : function() {

   var fields = this.$("form").serializeArray();

   function compose(obj, field) {
      obj[field.name] = field.value;
      return obj;
   }

   var attrs = _.reduce(fields, compose, {});

   var model = new EmployeeRecord(attrs);

   this.$(".error-message").text("");

   if (model.isValid()) {
      return model;
   }

   .each(model.validationError,
      this.displayValidationMessage.bind(this)
   );

   return model;
},
```

Populate a model and validate with each key up

Get a new model

Add model in the collection unless there are errors

If unsuccessful, return

Trigger a reset event

Reset the form and focus on the first field

Add form fields to an array

Callback function for reduce() to build an object using the form field array

Use reduce() to create the attributes object for your model

New model instance

If the model is valid, return for the collection

If the model isn't valid, pass each error to a display function

```
displayValidationMessage : function(err) {            ◄  Function to display
                                                         validation errors
    var selector =
    "[name='" + err.attr + "']+.error-message";

    this.$(selector).text(err.error);
  }

});

return Directory;
});
```

Backbone.js has a lot less magic going on than the other two MV* frameworks you're using. As you can see in the listing, all of the work focuses on maintaining the state of the form as the user types in information.

A.2.8   *entrylist.js view*

Interaction with your list of entries is done through your entry list's view (see the following listing). Here you declare a Backbone.js collection to manage your collection of entry models. You can think of a collection as a proxy to manage an internal array of models.

Listing A.8   entrylist.js view

```
"use strict";
define(["backbone", "views/employee"],
  function(Backbone, Employee) {

    var EntryList = Backbone.View.extend({        When a model is added,
      initialize: function() {                     call renderEntry()
        this.listenTo(this.collection, "add",   ◄
        this.renderEntry);
      },
      renderEntry: function(model, collection, options) {
        if(options.add) {

          var employee =
          new Employee({ model: model });       ◄  New view instance with
                                                   the model passed in
          this.$el.append(employee.render().el); ◄
        }                                           Render view
      }
    });

  return EntryList;
  }
);
```

In your view for the list of entries, you can listen to the Backbone.js collection and react whenever a new model is added. In this case, you're rendering each model that's added.

A.2.9 entries.js collection

This file is fairly simple, as you can see in the next listing. For your simple application, you need to define only a collection that will hold an `EmployeeRecord` model.

Listing A.9   entries.js collection

```
"use strict";
define([ "backbone", "models/employeeRecord" ],
  function(Backbone, EmployeeRecord) {

    var Entries = Backbone.Collection.extend({          Collection to hold models
          model: EmployeeRecord                          of type EmployeeRecord
    });

    return Entries;
  }
);
```

Make sure to include the model as a dependency. In the previous section, you saw that every time the form data is valid, one of these models is added to your collection.

A.2.10 employee.js view

You use the RequireJS text plugin to dynamically fetch and cache the employee template that contains placeholders for your model's data (see the following listing). Because you're performing template duty in this view, you're also relying on Underscore.js as the template engine.

Listing A.10   employee.js view

```
"use strict";
define([ "underscore", "backbone",
"text!templates/entrytemplate.html"],

  function(_, Backbone, templateHTML) {

    var Employee = Backbone.View.extend({              Element type used
        tagName: "li",
        template: _.template(templateHTML),
        render: function() {
          this.$el.html(this.template(this.model.toJSON()));
          return this;                                  Compile/render
        },                                              the template
        events: {
          "click .remove-entry": "removeEntry"          A click event to call removeEntry
        },
        removeEntry: function() {
          // its model
          this.model.destroy();                          Perform cleanup for the
          // this view                                    DOM and events
          this.remove();
        }
```

```
  });

  return Employee;
  }
);
```

In this view, you don't do any data validation. That's the model's job. The view is all about what the user sees and interacts with. In this case, it's just the employee entry itself. The view for the list will take care of the overall list UI. Here, you're just concerned with taking your model data and marrying it to your template.

You also have an event on hand to call the `removeEntry` function if the X button is clicked by the user. Backbone.js has a little magic here for you. The `destroy` event is observed by your collection, which will remove the reference to the model. To round out the cleanup job, you also call `remove()` to remove any associated DOM element in the view and any event bindings associated with this view as well.

A.2.11   employeeRecord.js model

The following listing shows the employee model behind the view. Don't worry that it looks like a lot of code. It's a little verbose, but it's just the validation needed by the model.

Listing A.11   employeeRecord.js model

```
"use strict";
define([ "jquery", "backbone" ], function($, Backbone) {

  var validators = {                        ◄── Regular expressions
    "*": [ {                                      used by validation
      expr: /\S/,
      message: "Required"
    } ],
    "phone": [ {
      expr: /^[0-9]{3}-[0-9]{3}-[0-9]{4}$/,
      message: "Invalid"
    } ],
    "email": [ {
      expr: /^[a-z0-9!#$%&'*+\/=?^_`{|}~-]+(?:\.
      [a-z0-9!#$%&'*+\/=?^_`{|}~-]+)*@(?:[a-z0-9]
      (?:[a-z0-9-]*[a-z0-9])?\.)+[a-z0-9](?:[a-z0-9-]*
      [a-z0-9])?$/i,
      message: "Invalid"
    } ]
  };

  function validateField(value, key) {          ◄── List of your
                                                     validation rules
    var rules = validators["*"]
    .concat(validators[key] || []);
                                                ◄── Find the first
    var broken = _.find(rules, function(rule) {      broken rule, if any
      return !rule.expr.test(value);
```

```
        }
    );

    return broken ?
    { "attr": key, "error": broken.message } : null;
}
```

> Return a description
> for a broken rule or null

```
var EmployeeRecord = Backbone.Model.extend({
    validate: function(attrs) {
```

> Validate each field

```
        var validated = _.mapObject(attrs, validateField);
```

> Compile a list
> of errors minus
> any nulls

```
        var attrsInError = _.compact(_.values(validated));
```

> Return an array
> of errors or null

```
        return attrsInError.length ? attrsInError : null;
    },
    sync: function(method, model, options) {
```

> Sync to the server not implemented,
> so invoke success immediately

```
        options.success();
    }
});

    return EmployeeRecord;
});
```

Obviously, the main event in this model is the validation you're doing. In Backbone.js, you can validate any way you want. The only thing you have to do if you want to make your errors available outside the model is to return them from the model's `validate` method.

A.2.12 entrytemplate.html

You finally see the template for the employee's data in the following listing. This file is nothing more than a snippet of HTML with template markup embedded. These snippets of HTML are also called *partials* or *fragments*.

Listing A.12   entrytemplate.html

```
<button type="button" class="remove-entry">
    &#9587;
</button>

<%= lastName %>, <%= firstName %><br />

Title: <%= title %><br />
Phone: <%= phone %><br />
Email: <%= email %>
```

> <%=%> is the Underscore.js
> syntax to indicate where model
> data should be inserted

As you may remember from chapter 2, the `<%=%>` mark the spots where your model's data will be inserted. When the template engine "compiles" the template, it's just turning the text string into a reusable function for generating the resulting view. When the view is rendered, the model's property values are inserted for its final presentation state. Keep in mind that Backbone.js is open minded when it comes to template engines. I'm using Underscore.js here, but many more options are available. Another popular choice is Handlebars.

A.3   *Knockout example*

Your second POC (proof of concept) was created using Knockout, which is squarely in the MVVM camp. Although it excels at data binding, you'll have to seek out other frameworks/libraries (such as Durandal) to fill any other SPA needs you have. Knockout sticks mainly to what it's great at: binding. For those who'd rather not have a magic black-box solution to MV* and would rather take an a la carte approach, Knockout is a perfect choice. For this POC, you'll incorporate a few of the same extra-helper libraries that you used in our Backbone.js version.

A.3.1   *Downloading your dependencies*

Here's the list of what you need for this POC. If you've already downloaded some of these for the Backbone.js POC, there's no need to download them again. You can use them again here (see table A.2).

Table A.2   Dependencies for the Knockout version of the example

Framework/library	URL	Comments
Knockout	http://knockoutjs.com	As with Backbone.js, you can select either the minified (compact) version or the nonminified (readable) version. Remember, the readable version is only for understanding the source code and debugging. For deployment, always use the minified version.
Knockout Validation plugin	https://github.com/ Knockout-Contrib/ Knockout-Validation	Because Knockout doesn't come with any kind of validation functionality built in, you can either roll your own or use a plugin. Feel free to create your own if you prefer. For this example, you're using a popular plugin that's easy to use and devoted to validating your ViewModel's data.
jQuery	http://jquery.com	A great overall utility library that excels at DOM manipulation and event handling.
RequireJS	http://requirejs.org	I discuss RequireJS in chapter 3. For now, just know that it's used for asynchronous JavaScript module loading and dependency management. Using it, you'll create code using the AMD specification (also discussed in chapter 3). You're also using two RequireJS plugins: domReady.js, which makes sure the DOM is ready before your JavaScript code acts on it, and text.js, which asynchronously downloads templates. Both plugins can be found at http:// requirejs.org/docs/download.html.

A.3.2 Directory structure

As before, you'll keep the directory structures fairly similar among the three versions but use framework-specific folders where it makes sense (see figure A.3).

This directory structure is, again, by feature, as covered in chapter 1. Your feature is still a directory, and the rest of the structure represents a somewhat typical Knockout layout.

Figure A.3 Directory structure for the Knockout version of the application

A.3.3 The shell

In typical SPA fashion, your index.html welcome file, shown in the following listing, is almost bare. Its main features are the style-sheet reference, the shell DIV for the application, and the RequireJS entry to kick-start the application.

Listing A.13 index.html

```
<!DOCTYPE html>
<html>
<head>
    <link rel="stylesheet" href="app/css/default.css">      SPA's style sheets
    <link rel="stylesheet" href="app/css/entries.css">
    <!--[if IE]>
    <script>
        document.createElement("main");
    </script>                                                IE HTML5 fix
    <![endif]-->
</head>
<body>
    <main />
    <script                                                 RequireJS
        data-main="app/components/main.js"                  configuration file
        src="app/components/thirdParty/require.js">
    </script>                                               Reference to
</body>                                                      RequireJS itself
</html>
```

As with Backbone.js, you're using RequireJS to manage your dependencies for you.

A.3.4   *main.js*

This file provides the configuration preferences for RequireJS, as shown in the following listing. Here you define a base URL and the paths relative to that where RequireJS can download each file and assign an alias to that path.

Listing A.14   main.js—RequireJS configuration

```
"use strict";
requirejs.config({
    baseUrl: "app/components",          ◄────── Base URL for your SPA
    paths: {
        // third party
        jquery: "thirdParty/jquery.min",
        domReady: "thirdParty/domReady",      ◄────── File paths and their aliases
        text: "thirdParty/text",                     (relative to base URL)
        knockout : "thirdParty/knockout.min",
        knockout_validation: "thirdParty/knockout-validation.min",

        // application
        viewmodels : "directory/viewmodels",
        templates : "directory/templates",
        partials : "directory/partials",
    },
    shim : {                               Declare that the plugin requires
        "knockout_validation": {           Knockout to be loaded
            "deps": ["knockout"]    ◄──────
        }
    }
});                                    Kick-off point
                                       and dependencies
require([ "app" ], function(app) {   ◄──────
    app.init();
});
```

The shim section is a special RequireJSism for helping non-AMD modules play well with the AMD ones. It can also be used to define other load properties, such as dependencies. The last line is the starting point for the SPA. RequireJS makes sure that app.js is loaded before calling your application's init() function.

A.3.5   *app.js*

Your app.js file, shown next, loads the user's first viewable area with the SPA's first HTML content file. The file doesn't have to be called app.js, but that's a typical naming convention for the first real code file. Any kind of pre-application work or setup goes in this file.

Listing A.15   app.js

```
"use strict";
define([ "jquery",
"text!partials/directoryContent.html",        ◄────── text.js plugin used to download
    "viewmodels/directory", "domReady" ],              a non-JavaScript file
```

```
function($, directoryHTML, directoryViewModel, domReady) {

   function init() {
      $("main").html(directoryHTML);           ◀──  Use jQuery to insert
                                                     the downloaded HTML
      domReady(function() {                           fragment (partial)
         directoryViewModel.init();
      });
   }

   return {
      init: init
   };

}

);
```

RequireJS downloads all dependencies in your list to begin with. After the dependencies are in place, the application's init() function is called. Here, you use jQuery to insert your first HTML content. When the DOM is ready, you call the init() function inside your ViewModel's JavaScript model.

Because you're creating your RequireJS modules as singletons (only one instance), creating a function that doesn't get called repeatedly is a nice place to put your call to apply the ViewModel's bindings. It doesn't have to be called init(); that's just what I called it.

Remember, you want to apply bindings only once for any given DOM element. Unlike Backbone.js, where templates are re-created for each new data set, ViewModels normally live perpetually. Making the call to apply bindings multiple times leads to memory leaks, because you're replicating event handlers with each call.

TIP Call applyBindings() or applyBindingsWithValidation() only once per subtree inserted into the DOM to avoid duplicating event handlers.

A.3.6 *directoryContent.html*

Your HTML file, shown in the following listing, doesn't mix in any JavaScript, but as you can see, it's a little more verbose than the Backbone.js file. As in most of life, there's a trade-off: with Knockout, your JavaScript might be a little lighter, but adding the custom Knockout attributes (called *declarative bindings*) makes the HTML a little heftier.

Some people prefer cleaner code if the only trade-off is a little more verbose HTML. Others don't like the idea of attributes from the framework being added to the HTML. It's all subjective. But then again, that's why it's a good idea to do little POCs like this so you get hands-on experience with a few of your top choices and can decide what's right for you.

> **Listing A.16   directoryContent.html**

```html
<header>Directory</header>

<section class="entries" id="directoryContent">       ◀──  The input form
   <form name="entryForm">                                 for the application
```

```
<p>
   <label for="firstName">First Name:<br/>

     <input id="firstName" type="text"
       name="firstName" placeholder="First Name"
       data-bind="hasFocus: isFocused,
       value: entry.firstName, valueUpdate: 'afterkeydown'" />

     <span class="error-message"
       data-bind="validationMessage: entry.firstName">
     </span>
   </label>
</p>
<p>
   <label for="firstName">Last Name:<br/>
     <input id="firstName" type="text"
       name="firstName" placeholder="Last Name"
       data-bind="value: entry.lastName,
       valueUpdate: 'afterkeydown'" />

     <span class="error-message"
       data-bind="validationMessage: entry.lastName">
     </span>
   </label>
</p>
<p>
   <label for="title">title:<br/>
     <input id="title" type="text"
       name="title" placeholder="Title"
       data-bind="value: entry.title,
       valueUpdate: 'afterkeydown'" />

     <span class="error-message"
       data-bind="validationMessage: entry.title">
     </span>
   </label>
</p>
<p>
   <label for="title">Phone:<br/>
     <input id="phone" type="text"
       name="phone" placeholder="555-555-5555"
       data-bind="value: entry.phone,
       valueUpdate: 'afterkeydown'" />

     <span class="error-message"
       data-bind="validationMessage: entry.phone">
     </span>
   </label>
</p>
<p>
   <label for="email">Phone:<br/>
     <input id="email" type="text"
       name="email" placeholder="youremail@address.com"
       data-bind="value: entry.email, valueUpdate: 'afterkeydown'" />
     <span class="error-message"
```

Bind the ViewModel data form fields

Binding for the validation plugin's error message

```
                    data-bind="validationMessage: entry.email">
              </span>
           </label>
       </p>
       <p>
          <button id="add"
            data-bind="click: addEntry,
              enable: isValidForm" >Add</button>        ◀─────  Add a new entry to the list

          <button id="clear"
            data-bind="click: clearForm">Clear</button>  ◀─────  Clear the form
       </p>
       </form>

       <ul class="entry-list" id="entryList"
         data-bind="foreach: entries">
       </ul>
</section>
```

The HTML looks a little more verbose than it is, because I'm trying to fit it within the width of this book's page. When you try the source code, feel free to adjust the formatting so it's the way you like it.

A.3.7 *directory.js*

In this POC, the module containing your ViewModel has the most code (see the following listing). Not all ViewModels will be exactly like this. Some, dealing only with the data, might be small. Others, with lots of logic, might be large.

Listing A.17   directory.js

```
define([ "jquery", "knockout",
     "text!templates/entrytemplate.html", "domReady",
     "knockout_validation" ],

  function($, ko, entryHTML, domReady, validation) {

     var emptyString = "";
     var astMsg = "Required";
     var invMsg = "Invalid";                            Regular expressions
                                                        for validation
     var emailRegX = /^[a-z0-9!#$%&'*+\/=?^_`{|}~-]+(?  ◀
       :\.[a-z0-9!#$%&'*+\/=?^_`{|}~-]+)*@(?:[a-z0-9](?:
       [a-z0-9-]*[a-z0-9])?\.)+[a-z0-9](?:[a-z0-9-]*
       [a-z0-9])?$/i;

     var phoneRegX = /(?:\d{3}|\(\d{3}\))([-\/\.])\d{3}\1\d{4}/;

                                                        ViewModel observables use
     var directoryViewModel= function() {               validation plugin extenders
        var self = this;                            ◀
        self.entry = {
           firstName : ko.observable().extend({
              required : {
```

Start of the
ViewModel

```
            params : true,
            message : astMsg
         }
      }),
      lastName : ko.observable().extend({
         required : {
            params : true,
            message : astMsg
         }
      }),
      title : ko.observable().extend({
         required : {
            params : true,
            message : astMsg
         }
      }),
      phone : ko.observable().extend({
         customRegEx : {
            regX : phoneRegX,
            blankMsg : astMsg,
            invalidMsg : invMsg
         }
      }),
      email : ko.observable().extend({
         customRegEx : {
            regX : emailRegX,
            blankMsg : astMsg,
            invalidMsg : invMsg
         }
      })
   };

   self.entries = ko.observableArray();

   self.isFocused = ko.observable(false);

   self.addEntry = function(e) {

      var newEntry = {
         firstName : self.entry.firstName(),
         lastName : self.entry.lastName(),
         title : self.entry.title(),
         phone : self.entry.phone(),
         email : self.entry.email()
      };

      self.entries.push(newEntry);
      self.clearForm();
      self.isFocused(true);
   };

   self.isValidForm = ko.computed(function() {
      if (self.entry.firstName.isValid()
            && self.entry.lastName.isValid()
            && self.entry.title.isValid()
```

Custom extenders for email and phone

Observable array for entry list

Add new entries to list

computed observable for validation

```
                    && self.entry.phone.isValid()
                    && self.entry.email.isValid()) {
            return true;
        } else {
            return false;
        }
    }, this);

    self.removeEntry = function(entry) {                    Remove an entry
        self.entries.remove(entry);
    };

    self.clearForm = function() {
        self.entry.firstName(emptyString);                 Clear your form entries
        self.entry.lastName(emptyString);
        self.entry.title(emptyString);
        self.entry.phone(emptyString);
        self.entry.email(emptyString);
    };

}
                                                            So validation plugin doesn't
function getValidationConfig() {                            automatically add the validation text
    return {
        insertMessages : false
    };
}
                                                            Configuration for
function createCustomValidationRule() {                     custom extenders
    ko.validation.rules["customRegEx"] = {
        validator : function(userInput, ruleObj) {
            if (!userInput || userInput.length == 0) {
                this.message = ruleObj.blankMsg;
                return false;
            }
            if (!ruleObj.regX.test(userInput)) {
                this.message = ruleObj.invalidMsg;
                return false;
            }
            return true;
        },
    };
                                                            Register extenders
    ko.validation.registerExtenders();
}

function init() {                                           Add template
    $("#entryList").html(entryHTML);

    createCustomValidationRule();
                                                            Add custom validation
    domReady(function() {                                   (via extenders)
        ko.applyBindingsWithValidation(
            directoryViewModel,                             Apply binding
            $("#directoryContent")[0],
```

```
            getValidationConfig());
        });
    }
    ;

    return {
        init : init
    };

    }
);
```

Remember that in MVVM, the observable wrapper around the POJO (plain old Java-Script object) property establishes the magic link between it and the form. The entire first half of the ViewModel is the binding of your form's entry fields so you can interact with them.

The observables look a little different only because there's a little extra information in there to tell the validation plugin how the property should be validated. The required option is a validation type that comes with the plugin. The validation information for the phone and email are for a custom validator I built for this specific type of UI design. The plugin has some options for phone and email, but they weren't exactly what was needed. Fortunately, the plugin is extremely flexible, and you can create your own.

One thing I haven't talked about is a type of Knockout observable called a computed observable. This isn't specifically MVVM but rather Knockout-specific (though other MVVM frameworks may include this). This is just a fancy term to mean the value is derived programmatically, rather than as a straight assignment. This code determines whether the observable gets a value of true or false.

> **TIP** Use a computed observable if the value of the observable needs to be programmatically derived, rather than a simple assignment.

After the assignment portion of your ViewModel and the validation, you have some bindings to handle the adding and removing of list entries. You also have one to remove an entry for the list. The interesting part here is that the declarative part of the binding (attribute in the HTML) is doing the heavy lifting of looping through the list of values in your array and making sure the UI reflects its current state. You don't have to code that part yourself.

Thanks to the two-way syncing going on, Knockout keeps track of everything that's happening with your observable array and updates the DOM and the ViewModel accordingly. All you have to do is add and delete entries, and Knockout takes care of the rest. Neat, huh?

The section of code added to create the custom validation rule is specific to the validation plugin. You're following the rules from the website on how to define your own validator. You're telling the plugin that if the field is empty, it's invalid and to use the blank message (the word Required). If the field isn't blank but is still invalid, use the invalid message (the word Invalid).

The validator is robust. You can use a ton of other features in your own SPA. Follow the same link as the dependency download to learn more.

The last part of your module is its `init()` function. Remember, this code runs only once. That makes it ideal for any setup work. Here you're using jQuery to add the template to the DOM and apply your bindings. Normally, the Knockout function to call is `applyBindings()`, but with the validation plugin, you need to call `applyBindingsWithValidation()`. You're passing in three parameters: the ViewModel itself, the DOM node where the bindings should be applied, and the configuration for the validation plugin.

A.3.8   *entrytemplate.html*

Your last listing, shown next, is the template for the employee's data. This file is nothing more than a snippet of HTML with template markup embedded. These snippets of HTML are also called *partials* or *fragments*.

> **Listing A.18   entrytemplate.html**

```
<li class="entry">
   <button type="button" class="remove-entry"
     data-bind="click: removeEntry">
     &#9587;                                      ◄──  Removes the entry
   </button>

   <span data-bind="text: $data.lastName"></span>,
   <span data-bind="text: $data.firstName"></span><br />

   <span>Title:</span>
   <span data-bind="text: $data.title"></span><br />

   <span>Phone:</span>
   <span data-bind="text: $data.phone"></span> <br />

   <span>Email:</span>
   <span data-bind="text: $data.email"></span>
</li>
```

As with your Backbone.js template, this file is fairly simple. One stark difference with MVVM is the use of declarative bindings (special attributes). Remember that Backbone.js uses placeholders to mark where the template engine will insert data and create a new view. With MVVM, the template and the view are one and the same. The custom Knockout attributes link this section of the DOM with properties from the ViewModel. Knockout handles the data sync going on under the covers.

A.4   *AngularJS example*

One thing you'll notice immediately about AngularJS is the reduction in the number of files you need. One reason is all the out-of-the-box magic that comes with the framework.

A.4.1 *Downloading your dependencies*

One thing you won't be using with AngularJS is RequireJS. In the pre-version-2 Angular-JS, the framework has its own proprietary module system. So to keep things in line with "the Angular way," you'll use AngularJS modules (see table A.3). This also further reduces the number of dependencies.

Table A.3 Dependencies for the AngularJS version of the example

Framework/library	URL	Comments
AngularJS	https://angularjs.org	Because it's an all-in-one system, this download covers most MV* requirements you have.
jQuery	http://jquery.com	A great overall utility library that excels at DOM manipulation and event handling.

> **NOTE**   AngularJS comes with a subset of jQuery called *jqLite*. If jQuery isn't present, AngularJS falls back on its own version; otherwise, the full jQuery is used.

A.4.2 *Directory structure*

Figure A.4 illustrates your nominal directory with AngularJS. Even using AngularJS, you can still have a "by feature" directory structure.

A.4.3 *The shell*

Again, your index.html file (see listing A.19) is minimal. Notice, however, that in the AngularJS version you need to define where the overall SPA begins by using the ng-app directive. Remember that directives are special HTML attributes that tell AngularJS what you want to do. From the AngularJS documentation:

> *Use this directive to auto-bootstrap an AngularJS application. The* ngApp *directive designates the root element of the application and is typically placed near the root element of the page—for example, on the* <body> *or* <html> *tags.*

```
app
  components
    directory
      controllers
        controllers.js
      partials
        directoryContent.html
      templates
        entrytemplate.html
  thirdParty
    angular.min.js
    jquery.min.js
  app.js
  css
    default.css
    entries.css
index.html
```

Figure A.4 Directory structure for the AngularJS version of the application

---

Listing A.19   index.html

```html
<html ng-app="DirectoryApp">

<head>
<link rel="stylesheet" href="app/css/default.css">
<link rel="stylesheet" href="app/css/entries.css">
</head>
<body>
```

Define where the application begins

```
<main id="directoryShell"
    class="container"
    ng-include
    src="'app/components/directory/partials/directoryContent.html'">
</main>

<script src="app/components/thirdParty/jquery.min.js"></script>
<script src="app/components/thirdParty/angular.min.js"></script>
<script src="app/components/app.js"></script>
<script src="app/components/directory/controllers/controllers.js"></
    script>

</body>
</html>
```

Directive to dynamically fetch the file

You're also using an AngularJS directive to tell AngularJS to dynamically fetch your SPA content for your shell.

One thing to take note of here with your index.html page is that AngularJS will manage only its own JavaScript modules. If you have other third-party libraries to include, you'll need to use a standard SCRIPT tag.

A.4.4 *app.js*

Your app.js file, shown next, is miniscule. There seem to be a million different ways to structure your AngularJS code. Feel free to do things your own way. Despite being a magic framework, AngularJS is flexible on this point.

Listing A.20   app.js

```
angular.module("DirectoryApp", [
  "DirectoryApp.controllers"
]);
```

Your single dependency

As mentioned, there are many ways to configure your AngularJS project. For larger projects, keep modules in separate source files. This makes development and maintenance much easier. In chapter 9, I discuss build processes to minify and combine your files into as few files as possible. For this simple application, you didn't need to do anything elaborate.

A.4.5 *directoryContent.html*

Like your Knockout content, the AngularJS version is verbose, as you can see in the next listing. You're using a lot of built-in AngularJS directives to take care of some of the plumbing for your UI's behavior.

Listing A.21   directoryContent.html

```
<header>Directory</header>

<section class="entries"
  ng-controller="DirectoryController">
```

Context for your controller

```
<form name="entryForm">

    <p>
        <label for="firstName">First Name:<br/>
            <input id="firstName" name="firstName" type="text"
            ng-model="formEntry.firstName"
            required placeholder="First Name"/>
```

ng-model binds the input field with the model

```
            <span class="error-message"
            ng-show="entryForm.firstName.$error.required">
            Required
            </span>
        </label>
    </p>
    <p>
        <label for="lastName">Last Name:<br />
            <input name="lastName" id="lastName" type="text"
            ng-model="formEntry.lastName"
            required placeholder="Last Name"/>

            <span class="error-message"
            ng-show="entryForm.lastName.$error.required">
            Required
            </span>
        </label>
    </p>
    <p>
        <label for="title">Title:<br />
            <input name="title" id="title" type="text"
            ng-model="formEntry.title"
            required placeholder="Title"/>
            <span class="error-message"
            ng-show="entryForm.title.$error.required">
            Required
            </span>
        </label>
    </p>
    <p>
        <label for="phone">Phone:<br/>
            <input name="phone" id="phone"
            ng-pattern="phoneRegX"
            type="text"
            ng-model="formEntry.phone"
            required placeholder="555-555-5555"/>

            <span class="error-message"
            ng-show="entryForm.phone.$error.required">
            Required
            </span>
```

Different validation message for invalid input

```
            <span class="error-message"
            ng-show="entryForm.phone.$error.pattern">
            Invalid
            </span>
        </label>
```

Display the errors related to required fields

```
            </p>
            <p>
                <label for="email">Email:<br />
                    <input name="email" id="email" type="email"
                      ng-model="formEntry.email"
                      required placeholder="youremail@address.com"/>

                    <span class="error-message"
                      ng-show="entryForm.email.$error.required">
                      Required
                    </span>

                    <span class="error-message"
                      ng-show="entryForm.email.$error.email">
                      Invalid
                    </span>
                </label>
            </p>
            <p>
                <button id="add"
                  ng-click="addEntry(formEntry)"
                  ng-disabled="entryForm.$invalid">
                  Add
                </button>

                <button id="clear"
                  ng-click="clearForm()">
                  Clear
                </button>
            </p>
        </form>

    <ul class="entry-list"
      ng-include
      src="'app/components/directory/templates/entrytemplate.html'">
    </ul>
</section>
```

Different validation message for invalid input →

Enable button if all form entries are valid, add the entry ←

Clear the form ←

Again, the HTML looks a little more verbose than it is, because I'm trying to fit it within the width of this book. It uses directives to do everything you did in the Backbone.js and Knockout versions. The `ng-model` is for the value binding, and `ng-click` is for the button clicks. For validation, you needed to add only the `required` keyword to tell AngularJS that the model is invalid if this field is empty.

Errors are tied to a particular model binding, so you can show/hide what's in your span tag by using a combination of the `ng-show` directive and `$error`. The keyword after `$error` is the type of validation that should trigger `ng-show`. In this case, the span with `required` will show when a required value is missing, and the span with `invalid` will show when a value the user types doesn't match the pattern.

A.4.6 *entrytemplate.html*

The following listing shows your template. As with the other two MV* examples, this file is a snippet of HTML (also referred to as a *partial* or *fragment*).

Listing A.22   entrytemplate.html

```
<li class="entry" ng-repeat="entry in entries">

    <button type="button" class="remove-entry"
      ng-click="removeEntry(entry)">
      &#9587;
    </button>

    {{entry.lastName}}, {{entry.firstName}}<br />

    Title: {{entry.title}}<br />
    Phone: {{entry.phone}}<br />
    Email: {{entry.email}}

</li>
```

Repeat binding for
your list of entries

Remove the entry
when clicked

{{}} indicate where model
data should be inserted

Like Backbone.js, placeholders mark where the framework will insert the data. You don't have to worry about writing any template instructions in your code, though. This is another facet of the process that's magically taken care of by AngularJS.

Finally, the following listing illustrates the controller for your application.

Listing A.23   controllers.js

```
angular.module("DirectoryApp.controllers", [])
.controller("DirectoryController", function($scope) {

    $scope.phoneRegX
    = /(?:\d{3}|\(\d{3}\))([-\/\.])\d{3}\1\d{4}/;

    $scope.entries = [];

    $scope.addEntry = function(entryToAdd) {
        $scope.errorMsg = "";
        $scope.entries.push(angular.copy(entryToAdd));
        $scope.clearForm();
    };

    $scope.removeEntry = function(entryToRemove) {
        var index = $scope.entries.indexOf(entryToRemove);
        $scope.entries.splice(index, 1);
    };

    $scope.clearForm = function() {
        $scope.entryForm.$setPristine();
        $scope.formEntry = '';
    };

});
```

Regular expression for
phone (email built in)

Array to hold
your entries

Add entries when
Add button clicked

Remove the entry
from the list

Clear the form, set back to pristine
(clean) state, clear the model

Remember that with AngularJS, your `$scope` is similar to a ViewModel.

A.5   Summary

The sample code in this appendix shows you not only how to approach your own POCs but also how differences in philosophies change the balance of where more verbosity lies, when it comes to model-to-view translation: the HTML or the JavaScript.

appendix B
Review of the
XMLHttpRequest API

This appendix covers

- A review of the XMLHttpRequest API
- The building of an XHR data source module

In this appendix, you'll review the low-level API for making a server call. In a real-world application, you'll likely rely on your MV* framework for XHR calls if it has this capability built in or a helper library such as jQuery if it doesn't. These frameworks and libraries often abstract away much of the boilerplate code and provide you with simple, easy-to-use methods instead. Even so, it's good to have at least a general idea of what's going on under the covers. That's why I'll stick with vanilla JavaScript here, so you can see basic XHR mechanics at work. I'll also *not* be using RESTful calls here, just to keep things fairly straightforward.

B.1 Using the XMLHttpRequest object

When you hear someone talk about making an *AJAX call*, they're usually talking about making an XHR call (*XHR* is short for *XMLHttpRequest*). *AJAX* (or Ajax) is short for *Asynchronous JavaScript and XML* and generally refers to using JavaScript to dynamically update a web page with the results of an XHR call. This section focuses solely on the XMLHttpRequest part of AJAX.

As I mentioned in chapter 1, the XMLHttpRequest functionality was originally created by developers at Microsoft. Eventually, it became a standard API with implementations in all the major browsers. This standard allows you to create an instance of the XMLHttpRequest object by using simple JavaScript, and the object will behave similarly across most modern browsers.

You start by creating an instance of the object. As long as the user is using a browser that supports the API, this one line of code is all you need to create the object:

```
var xhrObj = new XMLHttpRequest();
```

If you need to support Microsoft Internet Explorer prior to version 7, you should wrap your object's creation in a check for the XMLHttpRequest object and use an ActiveX object if the XMLHttpRequest object is not available. Microsoft recommends this approach:

```
function createXHRObject() {
    if (window.XMLHttpRequest) {
        return new XMLHttpRequest();
    }
    else {
        return new ActiveXObject("Microsoft.XMLHTTP");
    }
}
```

With an instance of the object created, you can now make an asynchronous request to your server.

B.2   *Making requests*

After you've created an instance of the XHR object, you can use its events, methods, and properties to customize your server call. The following is a list of the XHR concepts demonstrated in this section:

- onreadystatechange—This event fires when the state of the call changes. You assign your own function to handle this event. The most common use of this event is to see whether the call has completed. If so, you can subsequently check whether it succeeded or failed and react accordingly.
- open—This method assigns the request method and URL for the call. Many request methods exist, but not all of them may be supported by the technology you're using on the server. In chapter 7, we're using only GET, POST, PUT, and DELETE.
- setRequestHeader—With this method, you can specify the request headers for the request, such as the type of content you're sending and the type of content you'll accept in the response.
- send—This method fires the request. For requests that don't need a body, such as a GET request, you can pass in null or use the overloaded version of this

function that takes no parameters (this is the preferred approach). Otherwise, you use this method's parameter to pass data for the request body.

- readyState—This is the property you'll check when the onreadystate event fires to let you know what state the call is in. The readyState property has five basic values: 0 (UNSENT), 1 (OPENED), 2 (HEADERS_RECEIVED), 3 (LOADING), and 4 (DONE). For most situations, you'll need only to check for a value of 4 to make sure the call has finished.

- status—You'll check this property when the call completes to see whether it succeeded or failed. Status codes in the 400s and 500s represent errors. You can find a complete list of the status codes at www.w3.org/Protocols/rfc2616/rfc2616-sec10.html.

- responseText—This property contains the response body as a string. For JSON calls with no errors, the JSON text will be found here. In an error situation, it's up to the creators of the server-side code to determine what's written in the response body.

- responseXML—This property contains a Document object if the response can be parsed as XML or HTML. Otherwise, this property is null.

I'm covering only the basics here, but a full listing of the XMLHttpRequest API can be found at www.w3.org/TR/XMLHttpRequest.

B.2.1 Using URL parameters

When retrieving information using a request with a simple payload or no payload at all, the GET method is a good choice. In this type of request, no body is sent. Instead, URL parameters are appended to the URL itself when information needs to be sent. In our first example (see listing B.1), you'll use a simple GET request with a single URL parameter (the ID of the shopping cart) to retrieve the contents of a shopping cart.

In the shopping cart application for chapter 7, you use AngularJS to bind the data returned to the view. Here, you write things out to the console to get a better understanding of what's going on with each request.

Listing B.1   XHR call using GET and URL parameters

```
function getCart(){
    var xhrObj = createXHRObject();

    xhrObj.onreadystatechange = function () {

        if (xhrObj.readyState == 4) {
            var response = "\nreadyState: "
            + xhrObj.readyState
            + "\nstatus: " + xhrObj.status
            + "\nstatusText: " + xhrObj.statusText
            + "\nresponseText: " + xhrObj.responseText;

            if (xhrObj.status == 200) {
                response = "Success:" + response;
```

Create the XHR object

Do something only if the state has changed to 4 (complete)

Prefix console text with Success for an OK status (200); otherwise, Error

```
                      } else {
                          response = "Error:" + response;
                      }

                      console.log(response);

              }
          };
```

Define request as a GET and include the URL parameter cartId

```
      xhrObj.open("GET",
      "/SPA/controllers/shopping/getCart?cartId=123",
      true);
```

Make the request

```
      xhrObj.setRequestHeader("Accept", "application/json");
```

Tell server you're interested in JSON as the format of the response

```
      xhrObj.send();
}
```

After the request completes, the following information prints to the console:

```
Success:
readyState: 4
status: 200
statusText: OK
```

The readyState is 4 for complete, and the status of your call is 200/OK. You can also look at the Network tab in the developer tools of your browser to confirm the request URL and the request headers (see figure B.1).

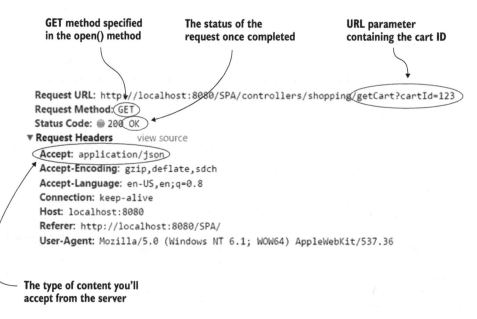

Figure B.1 Your request to get the shopping cart contents is successful. You use a GET request, passing a cart ID of 123 via a URL parameter.

While you're in the developer tools of the browser, you can also see the server's output in the console (see figure B.2).

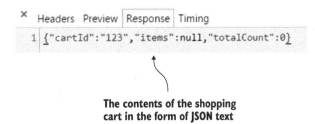

Looking at the response in the Network tab, you can see that you don't have any items in your cart.

To add a game to the shopping cart, you need

The contents of the shopping cart in the form of JSON text

Figure B.2 The server responds with your shopping cart's JSON-formatted text. You can see that the cart has no items.

only the cart ID and the ID of the game. You could continue to use URL parameters, but sending a more complex request payload might be a better choice. To send a more complex payload, you'll need to rely on the request body.

B.2.2 Using the request body

When you add a new item to your shopping cart, you'd like to send an object in the request. For this request, you'll convert your JavaScript request object into a JSON string and pass that via the request body. The following listing illustrates this technique.

Listing B.2 XHR call using POST and the request body

```
function updateCart() {
    var xhrObj = new XMLHttpRequest();

    xhrObj.onreadystatechange = function () {

        if (xhrObj.readyState == 4) {
            var response = "\nreadyState: "
            + xhrObj.readyState
            + "\nstatus: " + xhrObj.status
            + "\nstatusText: " + xhrObj.statusText;
            + "\nresponseText: " + xhrObj.responseText;

            // 200 is OK
            if (xhrObj.status == 200) {
                response = "Success:" + response;
            } else {
                response = "Error:" + response;
            }

            console.log(response);

    };
    xhrObj.open("POST",
    "/SPA/controllers/shopping/addToCart",
    true);

    xhrObj.setRequestHeader("Accept", "application/json");
```

Create the XHR object

Do something only if the state has changed to 4 (complete)

Prefix console text with Success for an OK status (200); otherwise, Error

Define request as a POST

Tell server you're interested in JSON as the format of the response

Tell the server to expect JSON in request

```
xhrObj.setRequestHeader("Content-Type", "application/json");

var cartRequestObj = {
        cartId : "123",
        itemNum : "madden_nfl_15"
};

var cartRequestString = JSON.stringify(cartRequestObj);

xhrObj.send(cartRequestString);
}
```

Create the JavaScript request object

Convert the JavaScript object into JSON-formatted text

Pass the JSON text in the request body

NOTE   JSON.js can be used as a polyfill for the JSON object if older browsers must be supported.

Looking at the code, you'll see that this time you're using POST for your request method so you can use the request body. You're then using the JavaScript method JSON.stringify() to transform your JavaScript object into JSON-formatted text. Next, you pass the text into the send() method of your XHR object so the payload is sent in the body of the request.

Another thing to note is that this time, because you're sending JSON, you need to specify that as another request header. Let's see what the request looks like now in your Network tab (see figure B.3).

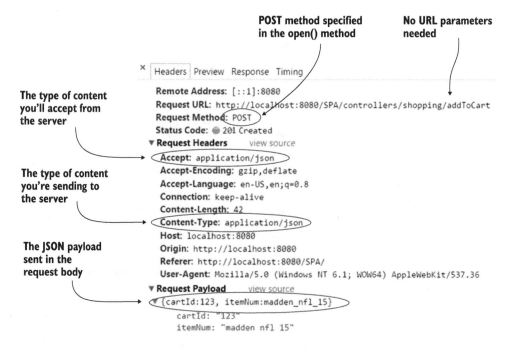

Figure B.3   You use the POST method to send complex request objects in the form of JSON-formatted text to the server from your SPA.

On the server, the code is written so that the entire cart is returned each time an addition or update is made. Checking the returned JSON, you can see that you have the item with the ID `madden_nfl_15` in the cart (see figure B.4).

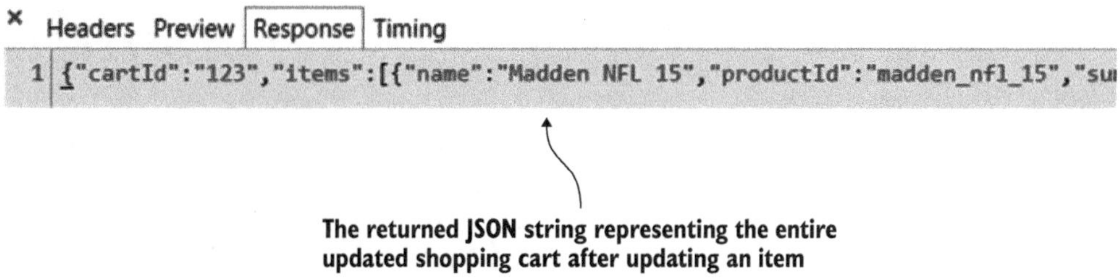

× Headers Preview | Response | Timing

1 | {"cartId":"123","items":[{"name":"Madden NFL 15","productId":"madden_nfl_15","su

The returned JSON string representing the entire updated shopping cart after updating an item

Figure B.4 After the new item is posted to the server, you have one game in your shopping cart.

appendix C
Chapter 7 server-side setup and summary

This appendix covers

- Working with server objects and tasks
- Setting up Spring MVC for the chapter 7 project
- Using Spring annotations in the chapter 7 project

As mentioned in chapter 7, you can choose to use any server-side technology you want for the end-of-the-chapter project. If you're interested in setting up Spring MVC for that project, this appendix provides details. It also covers the annotations used. The complete code is available for download.

In case you decide to use a completely different tech stack, this appendix also summarizes the task(s) each call is performing so it's easier to make the translation. Keep in mind that the project uses RESTful services, so the back-end technology you use must support REST either directly or indirectly via a third-party library/plugin.

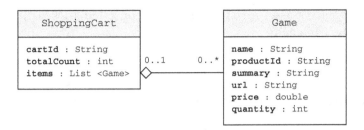

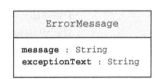

Figure C.1 The shopping cart has a list of items that holds a number of games ranging from 0 to *n*.

Figure C.2 The ErrorMessage object is used to relay errors back to the UI.

C.1   Server-side objects

Only two data objects are used in the project: a ShoppingCart object and a Game object. Each shopping cart holds a collection of games (see figure C.1). The Game object is standalone and can be used independently of the ShoppingCart object.

You also use an object on the server to hold information about any errors that occur (see figure C.2). The message field is for any error that's OK to display to the user. In addition to any server-side exception handling, exceptions are sent back to the UI in the exceptionText field.

Now let's summarize the calls that are made to the server. We'll do this before talking about Spring MVC. This will make it easier to digest what the back end is doing, regardless of the back-end technology you use.

C.2   Summary of server-side calls

This section generalizes the tasks the server is performing for a service call. I'll state the URL format, any object(s) used in the request and response, and a brief summary of what the server code does in each case.

C.2.1   Viewing the cart

This call is invoked whenever the user clicks the View Cart link. The braces { } indicate a path variable that contains the cart ID requested. Table C.1 contains its properties.

Table C.1 Call to get the cart identified by the path variable

URL	HTTP method	Request	Response
/shopping/carts/{cartId}	GET	Empty	Cart

Task list:

- *Get cart from memory*—If a cart is found in your static map that matches the requested cart ID, your code will return the matching cart. If there's no match, a new cart is created and added to the map of carts.

■ *Return the cart as JSON*—The retrieved cart is converted back to JSON and returned to the front end.

C.2.2   *Adding an item to the cart*

When a product item is added, you use the POST HTTP request, passing your cart ID and the ID of the product item. Table C.2 contains the call properties.

Table C.2   Call to add a product item for a given cart

URL	HTTP method	Request	Response
/shopping/carts/{cartId}/products/{productId}	POST	Empty	Cart

Task list:

■ *Add the item*—The cart is first checked to see whether the product being added from the product display view exists already in the cart. If it does, the count of the existing product is incremented by 1. If not, a new Game object instance is created by getting the requested game from the inventory. The total item count is also updated.

■ *Update the cart in memory*—The shopping cart in memory is updated to reflect the new state of the cart.

■ *Return the cart as JSON*—The retrieved cart with the updated product list and any quantity changes is converted back to JSON and returned to the front end.

C.2.3   *Updating the cart*

This call is used to update an existing product. Any update will submit the entire cart to the back end. Table C.3 contains the call properties.

Table C.3   Call to update the cart identified by the path variable

URL	HTTP method	Request	Response
/shopping/carts/{cartId}	PUT	Cart	Cart

Task list:

■ *Update quantities*—The entire cart is sent for an update. Because a scaled-down version of the cart is generated from the $scope of the shopping cart view, any missing information is regenerated from the static inventory list that's on the server. The total item count is also updated.

■ *Update the cart in memory*—The shopping cart in memory is updated to reflect the new state of the cart.

■ *Return the cart as JSON*—The retrieved cart with the updated item list and any quantity changes is converted back to JSON and returned to the front end.

C.2.4 Deleting an item

When an item is deleted, you identify both the cart and the item in the URL. You don't need to send any objects in the request body, because the resource to delete is perfectly identifiable using only the URL. Table C.4 contains the call properties.

Table C.4   Call to delete the item identified by the path variable

URL	HTTP method	Request	Response
/shopping/carts/{cartId}/products/ {productId}	DELETE	Empty	Cart

Task list:

- *Get cart from memory*—You use the information in the URL to get the cart from memory.
- *Delete the item*—In this call, you iterate over the items in the cart in memory until you find a match with the product ID in the URL. When the match is found, the item is removed.
- *Update cart total*—After the item is removed, the item count is recalculated.
- *Return the cart as JSON*—The retrieved cart with the updated item list and any quantity changes is converted back to JSON and returned to the front end.

Chapter 7 focused on only the shopping cart transactions to illustrate the concepts. In the project, you make a couple of other calls. From the product search view, the user can search for a game. When a game is found, it can be added to the cart via the button in the product display view.

C.2.5 Searching for a product

On the product search view, the user types in a search term. This search term is a simple string that can be the entire game title or just part of it (see table C.5).

Table C.5   Call to search for a game

URL	HTTP method	Request	Response
/games/search/{srchTerm}	GET	Empty	List of Game objects

Task list:

- *Search*—The search term from the URL path is compared with all the game titles in your inventory for at least a partial match. The number of matches can range from 0 to *n*. This call returns a list of Game objects as a result.
- *Return the list as JSON*—The retrieved list of games is returned as JSON to the UI.

C.2.6   *Displaying a product*

After a list of search results is presented, the user clicks a title to display its information (see table C.6).

Table C.6   Call to display the selected game's information

URL	HTTP method	Request	Response
/games/id/{productId}	GET	Empty	Game

Task list:

- *Retrieve game by ID*—In this call, the product ID is passed in the URL. The code behind the call uses the ID to find the matching game in your inventory.
- *Return the cart as JSON*—The retrieved game is returned as JSON to the UI.

C.3   *The project*

This section covers the server-side technologies used in our project and walks through the setup of Spring MVC. It also covers the Spring annotations used in our project.

C.3.1   *Prerequisites*

Feel free to substitute any particular technology with another if you already work with something else and would prefer it. This list was used to create the example:

- *Apache Tomcat*—Tomcat is a freely available server that supports Java EE.[1] Version 7 supports the Servlet 3.0 specification, which matches the needs for our server application (though higher versions should work as well). This version of Tomcat supports the Servlet 3.0 specification. You can download it from http:// tomcat.apache.org. Feel free to use something else if you prefer a different server, as long as it supports the Servlet 3.0 specification.
- *Apache Maven 3.2.1 or later*—Apache Maven is a software management tool. It can be found at http://maven.apache.org.

The following dependencies are managed by Maven:

- *Spring 4.1.6* (Core + MVC)—Spring (https://spring.io) is a Java-based application framework and inversion-of-control container. If you need to download the software directly, go to http://repo.spring.io/release/org/springframework/ spring to see a list of versions available for download.
- *Jackson*—Jackson is a fast, lightweight JSON parser. It'll also work by default with Spring MVC. The example uses version 2.5.3. It can be found at http://wiki .fasterxml.com/JacksonDownload.

---

[1] Tomcat supports only the Web Profile part of the Java EE specification, but this is enough for what you need here. Servers such as GlassFish, JBoss, WebLogic, and WebSphere support the whole specification.

- *Commons Logging* (required by Spring)—See http://commons.apache.org/ proper/commons-logging for more information. Download from http:// commons.apache.org/proper/commons-logging/download_logging.cgi. Version 1.2 is used in the example.

- *Commons Lang* (optional)—Lang is a suite of helper utilities, particularly useful for string manipulation. Version 3.4 is used, but 3 or higher is fine: http:// commons.apache.org/proper/commons-lang. Lang isn't a hard requirement. It's used in the code for convenience, but you can use vanilla Java instead.

It's also worth mentioning that Java version 8 is used. If you use a later version of any of the listed technologies, make sure that it's compatible with whichever versions of Java and Tomcat you're using.

Before you can get the application up and running, you need to work on configuring Spring MVC. Fortunately, the setup is minimal, because you won't be using a database or consuming any external web services.

C.3.2 *Spring MVC configuration*

To begin, you need to create a dynamic web project in your IDE. If you're using Eclipse, import the project and you're ready to go. If you're using another IDE, you can create a new dynamic web project in your IDE and copy the code from this archive. You can find everything you need, including pom.xml, in the downloadable source for chapter 7. See the readme.txt file for additional installation instructions.

After the workspace is set up, you can begin your configuration. In Spring 2.5.6 or higher, you can use either XML or Java classes for configuration. This example uses Java configuration. This is purely a design choice. Feel free to use XML configuration if you prefer (or mix the two). Starting with the Servlet 3.0 specification, you no longer even need a web.xml file, so this file isn't necessary. It's included in this case only to fulfill the Maven plugin's needs. Remember, though, your container also has to support this configuration. Check the documentation for the server you're using.

In our example, you'll go that route to keep your configuration code to a minimum. To get your web application up and running without a web.xml file, you need a class that implements the `WebApplicationInitializer` interface. This interface is available in Spring 3.1 or later. The following listing shows the class that implements this interface. The package it's placed in isn't important. It'll be detected automatically.

Listing C.1 WebAppInitializer.java

```
public class WebAppInitializer implements WebApplicationInitializer {

    @Override
    public void onStartup(ServletContext container)
    throws ServletException {                          ⟵ Web application context
                                                          and annotation support
        AnnotationConfigWebApplicationContext ctx
        = new AnnotationConfigWebApplicationContext();
```

```
            ctx.register(WebMvcConfig.class);                    ◄──── Register your class
Set the servlet   ctx.setServletContext(container);                   for MVC configuration
context for this
application        Dynamic dynamic
            = container.addServlet("dispatcher",
            new DispatcherServlet(ctx));              ◄──── Register the dispatcher servlet

            dynamic.addMapping("/controllers/*");     ◄──── Map all requests beginning with/
                                                            controllers/ (after root) with dispatcher
            dynamic.setLoadOnStartup(1);
        }
    }
```

All of your requests from the front end will come through Spring MVC's dispatcher servlet. To configure things purely in Java, without a web.xml file, you implement the WebApplicationInitializer interface and provide the implementation for the onStartup method. Spring hands the correct servlet context to this method. It's where you define any bootstrap code to be executed during the servlet container's start-up. You also need to let Spring know which class will be handling your MVC preferences. Listing C.1 defines WebMvcConfig as your MVC configuration class. The following listing contains its code.

Listing C.2 WebMvcConfig.java

```
                                    ┌─ Specify this is a configuration class
@Configuration
@EnableWebMvc                       ◄──┘
@ComponentScan(basePackages =
    { "com.gamestore.controllers", "com.gamestore.dataservices" })  ◄──┐
public class WebMvcConfig {}                                           │
                                          Enable component scanning ───┘
                                          for these packages
```

Enable Spring MVC →

Because you've defined WebMvcConfig as the MVC configuration class, you decorate it as such by using the @Configuration annotation. The class itself has no body. The real magic comes from the annotation @EnableWebMvc. This annotation sets up the Spring MVC defaults. If you need to override any of the defaults, you can implement WebMvc-Configurer in this configuration class and override any of its methods. Alternatively, Spring provides WebMvcConfigurerAdapter as a convenience to avoid having to implement all 16 WebMvcConfigurer methods. For your purposes, you need only a basic Spring MVC configuration so you'll use WebMvcConfigurerAdapter.

Finally, you use the @ComponentScan annotation to tell Spring where to look for the other components used in the application. You have controller components in the controllers package and a single service component in the data services package. You'll learn about both in the next section.

Figure C.3 shows your IDE's workspace with the complete project configured and ready to run.

C.3.3 *Annotations used in our project*

We've already discussed the annotations used in your Spring MVC setup. This section covers the other annotations you're using in your controllers and your service. To show the annotations in action, you'll use the shopping cart controller. You'll start at the class level and then work your way down to the method level.

CLASS-LEVEL ANNOTATIONS USED BY THE CONTROLLER

Your shopping cart controller class is decorated with two annotations: @RestController and @Request-Mapping (see the following listing). In Spring MVC, more than one can be used in combination.

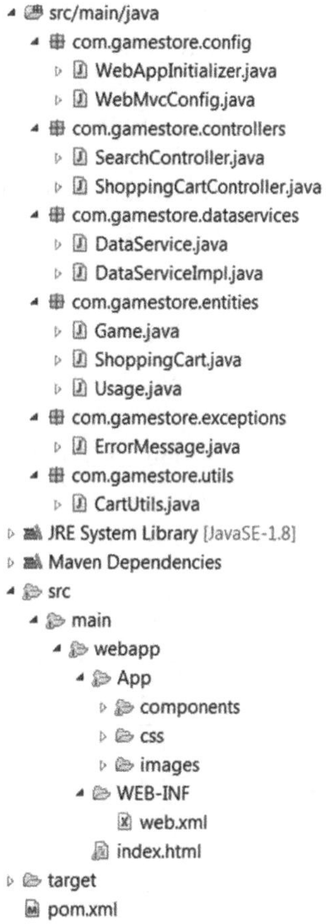

```
▲ 🖭 src/main/java
  ▲ ⊞ com.gamestore.config
    ▷ 🗋 WebAppInitializer.java
    ▷ 🗋 WebMvcConfig.java
  ▲ ⊞ com.gamestore.controllers
    ▷ 🗋 SearchController.java
    ▷ 🗋 ShoppingCartController.java
  ▲ ⊞ com.gamestore.dataservices
    ▷ 🗋 DataService.java
    ▷ 🗋 DataServiceImpl.java
  ▲ ⊞ com.gamestore.entities
    ▷ 🗋 Game.java
    ▷ 🗋 ShoppingCart.java
    ▷ 🗋 Usage.java
  ▲ ⊞ com.gamestore.exceptions
    ▷ 🗋 ErrorMessage.java
  ▲ ⊞ com.gamestore.utils
    ▷ 🗋 CartUtils.java
  ▷ ➡️ JRE System Library [JavaSE-1.8]
  ▷ ➡️ Maven Dependencies
  ▲ 📂 src
    ▲ 📂 main
      ▲ 📂 webapp
        ▲ 📂 App
          ▷ 📂 components
          ▷ 📂 css
          ▷ 📂 images
        ▲ 📂 WEB-INF
            🗙 web.xml
          📄 index.html
  ▷ 📂 target
  📄 pom.xml
```

Figure C.3   Complete project workspace

Listing C.3   Class-level annotations

```
                              ┌─ Applies @Controller and
                              │  @ResponseBody under the covers
@RestController          ◀────┘
@RequestMapping("/shopping")             ◀─── All URLs beginning (after the root) with
public class ShoppingCartController {          "/shopping" routed to this controller
```

The @RestController is a convenience annotation. It's the same as adding the annotations @Controller and @ResponseBody to the class.

The @Controller annotation lets Spring MVC know that this class is a controller and has methods to handle requests. With this annotation present, Spring MVC will scan your methods for request mapping annotations. We'll cover these shortly.

The @ResponseBody is used when you want the object returned in your method to be bound to the response body of the call. This annotation can be applied either at the class level or at the method level. When this annotation is added at the class level, every method in the controller follows this behavior, so it can be omitted at the method level. When your shopping cart objects are returned, they'll be sent back to the UI via the response body. Additionally, with the Jackson library in your classpath, it'll automatically convert them to JSON-formatted text.

The @RequestMapping annotation maps incoming requests to particular classes and/or methods. It can decorate the class, the method, or both. In the case of your shopping cart, it's defined at both places. This creates a kind of hierarchy in the request that's being mapped. The annotation defined at the class level maps this entire class to any URL that begins (after the root) with the string /shopping.

The @RequestMapping annotation elsewhere in your controller maps the other part of the request URL after /shopping with a particular method. I'll discuss these in the next section.

METHOD-LEVEL ANNOTATIONS

To see method-level annotations in action, you'll use your shopping cart update. It contains the gamut of annotations used in all of the methods (see the following listing).

Listing C.4   Method-level annotations

```
@RequestMapping(                                    ◄——— Maps a URL and request
    value = "/carts/{cartId}",                            type to this method
    method = RequestMethod.PUT)
public ResponseEntity<ShoppingCart> updateCart(
    @RequestBody ShoppingCart cart,        ◄——— Binds the request body to the cart parameter
    @PathVariable String cartId,
    HttpServletRequest request) throws Exception {   ◄——— Maps the path variable cartId to
                                                           the cartId method parameter

    authenticateRequest(request, cartId);

    ShoppingCart newCart = dataService.updateQuantities(cart);

    return new ResponseEntity<ShoppingCart>(newCart, HttpStatus.OK);
}
```

Decorating the method itself, you have the @RequestMapping annotation again. Its value is the part of the URL that's used to map the request to this specific method. With this annotation already defined at the class level with part of the URL, the full path for this method is /shopping/carts/{cartId}.

You'll also notice that, just as in the UI, you can define URL path parameters. They're denoted with brackets {} and correspond to method parameters decorated with the @PathVariable annotation. Finally, in @RequestMapping, you're defining the HTTP request method as PUT, because this is an update to your shopping cart.

@RequestMapping and @PathVariable allow you to easily define resources in the URL path through path variables and the type of HTTP request method for the method. As mentioned in chapter 7, the unique resource identifiers in the URL paths and the HTTP request methods that define the action requested come together to create a RESTful request.

The other method-level annotation you're using here is `@RequestBody`. It binds the method parameter decorated with it to the object being sent in the body of the request. In the case of a cart update, the entire shopping cart is being sent in the request body. This annotation binds it to the `ShoppingCart` parameter. Because you have the Jackson library in your classpath, Spring automatically converts the JSON-formatted text of the request body to a native Java `ShoppingCart` object.

You always hope that your calls will succeed, but in case there's an error, you can rely on annotations to turn the exception thrown into a meaningful response.

EXCEPTION-HANDLING ANNOTATIONS

Another part of the REST architecture is defining HTTP statuses to let the client know the outcome of the call. This is particularly important when errors exist. In Spring MVC, you can associate Java exceptions with particular responses by using annotations as well. Here's an example from the controller that takes any `UnauthorizedAccess-Exception` thrown and turns that into a proper response.

Listing C.5 Exception-handling annotations

Exception to handle →
```
@ExceptionHandler(UnauthorizedAccessException.class)
@ResponseStatus(value = HttpStatus.UNAUTHORIZED)          ◄── HTTP status to return
public ErrorMessage handleUnauthorizedException
    (UnauthorizedAccessException e) {
        return new ErrorMessage(
        "Unable to complete user request."                Return new instance of your
        , e.getMessage());                                custom ErrorMessage class
}
```

The `@ExceptionHandler` annotation can be used to specify what should be returned for a particular exception. In your shopping cart, you have a simplistic pseudo-authentication method you're using in lieu of an action login. You're comparing the ID of the cart passed in the request to the one stored on the session to demonstrate the use of exception-handling annotations. If any of the requests fail this check, the associated methods in your shopping cart controller throw the `UnauthorizedAccessException`, and this method automatically gets invoked. It returns a custom object you've created that holds a user-friendly message and the exception thrown. You've defined the 401/Unauthorized status as the status in this case by using the `@ResponseStatus` annotation.

The last couple of annotations you'll look at are used to ask Spring to inject the data services component into your shopping cart controller.

SERVICES AND AUTOWIRING

In chapter 7, you moved your dummy data from the UI to the server-side code. You placed it into a class called `DataServiceImpl`. You're using this class as a data store, a service, and a data access object (DAO) all rolled into one. Normally, your services create uniform APIs for any business-layer code, which, in turn, uses DAOs and other services to access the application's data. Because you're not using a database or any other web services, this class will assume multiple roles for simplicity's sake.

Because this class is also used in the other controller you have for searching and displaying games, you don't create a new instance of it directly in the shopping cart controller. Instead, you let Spring manage it and inject the service to whichever controller needs to use it.

This class itself doesn't do anything special except provide methods to search and access your static inventory data and your users' shopping carts. The source can be downloaded if you want to analyze it. What I want to point out here are the annotations used.

To define this class as an injectable service, you decorate your class with the @Service annotation. This allows it to be detected by Spring automatically when it performs its component scanning:

```
@Service
public class DataServiceImpl implements DataService {
```

To use the service, you can decorate either a setter method or an instance variable with the @Autowired annotation in whichever class it's to be injected into. Note that for autowiring, you use the class's *interface*. In your shopping cart, you've defined an instance variable as the interface type DataService and you've decorated it with this annotation:

```
@Autowired
private DataService dataService;
```

When Spring finds this annotation, it automatically assigns an instance of this service to this instance variable for you to use.

This project just scratches the surface of Spring MVC. If you want to know more, you can start with the friendly introduction at http://docs.spring.io/spring/docs/current/spring-framework-reference/html/mvc.html.

appendix D
Installing Node.js
and Gulp.js

This appendix covers

- Installing Node.js
- Installing Gulp.js

Gulp.js is a JavaScript-based tasked runner that runs in Node.js. This appendix guides you through installing these two applications.

D.1 Installing Node.js

Apart from Gulp.js, chapter 9 has another fundamental requirement. Gulp.js runs on Node.js, so you need to have that installed to follow along. You can find Node.js at https://nodejs.org/download. At the Node.js site, you can also find the installer that matches your system. After you've installed it, you can verify its installation by typing node -v from the command line:

```
C:\> node -v
V0.12.2
```

This tells you the version that was installed, and getting a proper response confirms the installation. With Node.js installed, you're ready for your first look at Gulp.js.

D.2   Installing Gulp.js

To get started with Gulp.js, you first need to install it. With Node.js installed, this is easy. You'll use the package manager (npm) that comes with Node.js (version 0.6 or higher). With npm, you can use a simple command from the command line to download and install Gulp.js.

In npm, what you install is called a *package*. Packages can be installed locally or globally (or both). You'll use the -g option to install Gulp.js globally so you can run its commands from any directory. From the command line, run `npm install -g gulp`.

> **NOTE**   If you're using OS X or Linux, it's recommended that you avoid using `sudo` when installing packages. See https://docs.npmjs.com/getting-started/fixing-npm-permissions.

If the process is successful, you should see output in the console similar to figure D.1.

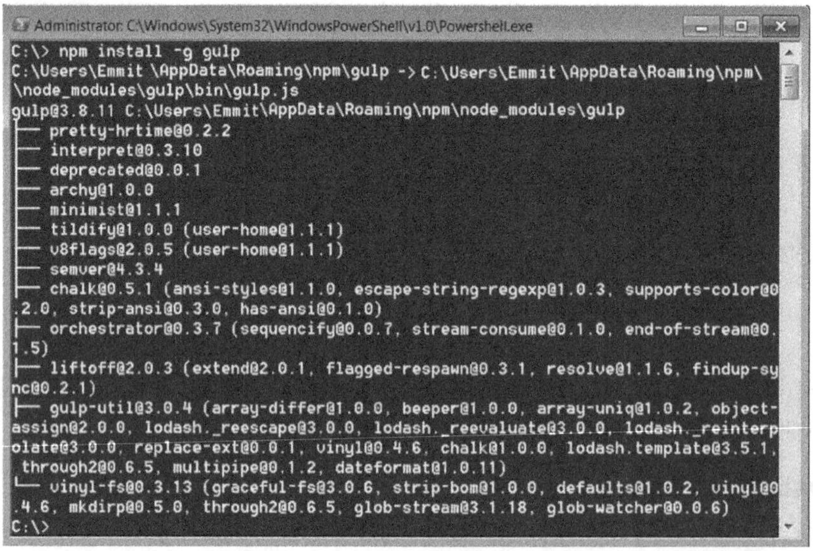

```
Administrator: C:\Windows\System32\WindowsPowerShell\v1.0\Powershell.exe

C:\> npm install -g gulp
C:\Users\Emmit \AppData\Roaming\npm\gulp -> C:\Users\Emmit \AppData\Roaming\npm\
\node_modules\gulp\bin\gulp.js
gulp@3.8.11 C:\Users\Emmit\AppData\Roaming\npm\node_modules\gulp
├── pretty-hrtime@0.2.2
├── interpret@0.3.10
├── deprecated@0.0.1
├── archy@1.0.0
├── minimist@1.1.1
├── tildify@1.0.0 (user-home@1.1.1)
├── v8flags@2.0.5 (user-home@1.1.1)
├── semver@4.3.4
├── chalk@0.5.1 (ansi-styles@1.1.0, escape-string-regexp@1.0.3, supports-color@0
.2.0, strip-ansi@0.3.0, has-ansi@0.1.0)
├── orchestrator@0.3.7 (sequencify@0.0.7, stream-consume@0.1.0, end-of-stream@0.
1.5)
├── liftoff@2.0.3 (extend@2.0.1, flagged-respawn@0.3.1, resolve@1.1.6, findup-sy
nc@0.2.1)
├── gulp-util@3.0.4 (array-differ@1.0.0, beeper@1.0.0, array-uniq@1.0.2, object-
assign@2.0.0, lodash._reescape@3.0.0, lodash._reevaluate@3.0.0, lodash._reinterp
olate@3.0.0, replace-ext@0.0.1, vinyl@0.4.6, chalk@1.0.0, lodash.template@3.5.1,
 through2@0.6.5, multipipe@0.1.2, dateformat@1.0.11)
└── vinyl-fs@0.3.13 (graceful-fs@3.0.6, strip-bom@1.0.0, defaults@1.0.2, vinyl@0
.4.6, mkdirp@0.5.0, through2@0.6.5, glob-stream@3.1.18, glob-watcher@0.0.6)
C:\>
```

Figure D.1   Installing Gulp.js

As you did with Node.js, you can confirm the installation by checking the version installed via the -v command: `gulp  -v`. With the ability to run Gulp.js commands from anywhere, switch to your project directory. Here you'll install any packages specifically needed for your project.

> **NOTE**   To include metadata about your Node.js project, including information about your build's dependencies and their versions, you'll need to create

a package.json file. The npm package manager can use the version field in this file to make sure the correct version of your packages gets installed. Additionally, if this file is present, information about the package being installed will be added to a list of dependencies if you use the `--save` or `--save-dev` options with the `npm install` command. The `--save` option can be used to specify runtime dependencies (when the application is used, such as your MV* framework), and the `--save-dev` option is for development dependencies. Although the dependency listings inside the file will be updated automatically during the installation of your packages using the options mentioned, you'll need to create the initial package.json file. You can do that manually or use the command `npm init`. If you need guidance in creating the package.json file, this command will walk you through the process by asking several questions. Feel free to edit the generated file as needed. After the process has completed, you'll have the initial package.json file created with the defaults you specified.

index

MORE TITLES FROM MANNING

The Design of Web APIs
By Arnaud Lauret

ISBN: 9781617295102
392 pages
$44.99
October 2019

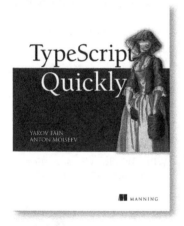

TypeScript Quickly
By Yakov Fain and Anton Moiseev

ISBN: 9781617295942
488 pages
$49.99
February 2020

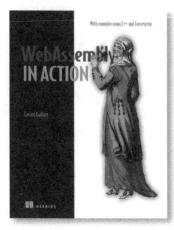

Web Assembly in Action
By Gerard Gallant

ISBN: 9781617295744
448 pages
$49.99
November 2019

For ordering information go to www.manning.com